Events That Changed
Ancient Greece

Events That Changed
Ancient Greece

Written and edited by
Bella Vivante

GREENWOOD PRESS
Westport, Connecticut • London

Library of Congress Cataloging-in-Publication Data

Vivante, Bella.
    Events that changed ancient Greece / written and edited by Bella Vivante.
      p. cm.
    Includes bibliographical references and index.
    ISBN 0–313–31639–2 (alk. paper)
    1. Greece—History—To 146 B.C.   2. Greece—History—146 B.C.–323 A.D.
  DF214.V58 2002
   938—dc21   2001033718

British Library Cataloguing in Publication Data is available.

Library of Congress Catalog Card Number: 2001033718
ISBN: 0–313–31639–2

First published in 2002

Greenwood Press, 88 Post Road West, Westport, CT 06881
An imprint of Greenwood Publishing Group, Inc.
www.greenwood.com

Printed in the United States of America

∞™

The paper used in this book complies with the
Permanent Paper Standard issued by the National
Information Standards Organization (Z39.48–1984).

10 9 8 7 6 5 4 3 2 1

Contents

Maps and Illustrations

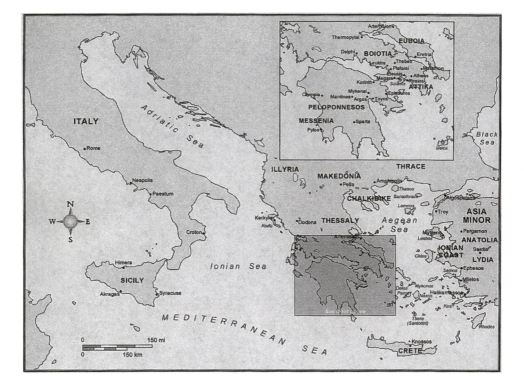

Map 1. Ancient Greece.

Introduction

Evidence of settlement of the mountains, plains, coasts, and islands of the northeastern Mediterranean lands we today call Greece dates back to Neolithic times (7000 B.C.E.). The connection of these early inhabitants with the Greeks of the later historical period is unknown. Ancient Greek recorded history spans about 1,500 years, from the earliest known Greeks, the Mycenaeans, sixteenth-century B.C.E., to the death of Kleopatra VII, the last Ptolemaic ruler of Egypt, 30 B.C.E. Her defeat marked the fall of the last of the Hellenistic empires to Roman conquest.

Greek time periods are roughly divided as follows:

3500–1400 B.C.E.	Minoan
16th–12th centuries B.C.E.	Mycenaean
11th–9th centuries B.C.E.	Dark Age
8th–6th centuries B.C.E.	Archaic
5th–4th centuries B.C.E.	Classical
3rd–1st centuries B.C.E.	Hellenistic

Periods from the Archaic are called *historical*, meaning from the introduction of written documents. Although the Mycenaeans used writing for some purposes, their form of writing did not survive the fall of Mycenaean civilization, nor did it provide the extensive literary, historical and other documents that emerged in later Greek writing. For all of Greek history, especially for the earlier periods, archaeology and art history provide major resources.

During this long time span, the lands defined as Greece shifted, as did the political, religious, and cultural centers. While the borders of the modern Greek nation formed the core through most of antiquity, its ancient limits were often both greater and less clearly defined. From the earliest recorded period, expanding cities on the Greek mainland sent colonies to the east, along the west coast of modern Turkey, in antiquity known as Asia Minor, or eastern Greece. These cities, especially those in the central region known as Ionia, benefited from influences of the Near Eastern civilizations with which they had contact, and they became the center for Greek cultural and political resurgence in the Archaic period. Other Greeks moved west, establishing colonies in Sicily and southern Italy, also called western Greece. Colonization continued throughout Greek history, including Massala (modern Marseilles, France) and eastern Spain, Kyrene, North Africa, and, with Alexander's conquests, Alexandria, Egypt, and cities as far east as the Indus River.

Ionian was also the designation for a particular group of Greeks, generally called "eastern." The southern region of Asia Minor was settled by Dorians, or "western Greeks," a second major group who were believed to have migrated into mainland Greece at a later date, populating the Peloponnesos and western Greece. Each group had its own Greek dialect, and often differing political, cultural, and religious practices. Cultural differences caused friction between Ionians and Dorians, as they sought to define an overarching Greek identity. Principal representatives of these groups were Ionian Athens and Dorian Sparta. The most powerful of ancient Greek city-states, these two cities played key roles through much of ancient Greek history. Hence, they serve as the main focus in many chapters, with attention given where appropriate to other important cities: Korinth, Thebes, Miletos, etc.

From the Mycenaean period to the mid-fourth century, political systems were defined by the power of individual centers, whether the Mycenaean palaces or later cities. These might become strong enough to impose their rule on other areas, but each still maintained its autonomy in some way. Shifts began with Sparta's conquests in the seventh and Athens's in the fifth centuries, where each imposed, with varying success, their rule over other regions. But the fourth-century conquests of Philip II of Makedon, his son Alexander the Great, and Alexander's followers decisively changed the earlier political concept of competing autonomous cities to that of empire, ruled by a king with full, autocratic power. Cities were submerged within empire, ruled by the king's appointed governors. From its original center in Makedonia, Alexander expanded the Greek empire to its greatest extent, east to northwest Afghanistan, south to the Persian Gulf, west to Egypt and North Africa. After Alexander's death, with some modifications, these areas continued to be ruled by Hellenistic Greek dynasties until each was conquered by Rome.

A significant aspect of Greece's development throughout the historical period is the close intertwining of religious, political, military and cultural activities. Not only were rulers interested in achieving military might and political dominance, but they also put major effort into expanding their city's cultural prominence, which was itself often an expression of their belief in deity. Hence, cultural developments were integrally tied to the political and military events marking Greek history.

This book's focus on political and military events—and cultural activities that formed part of major political endeavors—means that its concern is with typically male areas of activity, where women have only occasional roles. It should be noted, however, that, for ancient Greece, as for many societies, women had areas of activity that were also of major importance to the culture, notably in religion, the economy, and the home, considered central to ancient Greek society. Hence this book's attention to certain types of activity that provide historical understanding does not mean that these areas or the individuals important in them were the only ones considered significant in the ancient culture.

A note on orthography ("spelling") and dating. Recent direction in classical studies is to literally transliterate ancient Greek names, as a way of more accurately preserving ancient Greek legacy. This entails spelling Greek names according to their ancient Greek letters, rather than by their Latinate spelling, which is what has customarily been done. Typical changes are: k for c, as in *Sokrates* and *Kleopatra*; suffix in *-os* for *-us*, as in Herodotos; *ai* for *ae*, Mykenai. Nevertheless, some Latinate spellings remain, often because of multiple changes and reference accessibility, such as the writers Aeschylus and Thucydides. The dating designation, B.C.E. and C.E. (Before the Common Era and Common Era) is the preferred historical usage, equivalent to B.C. and A.D.

Part I

The First Greeks
(18th–12th century B.C.E.)

Figure 1. Warrior vase from Mykenai, ca. 1300–1100 B.C.E. Ceramic. National Archeological Museum, Athens, Greece. Photograph courtesy of Art Resource.

1

The Mycenaeans: Early Greek Civilization

INTRODUCTION

Where the Mycenaeans came from is uncertain. It is unlikely that the peoples living in Greek lands since Neolithic times (7000–3000 B.C.E.) were direct ancestors of the later Hellenes, what the Greeks called themselves. The first clear evidence of Greek speakers in this region are the documents left by the wealthy, centrally organized settlements from about 1600 to 1100 B.C.E., called the Mycenaean civilization.

Linguistically, Greek is an Indo-European language, related to the Sanskrit of the Aryan settlers in India, and to Latin and the Germanic languages of Europe. Like the Aryans, the early Greek speakers settled among and possibly conquered the earlier populations of the region. The Greek language of Linear B, the writing system of the Mycenaeans, shows linguistic affinities and dialectical distinctions with later Greek forms that indicate the presence of Greek-speaking people in Greece for some time. This idea contrasts with the belief, originating with the historical Greeks, that they arrived in the area in Mycenaean times when they subdued the pre-Greek populations. Such settlement, colonization, and conquest may well have happened earlier in the third millennium B.C.E. What does emerge from the archaeological record is that in the sixteenth century, sites growing in size and importance began to form powerful centers of Mycenaean civilization. All were destroyed or suffered decline from about the twelfth century, though some, like Athens, Sparta, and Thebes, continued to be inhabited or were re-established later, continuing into historical Greek, Roman, and even contemporary times.

This second millennium period and its culture were dubbed Mycenaean by the nineteenth century archaeologist Heinrich Schliemann, who discovered and made the first excavations at the sites of Mykenai (Mycenae) in the northeastern Peloponnesos and Troy at the mouth of the Hellespont. Schliemann's discoveries gave historical validity to Homer's epic poems, *The Iliad* and *The Odyssey*; his unearthing of numerous, elaborate gold finds in the shaft graves within the walls of Mykenai revealed a wealthy and powerful society. Archaeologists have since found and excavated numerous Mycenaean sites throughout mainland Greece, the Aegean islands, and Crete.

The splendid array of wealthy objects and burial patterns excavated at Mykenai suggests its importance, as do the network of roads and water systems that radiate out from it. While the name *Mycenaean* serves as a convenient designation, it probably does not reflect how the people of the age thought of themselves. Each major Mycenaean site functioned as its own powerful political center, ruling over, protecting, and receiving taxes from the surrounding populations. People identified with the region they lived in, and the other Mycenaean centers would not have considered Mykenai as ruling over them. Some of the distinctive Mycenaean features originated elsewhere. The earliest tholos tombs, elaborate beehive-shaped royal burial chambers, are found in Messenia in the southern Peloponnesos, while the earliest examples of Mycenaean palace architecture were built at Therapne, the Mycenaean settlement just south of Sparta, and at Tiryns, south of Mykenai.

Particularly valuable are the clay tablets found at numerous sites, most abundantly at Pylos in the southwestern Peloponnesos, that are inscribed with Linear B writing, which unmistakably identifies the Mycenaeans as Greek. But the distinctive "Lion Gate" relief sculpture at the fortified entryway to the hilltop palace complex—and which probably served as a symbol of royal power—has been found only at Mykenai. Thus, Mykenai may have become one of the most powerful of the Mycenaean sites, and may fittingly lend its name to the period.

Trade with the wealthy civilizations of the Near East and Egypt was apparently the impetus that led to the sudden rise of many Mycenaean centers in the sixteenth century. The resulting accumulation of wealth enabled a few powerful men to establish themselves as the ruling nobility over their respective areas, to embark upon extensive building programs, and to exhibit their power through newly developed, elaborate burial rituals. Once begun, this thirst for wealth fueled the development of the Mycenaean culture over the next few centuries. Military might and acquisition of wealth became the hallmarks of Mycenaean civilization, represented both in the artistic and archaeological finds of the Mycenaean age and glorified in later Greek epic stories, which extol the exploits of the period. Indeed, in *The Odyssey*, Homer regularly refers to the hero Odysseus as a "raider of cities."

This military activity and seeking after material wealth have been among the most enduring legacies of the Mycenaean age. The images portrayed in later Greek epic poetry and other literature formed the basis for the development of the political, social, and cultural systems of the Greek Archaic age (see Part 2). Virtually all Greek legendary tales have their historical roots in the Mycenaean period: the heroes Herakles (the Roman Hercules) and Theseus, the Oedipus cycle of tales, and most especially, the Trojan War. Some of these tales may reflect historical migrations of people, such as the return of the children of Herakles to resettle the Peloponnesos, identified by some with the Dorian migrations into the region, which probably occurred later. Tales of the Athenian hero Theseus credit him with consolidating the political units of Athens and the surrounding area of Attika, and founding the major Ionian festival to Apollo on the island of Delos. Tales of the Trojan War have historical roots, and the stories of the royal families at Mykenai—King Agamemnon, Queen Klytaimnestra, and their kin—and of Oedipus' royal family at Thebes may well reflect the political in-fighting and criminal excesses of their cities' ruling dynasties. Although the historical events of the Mycenaean age were largely forgotten by the later Greeks, the impact of these tales, as they came to be elaborated in Greek poetry and drama, was central to the development of Greek culture and identity.

While the historical and cultural events of the Mycenaean age may be seen to have these far-reaching effects, in other respects the Mycenaeans were themselves highly influenced by the pre-Greek peoples they settled among and eventually conquered. In the areas of religion, artistic activity, and possibly also of women's roles, what the Mycenaeans adapted from the non-Greek populations was to have enormous impact on the evolution of these activities in later Greece. Most apparent is their debt to the Minoan civilization centered on Crete. The art and archaeology of the Minoan centers on Crete, principally at Knossos and Phaistos, and on the island of Thera (modern Santorini) reveal a highly evolved society with a centralized governmental system, elaborate ritual life, possibly influenced by Egyptian ritual, highly developed artistic skill, a valued status of women in the culture, and a writing system called Linear A.

All of these elements of Minoan culture can be seen in the development of Mycenaean civilization. Mycenaean Linear B is clearly founded on the still undeciphered Linear A, as is the inheritance of artistic subjects and styles; very likely the artisans themselves were Minoans. Trade in Mycenaean goods seems to have taken over and expanded the extensive Minoan trade networks. The Mycenaean continuation of Minoan ritual subjects in their art suggests that they may have adopted some Minoan religious beliefs, and possibly also a more positive attitude toward women's roles, in the development of Mycenaean culture. These influences can be seen in Greek ritual practices of historical times (see Chapter 3).

It is not known what led to the decline of the Mycenaean civilization. Almost all Mycenaean sites were destroyed, mostly by fire, in the twelfth century B.C.E., the same period in which the Trojan War of legendary fame took place. Although various theories have been advanced for this widespread destruction, which also affected major centers of Egypt and of the Near Eastern Hittite and Phoenician civilizations, no clear cause is known. Some sites were rebuilt and had continuous habitation after this principal destruction, but the wealth and power of the Mycenaean age seems to have been broken. Settlements decline, wealthy burials cease, and artistic activity all but disappears. The end of Mycenaean civilization is shrouded in as much mystery as its beginning, and the Greek historical record enters a period called the Dark Age due to the much fewer and inferior archaeological finds of the next few centuries.

Although the documentary evidence declines, the memory of the Mycenaean period experiences its own renaissance through the tales transmitted in the oral storytelling tradition. In the Archaic age, the Greeks will resurrect these tales as they endeavor to fashion a new cultural heritage based on their dimly remembered but gloriously rendered heroic past. Moreover, the significance of the Mycenaean legacy continued far beyond the ancient Greeks, as it was passed on through the Romans and became instrumental in the development of the Western European cultural tradition. So we might validly assert that the significance of the events of the Mycenaean age is still being felt today.

INTERPRETIVE ESSAY
Carol G. Thomas

INTRODUCTION

The most exciting point to make about the Mycenaeans is that they actually existed. Equally surprising is that they created a civilization similar in many ways to that of their better-known contemporaries in Egypt, the Near East, and Anatolia (Asia Minor, or modern Turkey). These facts have only recently been demonstrated. Only fifty years ago, many people would have agreed with the view of classical scholar Samuel Bassett that the persuasively realistic heroic world of *The Iliad* and *The Odyssey* was merely a sublime fiction. That such an opinion persisted until the middle of the twentieth century seems strange in light of increasing archaeological discoveries in the Aegean area from the last decades of the nineteenth century. Heinrich Schliemann, trusting that Homer sang of real people and events, followed clues in the poems to locate Troy and Mykenai and other impressive sites. Sir Arthur Evans uncovered the labyrinthine palace of Minos and his alleged Minotaur at Knossos, while other explorers were bringing to light ancient settlements in Crete, the Aegean islands, and the Greek mainland. The dating of these recovered sites was problematic, as was their connection with Greeks of the familiar Classical age, for the people associated with these finds could have been colonists from Egypt, the Near East, or elsewhere.

In 1953 the script incised on the clay tablets preserved at several Mycenaean sites was deciphered, its language found to be an early form of Greek. The people, then, were Greek speakers—one problem solved. At the same time, new dating techniques placed the settlements in the Bronze Age (ca. 3000–1150 B.C.E.). Thus the second objection to inserting a new period into Greek history was removed. Greeks of the classical age could legitimately trace their story to a much earlier time. A rich legendary past is welcome but a flourishing historical past is preferable, especially when it was, in many respects, an age of heroes.

HISTORICAL PICTURE

This sea change in opinion defines the arrival of Greek speakers to the land they called Hellas as a major event that changed ancient Greece. Dating that arrival, however, is not an easy matter, and agreement still does not exist.

Archaeological evidence confirms that human ancestors lived in Greece as early as 200,000—perhaps even 400,000—years ago. The process of managing the environment that describes the human story during the stone age was especially difficult in Greece. Mountains fill 75 percent of the land, the soil—even in the plains—is relatively thin, sources of water are limited in many places, and earthquakes and volcanic eruptions are frequent. Coming to terms with these conditions demanded thousands of years of biological, technological, and social adaptations. A decisive leap forward sprang from the revolution associated with the domestication of plants and animals. In the Mediterranean region, this revolution began near 10,000 B.C.E. in the fertile crescent which extends along the east coast of the Mediterranean around the northern reach of Mesopotamia and southward along the eastern hills bordering the valleys of the Euphrates and Tigris rivers. Gradually, the agricultural, herding life spread, becoming increasingly prevalent in northern Greece by 7000. One opinion argues that the language of the earliest farmers was Indo-European, eventually a large, interrelated family of languages to which Greek belongs. If this theory is correct, arrival of the Greeks could be dated to 7000 B.C.E.

However, this theory has not won wide support. More traditional reconstructions of events bring the first Greek speakers to Greece five millennia later, about 2000 B.C.E. or mid-point in the Bronze Age. If this date of arrival is accurate, Greek speakers found a vigorous, established way of life in their new Aegean home of numerous farming villages with expanding populations. Trade with other areas, between sites and by sea, was growing. Archaeological evidence reveals a considerable advance in material culture resulting from local production and encouraged by the skills of other, more sophisticated cultures. The large island of Crete, stretching across the southern Aegean, had already developed a rich, complex way of life, known as the Minoan civilization.

Construction of elaborate fortifications around the more important towns on the Greek mainland was another feature the newcomers encountered: the leaders of individual settlements knew the wisdom of protecting themselves—and their wealth—from would-be attackers. The entering Greeks confirmed the wisdom of the earlier inhabitants' precautions: between 2100 and 1900, many sites were destroyed. One important fortified town—Lerna in the eastern Peloponnesos—was thoroughly burned but later rebuilt without fortifying walls around simple new houses with little sign of traded objects in the new settlement. In fact, the cultural level throughout much of the mainland plummeted. Archaeologist Emily Vermeule, in her book *Greece in the Bronze Age*, writes of "extreme poverty," the "kennel-look of architecture," "pathetic tools," and a "farmyard quality" (1964, 73–75, 77). All these clues point to newcomers at a lower level of sophistication than the existing population who, furthermore, seem to have prevailed by might. Yet not all earlier inhabitants were eliminated; newcomers mixed with existing peoples who instructed them in the arts of farming and herding, production of specialized goods, and trade by sea—a learning experience that took 400 years.

Fruits of the long tutelage suddenly ripened shortly after 1600, particularly at one site, Mykenai. Two circles of graves sunk into the ground as deep shafts had escaped plundering by later treasure seekers and, thus, retained their original grave offerings. When Heinrich Schliemann discovered the circle on the Akropolis heights, he found bodies "literally laden with jewels"; gold objects shaped as animals, diadems, masks, and vessels; masses of amber beads; ivories; rock crystal goods; and engraved gems. Indeed, such wealth and its early dating combined to bestow the name *Mycenaean* on the whole mainland culture from 1600 to 1150 B.C.E. It is important to remember, however, that other centers such as Pylos in the southwestern Peloponnesos, Tiryns near Mykenai, Thebes and Orchomenos in central Greece, and Athens experienced a similar, independent surge in prosperity and political/social organization about the same time.

The first century of the Mycenaean age witnessed the consolidation of local power centers as successful leaders extended their control over more territory and people. Trade resumed westward across the Adriatic, easterly into the Aegean and, what was to be most significant, southward to Crete, already a land of palace centers and far-reaching contacts with Egypt and the Near East. In tools of complexity, Crete led the mainland to a level of sophistication that deserves the title of "civilization."

The Cretans initiated contact as Minoan ships found their way to the newly resurgent mainland centers. The products the travelers carried had a ready market, but exchange required goods to trade in return. The specialization evident in the later Mycenaean period was probably underway early on, as the fleece of sheep and goats was woven into fine textiles, olive oil perfumed, flax converted to rope and sails, and metals fashioned into sturdy swords and graceful vessels. Nature provided another form of contact in the late seventeenth century when a massive volcanic eruption exploded the Aegean island of Thera into three chunks surrounding a deep caldera. Crete, just seventy-five miles south of Thera, felt the effects: sites were weakened, if not destroyed, and fleets were sunk or severely damaged. Mainland Greeks took advantage of their neighbors' difficulties. The major palace center of Knossos appears to have fallen under Mycenaean control at the end of the sixteenth century. Moreover, the seventy-five years from 1500 to 1425 B.C.E. witnessed a decline of Cretan activity in the larger Aegean and Mediterranean sphere, while Mycenaean connections in the East expanded. The height of Mycenaean visibility and prosperity follows: during the two centuries from 1425 to 1230 B.C.E., Mycenaean Greeks were equal players—along with Egyptians, Hittites, and others—in an international scene of trade, diplomacy, and warfare.

WAY OF LIFE

The Mycenaean world was one of kingdoms—eventually seven or eight—centered on well-fortified citadel strongholds. For the realm attributed to Nestor in Pylos, a territory of approximately 600 square miles drew together inhabitants of some 200 villages. All together, the kingdom's population may have been about 41,000. Most lived like peasants of every period—in family groups in small villages. They raised basic crops—wheat and barley, olives, grapes, legumes, fruits—and tended a few animals. As central control increased, however, it issued regulations about what should be planted or herded and what secondary products should be created. Rules as well as goods flowed to and from the center in its role as coordinator of production within the territory. To ensure the smooth flow of goods and orders, a road system connected parts of the kingdom with one another and, more important, with the center.

Central officials had the greatest power: at the apex was a kingly figure known as the *wanax*. He was aided by other officials, some associated with military responsibilities, others with religious concerns. The *wanax* held his position both because he was personally powerful and because he was able to maintain the personal allegiance of his near-peers. The hierarchical organization was reflected in wealth, especially landholdings, and status. The size of the larger territory and the intricate links within it necessitated local leaders. For Pylos, we have evidence of two "provinces," each of which had its official and deputy official. Each major town was under the supervision of a local "mayor." Members of the higher levels of society lived in substantial houses within and outside the citadels. It may well be that merchants, too, were among the privileged ranks of the kingdoms, perhaps representing a middle class in the societal hierarchy. Below the peasants, who comprised the largest portion of the population, were numerous slaves assigned to specialized tasks.

We know such detail through the new tool that became essential to administrative control: the Mycenaeans developed a form of writing for managing their affairs. Called Linear B from the simple outline shape of its signs, the script was derived from the earlier, as-yet-undeciphered script employed on Crete, Linear A. Linear B consisted of three elements. Ninety signs represent syllables composed of a pure vowel or a consonant plus a vowel. Other signs are pictograms, and a third component is units designating numbers, weights, and measures. The script's function was accountancy and, apparently, nothing else. Scribes recorded information about such matters as personnel, livestock, agricultural produce, and land ownership on clay tablets, many very small and containing information about a single item. The tablets were unbaked, evidently to be discarded at the end of the year. They were preserved only through the fires that destroyed the palace centers where they were produced and, together with all signs of the palaces, Linear B disappeared.

The written records were clearly needed to coordinate the economic affairs of the kingdom whose long history displayed increasing complexity. The exchange of raw materials and manufactured goods had been part of Mediterranean history since the stone ages. Obsidian—the natural black glass found in volcanic areas—was sufficiently prized for its sharpness to draw travelers to the few locations where it was found as early as the seventh millennium. Since much of traveling at that time was undertaken by sea, seamanship and ship construction became important skills. Residents of the Aegean islands continued the seafaring that had originally brought their ancestors to these peaks of submerged mountains. Cretans followed suit, encouraged by their location and precocious development to extend their maritime activity by trading their own products as well as serving as carriers for others. Minoan goods from early in the second millennium have been found at many Aegean sites on both islands and the Anatolian mainland, in Egypt and the Near East, especially in Syria. As we have seen, those same goods were found in greater numbers at mainland Greek sites as the millennium advanced.

Thus, when the Mycenaeans emerged from their centuries of building a vigorous way of life, they discovered an intensive network of trade, and from 1500 they became ever more active participants in that trade network. The presence of mainland goods, and surely of mainlanders, extended eastward to the Anatolian coast and neighboring islands, southward to Crete, particularly Knossos, and on to Egypt and the Levant. Underwater excavation of a ship sunk off the southern coast of Anatolia about 1300 describes clearly the intense maritime interaction of the eastern Mediterranean. Judging from the goods being carried in a fifty-foot-long cargo ship, trade activity reached from Cyprus to Syria/Palestine, Egypt, Mesopotamia, the mainland of Greece, even into the distant Baltic Sea region. The excavator suggests that the crew would have been as mixed as the goods.

The rising momentum of trade activity and production for trade transformed Mycenaean society: the citadel centers became political, economic, and, probably religious hubs controlling a rising population composed of more and more specialists. In addition to the thousands of farmers, an army of workers was engaged in the production of textiles, olive oil, weapons and other metal goods, jewelry, pottery, and leather objects. Another army built furniture, ships, roads, buildings, and fortifications. Production occurred throughout the kingdom, but much activity was located at the center. Outside the central hall, or *megaron*, of each palace lay a maze of workshops and storage sheds filled with hundreds, even thousands, of the manufactured objects they hoped to sell to the Mediterranean markets. One storage closet in the Late Mycenaean center at Pylos held over 500 drinking goblets waiting to be painted.

Raw materials were allocated to craftspeople for creation of finished products. Land was distributed with fixed goals attached to its use. Labor was needed to build and maintain roads and the center's fortifications. At Mykenai, the lords showed their status in elaborate tombs, known as "beehive" tombs because of their shape. Estimates suggest that about 57,600 man-hours were required to fashion each tomb, a figure that does not include dressing the masonry. There were nine of these status symbols at Mykenai alone! Other duties, too, had to be directed. For example, the wool industry at Knossos under Mycenaean control rested on the proper care of 80,000 to 100,000 sheep whose fleece yielded thirty to fifty tons of wool each year. Production of textiles from the wool commanded the time of 1,000 women workers and 200 men. Similar statistics would have emerged from the other realms, had records been preserved. Some of the production was undertaken for local use, but much would be part of a flourishing system of trade.

Why did so many people march to carry out these duties? While the Linear B records do not record the inner thoughts of any Mycenaean, they imply the force of a firm administrative hand reaching out from the citadels, a hand that often carried a sword. Society was structured hierarchically; obedience to authority was the cement that held the structure together. The highest authority—the *wanax*—may also have enjoyed special status by right of his role in dealing with divinity. The tablets and the presence of shrines show that religious affairs revolved, like so much of life, around the central palaces.

Mycenaean religion was polytheistic, and certain of the deities named on the tablets are familiar from the Classical Greek pantheon. Zeus, Poseidon, Hera, Hermes, Artemis, and Dionysos are among Mycenaean divinities. Despite the similar names, however, their characters may have been quite different from their portrayals in Greek poetry. Joining them are others not present in later Greek religion; one name seems to translate into "she of the cow" and another "the long-haired goddess." Priests and priestesses and special "servants of the god or goddess" are listed in the tablets along with offerings to deities and special land-holdings given over to particular deities. Archaeological evidence confirms the integration of religious activity into other aspects of life in the kingdom. On the Akropolis at Mykenai, three levels of the southwestern hillside were dedicated to buildings containing clay figures, frescoes, altars, and various offerings that give the clear impression of ritual activity.

VIEW OF THEMSELVES

Wall paintings and decorated pottery frequently depict the activities of hunting and fighting (see Figure 1)—very like the heroic pastimes described in *The Iliad* and *The Odyssey*. Among the Mycenaeans' prized heirlooms were long antique spears, tall, tower-framed shields of cowhide; and carefully preserved helmets made of sliced boars' tusks, all perhaps for public appearances and special combats.

Military strength was needed to establish and preserve control over the extensive territory the citadel center ruled. It was also imperative in dealings between citadels, for although a common culture linked them, they remained independent political spheres of power. Clues indicate that preserving independence was not always easy: almost all of the citadel centers were heavily fortified. Linear B records indicate that chariots were constructed, repaired and stored in the centers and that groups of men with armor and weapons were dispatched to various places as rowers and "watchers"; even the art of the centers delighted in scenes of fighting. Moreover, a pattern of destruction at several important centers is visible for the whole of the Mycenaean era. Early in the fifteenth century, Knossos was brought under Mycenaean control; we do not know *which* Mycenaeans took the reins of power, but the successful group gained a huge advantage both in commanding local resources on Crete and, even more, in acquiring access to the trade network stretching from Knossos to the east. A century later, Knossos was destroyed, very likely by other Mycenaeans who had become envious of the lords at Knossos.

Back on the mainland, the center at Thebes experienced rapid commercial growth in the fourteenth century, until it, too, was attacked, perhaps as early as 1300 B.C.E. This date marks the burning, followed by rebuilding, of the palace center of Pylos. In every case, no foreign elements—weapons, for example—accompany the evidence of the destructions. And, in every case, legends describe the attackers as Greeks: Theseus of Athens overcoming the Minotaur of Knossos; the seven against Thebes; Neleos coming from northern Greece to Pylos, in search of a kingdom.

Other peoples of the eastern Mediterranean also knew the Mycenaeans as troublesome intruders. To the Egyptians they were, first, dwellers in the Great Green Sea and, later, part of a host of attackers described in Egyptian records as those "who came in warships from the midst of the sea." To the Hittites in central Anatolia, the other great power of the second millennium, they came from Ahhiyawa, perhaps a reference to Achaea—we remember that Homer calls his Greek hosts at Troy Achaians. Hittite documents refer to a quarrel over a place called Wilusa— possibly Ilium, an alternative name for Troy—and to a king of Ahhiyawa campaigning in person on the boundaries of the Hittite kingdom. A Trojan War, long thought to be just one more element in the fictitious past created by later Greeks, is a distinct likelihood. Mycenaeans were recognized by their contemporaries as warlike; archaeologists have produced Mycenaean finds at the site of Troy and current excavation there has shown it to be a fairly extensive citadel. At the base of the citadel spread a large city that was an important hub in the vast trading network that we have described. Not Helen's face, then, but knowledge of Troy's wealth may have launched the ships that carried the Greeks to the northwest corner of Anatolia.

COLLAPSE

There is no doubt that the site known as Troy was destroyed. In fact, it was devastated twice in the thirteenth century and again in the twelfth. Achaians may have been the aggressors on one, both or neither of these occasions. In the thirteenth century B.C.E., their civilization was vigorous and expansive. In the twelfth, however, the mainland Greek sites were pressed by difficulties occurring throughout the Mediterranean, difficulties that would put an end to the impressive cultures of the Bronze Age. In the eastern Mediterranean, these cultures would revive in a similar form. For Greece, however, revival would take a very different turn.

There is no doubt about the magnitude of problems erupting in the later thirteenth century B.C.E. Our understanding of the cause or causes is less clear. Until recently, archaeologists and historians sought answers for each affected area. Invasion by newcomers was posited as a frequent explanation. For Greece, the proposed invaders were Dorians, a branch of Greek speakers named after their particular dialect of Greek—Doric. They were thought to have lingered in the Balkans long after their relatives had entered Greece and begun building the Mycenaean civilization. Learning of the wealth of their southern relatives, or perhaps being propelled by others, the argument continues, they invaded and destroyed the Mycenaean kingdoms in the late thirteenth and early twelfth centuries B.C.E. It was often claimed that new cultural traits were introduced by the invaders, the most striking being iron technology, cremation burial, and geometric pottery. These features were believed to define a persuasive cultural "break" since they were associated with material, aesthetic, and religious characteristics.

Reassessment during the last two decades, however, has shown that these supposed signs of newcomers came into gradual use in the transitional years of the later Bronze Age. Iron technology was practiced in Anatolia in the mid-second millennium B.C.E. and spread gradually through the eastern Mediterranean; forged iron artifacts are found in Greece at the end of the Mycenaean period. Cremation, too, is known from the Bronze Age; in some late Mycenaean cemeteries, cremation burials began to occur side by side with the usual inhumations. Not a "break" but a continuous evolution also best describes the development of pottery, where the handmade, unburnished pottery thought by some to be the product of newcomers is found in fully Mycenaean levels, and the roots of the "new" geometric pottery are evident in Late Mycenaean ware. Finally, the eminent Linear B scholar John Chadwick further weakened the theory of a Dorian invasion by demonstrating the presence of features of Doric Greek in the Linear B tablets. Interestingly, the Doric elements suggest that Linear B was the dialect of the common people, whose presence is little attested to in the palace-oriented world of the tablets.

With the skepticism over the once-certain indicators of newcomers, practically the only archaeological evidence that may now be connected with the traditional Dorian invasion is the destruction and burning of Mycenaean centers. An important advocate of the Dorian invasion theory, Vincent Desborough, was increasingly troubled even by this evidence and in 1968 asked: "If [invaders] remained and settled, why have they left no trace? Can one only really suppose that they were so primitive as to leave no evidence, whether in some new custom or at the very least in some new artefact? . . . If they moved on, where did they go to? If they went back, why did they do so, leaving the good land which they could have occupied?" ("History and Archaeology in the Last Century of the Mycenaean Age," *Atti e Memorie del 1º Congresso Internazionale di Micenologia* (1968, 1076f.).

Agents of destruction need not have come from outside Greece. Civil war is not ruled out, nor is an attack by a coalition of Mycenaean powers moving against other mainland centers. The tales of the difficulties Agamemnon and Odysseus faced on their return from Troy may be remembrances of civil strife. Perhaps a great revolt was led by the merchants, by the free peasants, by the masses of slaves, or by several or all of these elements making common cause against the autocratic kings and nobles. Natural factors may have played a role. Could the deforestation that likely followed the construction boom and spreading agriculture have caused such serious erosion of the soil that famine produced revolution? Might there have been a widespread plague or series of epidemics, which could perhaps account for the increased practice of cremation burial?

All of these theories have proponents. However, rather than settling on one explanation for each area, it is sensible to consider the larger context. Just as the Mycenaeans were associated with other contemporary cultures through trade and warfare, so too were they caught up in a common challenge to the established way of life.

Egyptian records describe attackers in some detail. Libyans and various Northerners attacked the Delta region in 1231, and Libyans again joined forces with others attempting to invade Egypt early in the twelfth century. At least one group of would-be invaders is known to subsequent history: the "Peleset" eventually settled in Palestine and appear as the biblical Philistines. The weakened Hittite kingdom was destroyed near the end of the thirteenth century. Major towns in Syria were also beset, and many were destroyed around this same time.

Collectively, the attackers have been called "the land and sea peoples." Egyptian documents preserve the names of some of the motley hordes that comprised the Sea Peoples. Identification with known peoples, such as the Lycians, the Sardinians, the Tyrrhenians, and the Sicilians, have been proposed, although they remain tentative. Even if these equations are correct, the names may refer to places where certain groups eventually settled, not to their places of origin. Some scholars have suggested that even the Achaians-Mycenaeans are represented by a group called Akawasha, but it remains problematical whether Achaians joined the Sea Peoples in their attacks on the Near East or were themselves among the objects of these attacks. The wealthy Mycenaean citadels, most of them situated near the sea, must have been tempting targets in an era of large-scale piracy. The Linear B tablets from Pylos hint that all was not well just before the fire that destroyed the palace: rowers are stationed, watchers are dispatched, resources and manpower of the kingdom are being tabulated and special offerings are made to the gods.

Where did these people come from and what drew them to the eastern Mediterranean? Some were no doubt present in the area before the time of difficulties. Others were probably driven or drawn to the region as the spread and success of civilization drew new currents into its own. Trade, plunder, and opportunities all attract outsiders to a prosperous area. Some currents came from the west, where native cultures began to import and use Mycenaean pottery and blades. Others came from the Balkan region of northern Greece as far away as the Danube, where rich metal deposits and thick forests allowed other farming cultures to enter the fringes of Mediterranean trade with their own bronzework and weaponry. Some came from Africa south of the Egyptian kingdom; some, perhaps, from as far as the Black Sea. One theory is that recruits from the central Mediterranean were valuable as foot soldiers in the large armies of the Bronze Age kingdoms. Another thesis is that the Mediterranean experienced a major drought in the twelfth and eleventh centuries B.C.E. as melting polar ice altered the trade winds, bringing a warming trend and drying. Resulting famine drove starving people to seek better conditions for their farming and herding.

The wisest solution would take into account all these possibilities: the interlocked "system" of activity in the eastern Mediterranean underwent "systems collapse." The central administrative organs became top-heavy, too specialized to adjust to economic difficulties. Several years of crop failure or the interruption of essential trade would have strained a kingdom's entire structure. The ruling class would have lost power as it ceased to function efficiently; signs of the decline in management could be seen in unrest, lower production of basic products and specialized goods, movement of people, and even disease leading to population decline. The confusion would have been inviting to would-be invaders. In a word, there was probably no clear, single "cause" for the collapse.

An attractive feature of this explanation is that it allows for differing local conditions and reactions and it appropriately links events in Greece with those of the larger Mediterranean. The "land and sea peoples" may have been moving because they had experienced similar economic disasters; similarly, their movements may have precipitated fundamental upsets in the productive systems of the advanced cultures of the eastern Mediterranean. Certainly, the activities of marauders would have disrupted the international trade of the fourteenth and thirteenth centuries B.C.E., severely damaging the way of life of the Mycenaeans who were active participants in Mediterranean commerce.

Interruption of trade and crop failure do not explain the actual destruction of the palaces, but the collapse of the entire system does suggest an answer, since centralized administrations controlled the mechanisms of these redistributive economies. In this system center officials allocated goods, such as supplies of metal or quantities of wool, to workers in several parts of the kingdom to be made into specific finished products which then were returned to the center to be used there or redistributed. Agricultural goods, too, were brought to the palace to be distributed as rations, traded, or turned into secondary products such as perfumed olive oil from olives or wine from grapes. If the palace officials were unable to correct malfunctions, the local units comprising each kingdom could become severed from the administrative machinery and thrown back on their own resources. The Linear B tablets from Pylos signal such problems: taxes were in arrears, bronzesmiths were short of raw materials. Simultaneously, the palace appears to have been intensifying its control over production.

Most of the Mycenaean centers experienced difficulties and eventual destruction, but many left no tablets providing details about local conditions. The physical evidence indicates local differences in results, which suggests local differences in causes as well. There would have been no single, recognizable common enemy. The enemy was both external and internal, human and natural. As problems arising in one region spread to others, the situation worsened. So disastrous were the consequences for Greece, that the Age of Heroes became a legend. Its reality faded from view until the efforts of modern archaeologists, linguists, and historians restored it as the first civilization of Hellas.

AN EVENT THAT CHANGED ANCIENT GREECE

The most obvious proof that the Mycenaean accomplishment changed ancient Greece is the extension it has given to Hellenic history. Before the reality of the Age of Heroes was demonstrated, Greek history was usually taken to have begun in 776 B.C.E. with the first Olympic Games. Dating the arrival of the first Greek speakers to circa 2000 B.C.E. adds more than 1,200 years to the cultural tradition.

Furthermore, the form of Mycenaean culture was not insignificant. At its height, the Mycenaean age was a sophisticated civilization based on sizable kingdoms. Kings and other officials directed the lives of thousands of people from impressive citadel centers. A diversified economy based on use of basic commodities—olives, textiles, grapes—was capable of the production of specialized goods that found a market in a vast interlocking network, stretching around the eastern Mediterranean coastal area and beyond. Superpowers of the second millennium recognized the importance of Mycenaeans not only as traders but also as soldiers.

Paradoxically, another significance of the Mycenaean culture is that it so thoroughly collapsed at the end of the Bronze Age. Certainly not every skill and feature of that way of life disappeared, but the heritage was transformed during the four centuries known as the Dark Age. Most completely changed was the nature of community: kingdoms and kings, citadel centers with their administrators and records were replaced by small, independent communities in which ordinary peasant farmers participated in ordering the collective well-being. Without the "decapitation" of the central authority, the later democratization of Greece would have been delayed, if not prevented.

At the same time, memory of the glorious past was preserved in oral tradition—stories told and retold through the Dark centuries that culminated in the Homeric poems. *The Iliad* and *The Odyssey* seem to have been "fixed" in a new form of alphabetic writing in the second half of the eighth century B.C.E. The poems defined the values of later Greeks: their quest for *arête* (skill/virtue), a constant competitive spirit to achieve, realization that individual goals must be balanced with the larger goals of one's community. Successful citizens, like their heroic ancestors, must be doers of deeds and speakers of wise words. The poet Homer was regarded as the greatest poet, the leader in all civilizing arts.

The Mycenaean heritage itself was a source of pride to later Greeks. In his account of the Peloponnesian War (431–404 B.C.E.), the historian Thucydides begins with the Mycenaean age. Thucydides is particularly interested in the source of the military strength of Agamemnon, king of Mykenai, in the campaign against Troy. Actual products of the Bronze Age are prized as treasures in the present. "Golden Mykenai" shines in the National Museum in Athens; the "Trojan Gold" is a source of pride—

and contention over its "proper" location—today, as it was more than three thousand years ago.

SUGGESTIONS FOR FURTHER READING

Alexander, Caroline. 1999. "Echoes of the Heroic Age," *National Geographic* (December): 54–79. The first of three well-illustrated articles on ancient Greece.

Chadwick, John. 1976. *The Mycenaean World*. Cambridge: Cambridge University Press. An account of Mycenaean Greece as it emerges from the Linear B tablets. It is intended for students of the early phase of Greek civilization and also for more general readers.

———. 1987. *Linear B and Related Scripts*. Berkeley and London: University of California Press and the British Museum. A concise, clear discussion of the decipherment of the script and the nature of information provided by the tablets.

Fitton, J. Lesley. 1966. *The Discovery of the Greek Bronze Age*. Cambridge, Mass.: Harvard University Press. Recounts the story of unearthing the Greek heroic past.

Higgins, Reynold. 1967. *Minoan and Mycenaean Art*. New York and Washington: Praeger. A well-illustrated survey of the art and architecture of Aegean Bronze Age civilizations.

McDonald, William, and Carol Thomas. 1990. *Progress into the Past*. 2d ed. Bloomington and Indianapolis: Indiana University Press. The story of the pioneers who demonstrated the reality of the earliest civilizations, ending with developments through 1988 and current theories and problems.

Taylour, Lord William. 1990. *The Mycenaeans*. Rev. ed. London: Thames and Hudson. One volume in the expansive *Ancient Peoples and Places* series, it provides a succinct account of major aspects of Mycenaean civilization.

Vermeule, Emily. 1964. *Greece in the Bronze Age*. Chicago and London: University of Chicago Press. An archaeological study intended to give an impression of specific qualities of each phase of civilization on the Greek mainland between 6500 and 1100 B.C.E.

Warren, Peter. 1975. *The Aegean Civilisations from Ancient Crete to Mycenae*. Oxford: Phaidon. A readable account of the larger Aegean context of the Mycenaeans. Unfortunately it is now out of print.

Warry, John. 1995. *Warfare in the Classical World*. Norman: University of Oklahoma Press. A superbly illustrated, excellent description of all aspects of warfare in the ancient Greek and Roman world; see Chapter 1 on Homeric and Mycenaean warfare.

Wood, Michael. 1985. *In Search of the Trojan War*. New York and Oxford: British Broadcasting Corporation; Facts on File. A BBC television series and a book. These place the Mycenaeans in the larger context of the eastern Mediterranean during the second millennium B.C.E., examining the heights of the powerful civilizations as well as their collapse.

Part II

The Archaic Age
(8th–6th century B.C.E.)

Figure 2. Bronze statuette of a Lyre-player with a Companion. Photograph courtesy of The J. Paul Getty Museum, Los Angeles.

2

Epic Poetry, *Polis*, and Tyranny: Political Revolutions and Development of Ethnic Greek Identity

INTRODUCTION

After the collapse of Mycenaean civilization (twelfth century B.C.E.), some Mycenaean-style artifacts continued for two more centuries, although writing disappeared. The ensuing Dark Age yielded few items, and those few were of inferior quality. Recovery was slow, but the ninth and eighth centuries B.C.E. witnessed increasing creative momentum. Geometric pottery, so named for the abstract geometric designs covering the surfaces, became prevalent, and visual images returned, some poignantly depicting, on five- to six-foot-high funerary urns, scenes of the dead on a bier surrounded by women mourners. The Archaic age (8th–6th centuries B.C.E.) witnessed the forging of a new Hellenic identity in multiple ways: religion, politics, economics, poetry, art, and architecture. Reinforcing each other, together the changes in all these spheres shaped Greek history and identity. This chapter will examine significant political developments through the seventh century and the importance of Homeric poetry in the fashioning of a unified Greek identity.

The Archaic age witnessed a new surge in colonization. Under pressure of expanding populations, Greek cities sent out new colonies in many directions: west in Sicily, Italy, and as far as the coast of Spain and

Marseilles, France; south to the North African coast west of Egypt; and east to the Black Sea. These colonies possibly developed from, and certainly provided, solid Greek bases in trading routes. Although ties were to be maintained between the mother city and the colony, the exact nature of this relationship is not clear, and over time, most colonies saw themselves as independent of their founding metropolis.

Central to historical events of the Archaic age was the emergence of the *polis* ("city-state"; consider the words *politics, metropolis*), a political unit distinguishing Greek civic structures from those of other ancient societies. Shaped during the Dark Age, the *polis* became a political organization that oversaw political, economic, religious, cultural, and social affairs of a centralized city core and surrounding vicinity. Reflecting new power relationships after Mycenaean feudal monarchies declined, the *polis* distributed governance among defined groups of citizen men, usually determined by military status and land ownership, who conducted city affairs through councils, judiciaries, and governing offices. Individuals credited with establishing their cities' distinctive social system were memorialized. Thus, Athens esteemed the legendary king Theseus for bringing together the villages of Attika, the region around Athens, into a confederated political entity, and the two historical rulers Drakon and Solon as principal lawgivers. Spartans celebrated Lykourgos as their lawgiver, who was probably historical, but about whom no early evidence exists. While many early *poleis* (pl.) proclaim themselves as representing the people, nobles retained great influence, if not control; in some, notably Sparta, an active, though restrained, dual kingship continued with *polis* organization.

Contributing to the *polis* were important developments that would transform Greek society. Early on, the *polis* established control over new or expanded ritual institutions and cultural festivals. Enhancing their prestige, cities built great temples in honor of deities—hallmarks of ancient Greek architecture—and held celebratory festivals with poetic and dramatic contests as important elements that gained national and international reputations (see Chapter 3). The mythological stories presented in the poems recited at these festivals provided the widespread individual *poleis* with a unifying heritage known as Panhellenism (an "all-Greek" identity). Homer's epic poems, transmitting oral tales deriving from Mycenaean times about 500 years earlier, helped shape this newly fashioned, invigorated Greek identity. *The Iliad* and *The Odyssey*, and most subsequent Greek literature, depict a glorious heroic past as the basis for constructing a consolidated Greek identity. Writing's reintroduction in the eighth century expanded poetry's culturally significant role.

Adapting the Phoenician Semitic alphabet, by the seventh century, poets regularly wrote down their compositions. Homer's poems, orally composed throughout the long Dark Age, were set in semipermanent form in the late eighth century, thereby strengthening their Panhellenic cultural role.

Related to the development of the Greek *polis* was another political feature occurring in several Greek cities—tyranny. Initially, a *tyrannos* referred to an outsider who became king in an unusual way, whether peacefully, such as by marrying the queen rather than inheriting the throne, or by usurping the throne from those considered the traditional ruling powers. Hence, Sophocles' play, *Oedipus the King*, is called *Oidipous Tyrannos* in Greek, reflecting Oedipus' apparent status as a newcomer to Thebes. Tyrannies were not initially dictatorial, and many tyrants maintained *polis* governing codes. They often expanded the *polis* political reach, underwrote public works, temple building, and religious festivals, and promoted poetic competitions. The later, contemporary meaning resulted from the cruel actions of some tyrants and the influence of Plato's and Aristotle's negative views of tyrannies in their political philosophies.

The earliest, and longest-lasting, tyrant dynasty was that of Kypselos in Korinth (ca. 657–627), who overthrew the aristocracy of the Bakkhiadai, even though his mother may have been a Bakkhiad herself. Little is known of his activities while in power: he founded colonies in northwest Greece, and he built a treasury at Delphi, a visible marker of his success and gratitude for Delphi's support through favorable oracles, prophecies of the god Apollo. Kypselos reputedly went about without a bodyguard, which may suggest that he was regarded favorably and did not need one. But tyrannies met with mixed success in Greece: Theagenes, tyrant of Megara (ca. 640–620), was eventually banished, unable to hold onto power. Others, like the Athenian aristocrat Kylon, failed altogether in their attempts to seize ruling power.

In this environment developed the two *poleis* that would become most powerful in Greek history—Athens and Sparta. Considered a model of *eunomia* ("good social order") by other Greek cities, Sparta's civic structure functioned effectively for five centuries. One of the earliest *poleis* to emerge, Spartan power was distributed among a council of *homoioi* ("Equals"), a select core of Spartan citizen men, a dyarchy ("dual kingship")—no doubt according two former aristocratic families equal representation—and a very powerful council of elders.

Five villages formed the central *polis*, and some outlying areas retained independent trade and cultural relations. But Sparta conquered nearby

Messenia (late 8th–7th century B.C.E.) and enslaved its population, who were called helots. In contrast to the family-based system of slavery obtaining through much of Greece, the helots belonged to the *polis* and were kept in a particularly vicious and cruel system of slavery that was constantly threatened by revolt. Unable to conquer other Peloponnesian cities, Sparta made treaties that guaranteed allies' assistance in subduing helot revolts. This alliance, eventually called the Peloponnesian League, was the oldest and longest-lasting ancient Greek defensive pact. Through it, Sparta gained a reputation for ousting tyrannies from other Greek cities.

The elite Spartan social system depended on the forced labor of the helots, in making agricultural products, food preparation, and textile production. This slave-based economy freed Spartan citizens, male and female, to pursue the tasks deemed appropriate for each gender: for men, warfare and city governance, for which they underwent rigorous training and lived mostly in men's quarters—the only Greeks to have military training, hence the famed strength of their army; for women, bearing and nourishing the young, and educating girls into their societal roles, parallel to the boys' training. Although only men acted in Sparta's formal governing and military systems, elite Spartan women's roles may have been among the highest in ancient Greece: choral rituals prepared adolescent girls for their roles as adult women, a transition they celebrated in ritual festivals that publicly recognized women's importance to the community, independent of her marital status. Unlike Athens, Sparta had a word for female citizen, and many ancient writers commented on the independent and powerful status of Spartan women.

While Sparta long maintained its social organization, Athens' political development was more checkered, the result of political in-fighting among powerful aristocratic clans. From the early seventh century, three *archons* ("rulers," the principal city officials, later expanded to nine), ran city affairs. But a quarter of a century after Kypselos gained power in Korinth, Kylon, with the help of his father-in-law Theagenes, tyrant of Megara, and others, occupied the Akropolis in Athens intent on seizing control (ca. 632). Besieged by the Athenians, Kylon escaped, but many of his supporters were killed at an altar. Considered responsible for this sacrilege, the eponymous *archon* (that is, the ruler for whom the year is named and dated in the Athenian calendar), Megakles and his clan, the Alkmaionidai, were cursed and expelled from Attika. However, the deeply rooted power of the Alkmaionidai is shown by their return to influential governing positions in Athens in subsequent generations.

Another response to this political wrangling emerged about a decade later: Drakon is the first lawgiver of whom we have firm record, however meager. Although later depicted as imposing harsh laws, it is more likely that he codified in written form (ca. 621) existing custom and law. Only parts of his law on homicide have survived, which are concerned with defining both what the victim's relations are due and the punishment for the perpetrator. This first attempt at codification of the laws was not successful, as Athenian clan in-fighting continued well into the next century, prompting renewed attempts at legal and social reforms by Solon, elected sole *archon* (594), and at tyranny mid-century by Peisistratos (see Chapter 4).

INTERPRETIVE ESSAY
F. E. Romer

By the mid-eighth century B.C.E., Greeks were leaving new marks on the political landscape of the Mediterranean. Signs of the *polis* begin to appear in the record, and this new form of political organization lasted until the end of the Classical period. About the same time, *The Iliad*, and a generation later *The Odyssey*, began to be sung in forms more or less familiar to us, even though two more centuries would pass before these poems were written down. The reappearance of writing, colonization, the Homeric poems, and the emergence of the *polis* mark the beginning of the Archaic age (800–490 B.C.E.), and along with them come written law and the struggle for power within the emergent *polis*. The Archaic age falls into an earlier subperiod (800–600 B.C.E.), for which the record is more fragmentary, and a later one (600–490 B.C.E.), for which more information is available. The first of these two subperiods is the subject of this chapter.

The preceding Dark Age (1150–800 B.C.E.) is the germinal period of Greek civilization. It takes its name from the absence of writing, which was lost when Mykenai fell, and there are no historical personalities or datable events. A graffito scratched into a drinking cup sheds the first glimmer of new light. It says simply, "I am the well-drunk goblet of Nestor: Desire for fair-crowned Aphrodite will seize whoever drinks this." The inscribed cup was found at Pithekoussai (Ischia), an island in the Bay of Naples off the coast of Italy, well to the west of the Greek homeland, and its archaeological context is dated to circa 750–700 B.C.E. The spot where it was found reflects the wider geographic dispersion of Greek settlements, as does the east Greek lettering of the inscription, and

Pithekoussai actually is recorded as the first Greek colony in the west. The inscribed cup appears to speak in the imagined voice of Nestor's famous goblet, described in *The Iliad*. The epic allusion points to a poetic tradition that was increasingly Panhellenic, that is, shared by Greeks wherever they lived, but it also points to the heroic nature of the life of the colonists and the people who sent them out. Underlying both the graffito and other issues addressed in this chapter is the implicit question of how much continuity, if any, exists between the Archaic age and the Mycenaean period.

COLONIZATION

By the time of the graffito, Greeks were spreading around the Mediterranean. The eighth and seventh centuries B.C.E. were an age of colonization. The first thrust went westward, especially to Italy and Sicily, and the second went to the Black Sea. Greeks were trading at al-Mina (Greek name unknown) in Turkey as early as circa 800. In the next half-century, Chalcidians and Eretrians founded a trading station at Pithekoussai, and Chalcidians set up the first colony on the southern Italian mainland at Cumae circa 740, and the first one in Sicily at Naxos (Capo Schisò) in 734. Sicily was a busy center of colonization. A year later, Korinthians founded Syracuse, and in 729 Chalcidians from Naxos suppressed the native Sikels and established Leontinoi (Lentini). In southern Italy, exiles founded Sparta's only colony, Taras (Taranto), in 706 B.C.E., and Megara led the movement toward the Black Sea, with Chalcedon (Kadiköy) colonized in 685 and Byzantion (Istanbul) by 659. Islanders from Thera (Santorini) established Kyrene (Shahat) in North Africa circa 630, and a party of Phokaian colonists set up Massalia (Marseilles) circa 600. Shortly afterwards, Massalians based a small trading port at Emporiae (Empúries) in Spain, along with other trading stations down the coast at Hemeroskopeion (Denia), Alonae (uncertain), and Maenaca (Vélez-Málaga). By 600, Greeks also had an emporium at Naucratis in Egypt, and Samian merchants were sailing to the Tartessos region (Biblical Tarshish) of Spain near the Strait of Gibraltar.

Reasons are not given for the founding of most colonies, and there was no single cause. Trade, especially in metals, preceded colonization. The good new citizen (*politês*) required land to support his new lifestyle, and the all-but-universal need for more land was a factor, as were aggravating causes like overpopulation, poor farming conditions, and political turmoil. A colony was sent out under the leadership of an appointed *oikistês* (founder), who would ordinarily be its first *basileus* (a term to be defined momentarily), and one of the first duties of the *oikistês* was to see that land was distributed among the colonists. At Taras, the founding party consisted of expelled Partheniai, said to be the illegitimate offspring of Spartan women left at home while their husbands were fighting a protracted war in Messenia (735–716). The colonists of Kyrene were authorized by the Delphic oracle, which was, in turn, ratified by a decree of the Theran assembly, and we are reminded that colonies were sent out by mother cities (*mêtropoleis*) with preset constitutions, which reinforced the inchoate *polis* way of life.

THE EPIC TRADITION

The graffito from Pithekoussai raises other questions. Its reference to Nestor's goblet shows that this part of the epic tradition was known, whether or not the graffito alludes to our *Iliad*, a rival version, or other songs in the oral tradition. Archaeology has recovered from Mykenai, Pylos, and Troy material remains that illuminate the Bronze Age, but because of the level of the destruction at Troy and elsewhere, we cannot verify the details of the legendary Trojan War. In the twentieth century C.E., scholars reached a new understanding of both the oral tradition and the process of composition-in-performance to which the poems owe their existence. The poems are an amalgam of traditional poetic materials and of specific poetic gestures contributed by a number of individual bards over the course of numerous performances and many, many years. Even if specific details in the poems may go back to earlier times, the individual characters and their behaviors had to be believable to eighth-century B.C.E. audiences. In this way, the poems reveal more about how communities operated in the ninth and early eighth centuries than they do about the Mycenaean past.

The two Homeric epics are cultural artifacts by which Greeks developed a coherent sense of their shared culture and collective identity, but they were also produced by that same drive toward Panhellenization, which is most conspicuous in stories about the gods. For all Greeks, Homer and Hesiod "composed the divine genealogy . . . , gave the gods their titles, distinguished both their functions and spheres, and noted their outward forms" (Herodotos 2.53). The two poets were a powerful force for unifying Greek culture because epic poetry was recited at some festivals, but the process of Panhellenization is most visible when these two do not agree. In *The Iliad*, Aphrodite is the daughter of Zeus and Dione, but in Hesiod's *Theogony* she is a generation older than Zeus and miraculously born from the dripping blood of Ouranos's severed genitals. Hesiod's version, which eventually became Panhellenic, may sound more primitive, but it only entered the Greek world in the eighth century B.C.E. in the shadow of the Semitic (Phoenician) Ishtar/Astarte, while Homer's Zeus (Dios) and Dione (the female Zeus) have counterparts in the Diwos and Diwija of the Linear B tablets. The expanding notion of ethnic community caused the myths to be collected and retold until they were virtually all interlinked by common genealogical threads, but occasionally, as here, the seams show. The same articulated ethnic awareness lies behind the Olympic Games (traditionally established in 776 B.C.E.), where Greek competed against Greek in honor of the gods and on behalf of their own *poleis* (see Chapter 3). Greeks still lived in separate and distinct communities, but in recognizing their shared heritage they began to establish Panhellenic institutions.

In the Homeric poems, individual communities operated under a *basileus* (pl., *basileis*). The term *basileus* describes a large number of roughly equal individuals with important power in their respective communities. *Basileus* is often translated as "king," sometimes as "baron," but the best translation for this period is what anthropologists call a "chief." In *The Odyssey*, Penelope's suitors are all *basileis*, who have gathered for one purpose, to marry the former chief's wife and claim his position. They occasionally defer to one another, but each is intent on claiming a higher social position by defeating his peers. Chiefs claimed that their authority originated with the gods. In *The Iliad*, many chiefs are descended from gods, and one standard epithet for them is "Zeus-born" (*diogenês*). The Homeric *basileus* is, then, a "first among equals" and does not occupy the apex of a pyramidal social structure.

The role of public assemblies was still irregular, but their function was to mediate a proper working relationship between ruler and ruled. There was no claim to inherited succession. As *The Odyssey* opens, a public assembly is convened in Ithaka for the first time in twenty years. In that assembly, Antinoös, one of the suitors raiding Odysseus's larder, recognized the right of Odysseus's son to inherit his father's goods and his position among the local chiefs, but he questioned Telemakhos's ability to hold on to them. Leokritos said Odysseus had no automatic right to resume his position in society. The suitors were in competition for Penelope's hand, and Odysseus was expected to defeat them to regain his former pre-eminence in Ithaka, which he could maintain only as long as he was physically able.

In the same assembly, Mentor contrasted good chieftaincy and bad in no uncertain terms. He bemoaned the loss of Odysseus's kindliness, sense of justice, and paternal benevolence, and called for the opposite kind of leader—an unsympathetic chief who could right wrongs and restore order. Throughout *The Iliad*, the chief's most important role involves his fighting ability, and in the two Homeric poems military strength is the basis of the chief's power in society. But in Hesiod's *Theogony* the *basileis* are almost entirely describable in terms of their judicial functions. These functions, which did survive from the past, make it possible to detect a new step in the development of the *polis*, the restriction of the chief's power within the community.

Advisory councils have their own prehistory, and over time councils of elders, a venerable Indo-European institution, did check the powers of the chief. In Scheria, according to *The Odyssey*, the lesser Phaiakaian *basileis* used to summon their chief, Alkinoös, to council, and he was subject to the will of those over whom he presided. By contrast, Athena expected Telemakhos simply to call a council of Achaian heroes and announce his own plan. These councils work differently, but they represent alternate configurations of power within a homogeneous set of political and social arrangements. Limited chieftaincy is a key element in later reconstructions of the Greek past, and other factors, like the public assembly, played a part too. But the existence of these advisory councils is important, since political society—the life of the *polis*—required negotiation between ruling elements and thus, in the course of events, prevented absolute rule from being the norm.

POLIS AND TYRANNY

Only in the mid-seventh century (ca. 650 B.C.E.) does a constitutional law express the full political and legal concept of the *polis*. It first appears in an inscription from Dreros on the island of Crete, which shows how early this new form of governance had to grapple with regulating political succession and restricting continuous control of the city-state. After invoking divine protection, this law restricted the principal magistrate (*kosmos*; pl. *kosmoi*) in four important ways: (1) it prevented the magistrate from holding that office again until ten years had elapsed; (2) it fined violators double the amount of any judgments they had imposed; (3) it apparently made violators ineligible for any public office for as long as they lived; and (4) it abrogated any enactments put in force by the violators. These provisions were enforceable, on oath, by three groups, namely, the entire annual board of *kosmoi* (as most scholars believe), the *Demioi* (lesser magistrates representing the *dêmos*, or people), and the Twenty of the *Polis* (exact function unknown).

The injunction against repeated tenure of the principal magistracy, combined with the ten-year wait between successive terms of office, limited the power of specific individuals and particular interests within the ruling circle. The first editors of this law thought these restrictions showed that it was designed to prevent using the office of *kosmos* as a first step to becoming tyrant (*tyrannos*), but other scholars thought it was a deliberate check on the power of individual families. The distinction, however, between a law against tyranny and one designed to constrain powerful families is not absolute. Some tyrants, like Kypselos at Korinth, the unsuccessful Kylon at Athens, and—in the sixth century—Peisistratos at Athens, and perhaps even Pittakos in Mytilene, could claim a degree of aristocratic privilege, although they also may have been among the aristocracy's newest members. In addition, tyrants' families became involved in their rule, because tyrants "made provisions only for their own immediate interest as regards both their own persons and the greater glory of their families . . ." (Thucydides 1.17). Tyrants tried to legitimize themselves by establishing a fixed hereditary right of political succession within their families, and thus exceeded established practice.

In a sense, the law from Dreros resolved the problem of uncertain political succession that confronted Homeric chiefdoms like Odysseus's. The Homeric poems never use the words "tyrant" or "tyranny," as Hippias of Elis noted in the fifth century B.C.E., but they illustrate, as in Mentor's speech, the difference between abusive rulers and good ones. Chieftaincy was heritable in a limited way and defined by established privileges, but tyranny was not: "As Hellas became more powerful and acquired still more wealth than previously, tyrannies became established in most cities, while revenues became greater (but previously there had been hereditary chieftaincies [*patrikai basileiai*] based on fixed privileges) . . ." (Thucydides 1.13,1). In many *poleis*, tyranny existed side by side with the last stages of establishing strong political institutions, and tyrants, who ultimately relied on force, arguably prompted the final stage of *polis* development.

In the seventh century, civic magistrates had replaced chiefs at Dreros, Sparta, Athens, Korinth, and other places. Tyranny, however, reaffirmed and extended the old idea that the position of the chief was somehow heritable, by attempting to institutionalize their aristocratic family rule within the structure of the developed *polis*. This is the tyrant's dilemma. At Korinth, the founding tyrant, Kypselos, came to power because his father married into the ruling Bakkhiad clan. In the second generation, the tyranny degenerated because Periander, Kypselos's son, manifested several characteristics of the wicked tyrant: wanton use of force, abuse of women, and dogged determination to establish hereditary rule. To secure the succession of a powerful son, Periander wanted his own exiled younger son, Lykophron, to come home to rule. Periander used his daughter to plead with her brother because she literally embodied the family's interest in preserving its wealth and power intact. Lykophron agreed to switch places with Periander, but the terrified Corcyrans thwarted the plan by killing Lykophron, and the tyranny limped through its third and final generation.

In seeking the status of royalty in their own societies, the tyrants looked backward. They appealed to powers and privileges that belonged to a traditionally conceived past rather than to the new world in which institutions of state and written law were becoming increasingly important. Hence, tyranny was both destabilizing and retrogressive, often provoking a reaction that led to a more fully political society.

SPARTA

It is generally thought that the constitutional law inscribed at Dreros signals an era in which developing *poleis* concerned themselves with creating civil laws, whether these were written or not. Many *poleis* had legendary lawgivers (*nomothetai*) like Lykourgos at Sparta. The so-called Lykourgan reforms are dated to circa 650, in part because they represent a similar constitutional phase at Sparta. Nothing certain can be said about Lykourgos, not even whether he was divine or human, and very little is known about the reforms themselves. Spartan laws were unwritten, and only public officials needed to engage in acts of literacy.

According to tradition, Lykourgos made Sparta virtually into an armed camp. His laws supposedly provided the rigid structure of the educational system (*agôgê*), under which young Spartan males and females were trained to take their respective places in an authoritarian and militaristic state. But this description has been called a mirage. Tradition also identifies Sparta's constitution as a *rhetra* (Pronouncement) of Delphi, to which a rider, passed by the assembly, was added. But the authenticity of the oracle and its supposed rider, as reported by Plutarch, is dubious. Archaeology shows that the material and cultural life of Sparta was similar to that of other contemporary *poleis*, and the origin of this mirage is traceable to the fifth and fourth centuries B.C.E. when Sparta was more vulnerable to its enemies and propagandized on behalf of its self-proclaimed invincibility. Nevertheless, by the mid-seventh century B.C.E., Sparta had achieved its characteristic form of *polis*.

Sparta was distinctive. It was the single *polis* controlling the region called Lakedaimon, and Lakedaimonians had three castes. The Spartan elite formed the citizen body. At bottom was a "captive" population called helots. In between came the *perioikoi*, a free people "living throughout" Lakedaimon in towns that had autonomy over strictly local affairs, but deferred to Sparta in foreign relations and other matters. Sparta was famous for its rough treatment of helots, and a secret organization, the Krypteia, enabled young Spartan males to harass the helots and kill their outspoken leaders.

The first helots were a subject population in Lakedaimon, whose origin is lost in the Dark Age. But by 700 B.C.E., Sparta had expanded its territory across the mountains into Messenia and reduced its population to a condition of helotry. According to tradition, the first Messenian War occurred in 735–716, and afterwards the Spartan males returned home to find a generation of illegitimate children born to the Spartan women who had stayed behind. These offspring were the Partheniai, who were sent to found Taras in 706.

The Messenian territory was divided into lots that were assigned to individual male Spartans. Messenian helots worked these lots, and fixed amounts of foodstuffs were shipped to Sparta to support the citizen owner, the common mess to which he belonged, and any other family obligations he had. Whatever the Lykourgan Reforms were, Sparta's tripartite social stratification and characteristic political and social institutions were in place by circa 700 B.C.E.

The story of the Partheniai also reflects the independence of Spartan women, who enjoyed greater freedom and public prominence than their Athenian counterparts. Just as the Krypteia marks the evolution of a rite of passage for boys as they become men, so the maidensongs of Alkman describe rites of passage for girls as they become women. It is hard to generalize from the scraps of evidence, but the Hyakinthia festival, a rite of passage for both males and females, may reflect the greater importance of women here than elsewhere.

The developing *polis* checked the power of the chiefs first, and then transformed their power into a civic magistracy. Atypically, Sparta not only retained its chiefs, but developed a dual kingship (thus a dyarchy, not a monarchy). The two kings acted as a check on one another, and they participated in a council of elders, the *gerousia*, which provided a further check on their authority. The kings also answered to a board of five annually elected civic magistrates called *ephors* ("overseers"), who were elected by a popular assembly (*apella*) attended by any adult male Spartan. Since any adult male Spartan could also be elected *ephor*, this magistracy represents an antiaristocratic impetus within the *polis*. The structure of the ephorate addresses a problem like the one at Dreros, since nobody could be *ephor* twice. It is noteworthy, then, that tyranny never developed at Sparta and that, in the sixth century, Sparta acquired a reputation for suppressing tyrannies (see Chapter 4).

ATHENS

Athens was slow to experience certain major developments in the Archaic period. In the eighth century, a protracted war between Kalkhis and Eretria drew in Greeks from all over the world, but not from Athens. Despite widespread colonization after 750 B.C.E., Athens did not found a colony until the end of the seventh century. Overpopulation frequently motivated colonization, but population pressure in Attika was perhaps less severe because of its large territory and, possibly, because Athenians who failed to pay their debts were sold into slavery. In fact, the founding of a colony at Sigeion circa 600 may indicate that the population crisis had reached Attika, even though its first effects were offset, as the burial evidence suggests, by an epidemic that devastated the population and ultimately may have contributed to the end of debt-slavery. Athens also lagged behind in its internal development: the annual archonship had begun in 684/3, and tyranny succeeded there long after the rest of Greece.

The first recorded political event in Athenian history is an attempt at tyranny. In an Olympic year circa 632 B.C.E. and with the backing of the Delphic oracle, Kylon, a disaffected aristocrat and former Olympic victor, seized the Akropolis and tried to become tyrant with help from a band of supporters that included both his friends and foreign mercenaries supplied by his father-in-law, Theagenes, tyrant of nearby Megara. The attempt failed, and the usurpers were besieged on the Akropolis when the Athenians, who were celebrating a festival in the countryside, dropped what they were doing, and came on the run the minute the alarm was raised. After pinning down the rebels, the magistrates brought the sorry affair to a quick conclusion.

The magistrates tried to avoid the sacrilege of having the usurpers, who had sought asylum, die on sacred ground. They led the conspirators off under truce, presumably to stand trial, but the prisoners were killed, some while in custody, others at the altars of the Semnai Theai ("the Awesome Goddesses" Demeter and Persephone). Megakles, the eponymous *archon*, together with his family, the Alkmaionidai, was held accountable and eventually expelled from Attika as Accursed and Sinners Against the Goddess Athena. The living Alkmaionidai were driven out forever, and the bones of the dead were exhumed and deported beyond the border. Kylon's assault on the Akropolis, the composition of his band, the killing of his supporters, and the punishment of the Alkmaion-idai as a group, all suggest sharp in-fighting among the important aristocratic families of the day. Control of the Akropolis, the role of public office, and the magistrates' accountability to the goddess mark important new developments, but also highlight the continuing status of mixed divine and public institutions in relation to claims of aristocratic family privilege.

Athens had no written law code when Kylon stormed the Akropolis. Circa 621/0 B.C.E. Drakon drew up Athens's first written law code, and he simply systematized, codified, and wrote down the traditional practices of the oral law. In early times, when right was tied exclusively to birth, property, and wealth, the commonest penalty for any infringement was death. As a result, death was Drakon's most frequently specified punishment, and later generations claimed that his harsh code was written in blood. There is no reason to believe that Drakon's laws were accepted at once or were universally enforceable within their expected jurisdiction.

Drakon's one surviving law (on unpremeditated, involuntary murder) names the public agencies responsible for trying the case, lists the rights and privileges of the victim's next of kin and the order of their precedence, defines the role of the fictive kinship group (the phratry or brotherhood), and specifies the punishments. The law delineated the proper spheres of state and family in avenging murder and also penalized the killing of a homicide who had abided by the terms of his exile. Those families in Attika with established influence and those on the verge of earning it stood to gain or lose the most from Drakon's law. Kylon's revolt shows that some powerful families could still mobilize a significant military force in their private interest. Likewise, the powerful Alkmaionidai brought about their return from exile within a generation or two. Plutarch emphasized the hostilities of the powerful families, and he explained the aftermath of the revolt as the continuing struggle of a divided *dêmos* led by rival kin coalitions.

According to Plutarch, during the disturbances following the crisis, the Megarians seized Nisaia and drove the Athenians out of Salamis. The border dispute between Athens and Megara was a long, drawn-out affair, and as early as circa 632 B.C.E. the tyrant of Megara had intervened in Athenian affairs by backing Kylon. The costly war continued until Sparta intervened. The outcome of this intervention is uncertain, but the events contributed directly to Solon's rise to political power, which culminated in his eponymous archonship of 594/3. Thus, Solon's activity—

the last consequence of Kylon's conspiracy—occurred not much before 600. If the Alkmaionidai were exiled around the time Solon retook Salamis, that would explain why Solon also invited Epimenides the Cretan to conduct a ritual purification of Athens.

The expulsion of the Alkmaionidai also contextualizes Solon's later law requiring individuals to take sides openly in times of political crisis (*stasis*). Far more dangerous than being on the wrong side of a crisis in a politically conceived society is the opportunist who does not know what is worth fighting for and what is not. Solon's law on *stasis*, in effect, politicized the resolution of public quarrels by bringing differences out into the open, articulating the exact points of disagreement, and creating a political obligation to resolve them.

CONCLUSION

The Archaic age was a long period of important but slow change, with briefer, more intense moments of rapid social transformation at either end. It saw major innovations in society, religion (see next chapter), and technology. The development of *polis* institutions, and particularly of written law codes, undermined the aristocratic privileges of the old Homeric chiefdoms, as shown by the constitutional law from Dreros and by the invention of elective magistracies like the *kosmoi* (Dreros), *ephors* (Sparta), and *archons* (Athens), as well as by the so-called Lykourgan Reforms at Sparta and by Kylon's failure and the expulsion of the Alkmaionidai at Athens.

Drakon's law on homicide, with its firm demarcation of family and state roles in avenging the victim, addressed the same set of problems in aristocratic politics at Athens. It restricted retaliatory behavior between families and tried to regulate the endless cycle of blood feuds that disrupted the community from time to time. But as a written document, his code gave Athens a basis for even-handed and consistent treatment of similar acts over time. Law allows for social order, written law for measurable equity in similar cases, and political authority for both continuity and orderly change under the law. These concerns, which are implicit in Athens's first written law code (as they are also in the law from Dreros), became explicit in the programs, policies, and poems of Solon a generation later.

In the Archaic period, tyranny coincided with the emerging *polis*. Tyrants and would-be tyrants exerted force on their own behalf in a traditional aristocratic, and conceptually Homeric, manner of asserting family interest. But an ethnic, and eventually ethnocentric, vision of communal life surfaced as Greece transformed itself by inventing the *polis* and its institutions. In the sixth century B.C.E., Athens created a strong opposition between *tyrannos* and *basileus* that left a lasting mark in oratory and political philosophy, while Sparta managed to avoid tyranny at home and conspicuously resisted its establishment abroad. Through it all, the Homeric poems continued to be sung and to generate an idealized image of a Panhellenic past that united and identified Greeks everywhere.

SUGGESTIONS FOR FURTHER READING

Ancient Sources

Herodotos. *The Histories*. Translated by Robin Waterfield. 1998. Oxford and New York: Oxford University Press. A modern, readable translation with excellent notes.

Hesiod. *Theogony*. Translated by Apostolos Athanassakis. 1983. Baltimore: The Johns Hopkins University Press. A lively translation with excellent notes of Hesiod's account of the Greek gods.

Homer. *The Iliad*. Translated by Robert Fagles. 1982. New York and London: Penguin Books. An exciting modern translation of Homer's first great epic poem.

Homer. *The Odyssey*. Translated by Robert Fitzerald. 1990 (1969). New York: Vintage Classics. A moving modern translation of Homer's second great epic poem.

Thucydides. *The Peloponnesian War*. Translated by Robert B. Strassler. 1996. *The Landmark Thucydides: A Comprehensive Guide to the Peloponnesian War*. New York: The Free Press.

Modern Studies

Andrewes, Antony. 1956. *The Greek Tyrants*. London: Hutchinson's University Library. This small book is still the best and most concise introduction to tyranny in the Archaic period.

Calame, Claude. 1997. *Choruses of Young Women in Ancient Greece: Their Morphology, Religious Role, and Social Function*. Translated by Derek Collins and Janice Orion. Lanham, MD: Rowman & Littlefield. Calame concentrates on choruses of young women, but illuminates the broader development of Greek choral poetry generally. He treats non-Spartan and Spartan rituals to recapture the importance of women in Greek society.

Cartledge, Paul. 1979. *Sparta and Lakonia: A Regional History, 1300–362 B.C.* London and Boston: Routledge & Kegan Paul. A first attempt at a regional history, and not always easy to read, the first half of this book provides a rich and comprehensive analysis of the Spartan territory from prehistory to the end of the Archaic period.

Finley, M.I. 1978. *The World of Odysseus*, 2d ed. New York: Viking. Finley defends and augments his arguments about the social importance of gifts, concrete expressions of "honor," and the "post-Homeric" dating of the Homeric world.

Fisher, N.R.F., and Deborah Boedeker. 1998. *Archaic Greece: New Approaches and New Evidence*. Oakville, Conn.: D. Brown Book Co. The authors capitalize on the intersection between historical and archaeological studies, and indicate the new questions and methods that are emerging.

Fitzhardinge, L.F. 1980. *The Spartans*. London: Thames and Hudson. In clear terms, students can examine the paradox of the rich material and literary culture of Archaic Sparta and the later "myth" and "mirage" of Spartan invincibility.

Homan-Wedeking, Ernst. 1966. *Archaic Greece*. Translated by J.R. Foster. London: Methuen. A survey of basic artistic and other material remains necessary for understanding the period.

Morris, Ian. 1987. *Burial and Ancient Society: The Rise of the Greek City-State*. Cambridge: Cambridge University Press. A study of the scholarship about death and burial, analyzing the actual burial record, and relating changes in it to the development of the *polis*.

Murray, Oswyn. 1980. *Early Greece*. Atlantic Highlands, NJ: Humanities Press. "Early Greece" means more than the Archaic period in this detailed account of the evidence and the sophisticated methods scholars use to interpret the period.

Osborne, Robin. 1996. *Greece in the Making: 1200–479 B.C.* New York: Routledge. A richly illustrated examination of the epigraphic, archeological, and historical sources on early Greece.

Snodgrass, Anthony J. 1980. *Archaic Greece: The Age of Experiment*. London: J. Dent. This famous book used archaeology to answer historical questions and to demonstrate the nature of interactive change, while also presenting a unified interpretation of this period.

Starr, Chester. 1961. *The Origins of Greek Civilization 1100–650 B.C.* New York: Knopf. Starr modernized the study of the Dark and early Archaic periods by using pottery sequences to pin down relative chronology where there was no absolute chronology; he reframed the questions of historical continuity between the Mycenaean and Archaic periods.

———. 1986. *Individual and Community: The Rise of the Polis, 800–500 B.C.* New York: Oxford. Starr summarizes his thinking about the historical development of the *polis* as the social history of individuals and groups interacting in the midst of identifiable historical changes.

Figure 3. Cult statue of Zeus at Olympia, circa fifth century B.C.E. Reconstructed drawing by Friedrich Adler, from Alt-Olympia by Wilhelm Dörpfeld, Band 2, Appendix 22, originally published Berlin 1935, republished by Otto Zeller, 1966. Used by permission.

3 ————————————————————————————

The Olympic Games and the Rise of Greek Religious Institutions

INTRODUCTION

Development of religious institutions accompanied the political and cultural changes in the Greek Archaic age serving further to define Hellenic identity. The games for Zeus at Olympia date to 776 B.C.E., when recording of victors begins. These Olympic Games for Zeus were the most outstanding of numerous other competitions, many of which remained local. All were occasions for honoring the deity through excellence in athletic competition, which was only one of several forms of worship that developed in the Archaic period.

Religious belief and practice were at the heart of all Greek activities. Many religious practices had Mycenaean roots, notably the agricultural rites which include celebration of adult women's and men's sexuality and fertility, and the rites marking significant stages and transitions in a person's life. But the momentum of Panhellenism in the Archaic period, that thrust toward encompassing all Greeks in a distinct Greek identity, profoundly shaped evolving ritual practices. Besides the games honoring a deity, all the newly established or redefined practices—temple building and accompanying rites, hero cults, mystery rites, and hymn composition—also aggrandized nearby cities and the group's cultural identity. Sanctuaries became centers not only for religious devotion, but also for cultural definition. Originally, Olympia was principally aligned with western, Dorian Greeks—which may explain why the Dorian Spartans frequently won the earlier games, while eastern, Ionian Greeks held their cultural rites for Apollo, god of music, light, and prophecy, on Delos. The sanctuaries most attended by all Greeks were those for Apollo at Delphi and for Demeter, goddess of agriculture and the earth, and Persephone, goddess of the underworld and spring, at Eleusis.

Greek belief was polytheistic, worshipping a variety of deities for different occasions and purposes. Archaic literature establishes twelve principal gods as living on Mt. Olympos, the highest peak in Greece, who were collectively referred to as "the Olympian pantheon," meaning "all the gods." Zeus, god of the sky and thunder, was the ruler of the gods, accompanied by his wife, Hera, goddess of marriage. With the exception of Aphrodite, goddess of love and erotic desire, an early genealogy of the gods, the *Theogony* by Hesiod (late 8th century B.C.E.), portrays the nine other gods of the Olympian pantheon as either siblings or offspring of Zeus: Demeter; Poseidon, god of the sea, horses, and earthquakes; Athena, goddess of wisdom, the olive tree, victory in battle, and crafts; Apollo; Artemis, goddess of animals and the hunt; Hermes, the messenger god; Dionysos, god of the vine, wine, and the theater; Ares, god of war, and Hephaistos, god of fire and crafts. While the *Theogony* and other Greek literature present many stories about the deities, these stories do not always reflect their importance in actual worship. In fact, some stories appear to contradict the important role individual gods and goddesses held in the worship of the people. This is especially true when considering the worship of female deities, whose rites were highly significant, often central to life in the community, but the male-oriented stories often portray them as secondary figures. Hence archaeology and documentary evidence are essential for understanding ancient Greek religious practices and beliefs.

Some common features characterize the diverse forms of Greek worship developed in the Archaic religious renewal. Greek temple construction made the building the new center for worship in the deity's sanctuary. However, worshipers did not congregate inside the temple, which was literally the house of the deity, in which the deity resided and which held the cultic statue. Rituals took place outside, around the altar that stood at the eastern end of the temple. Although the games for Zeus at Olympia date to the early eighth century B.C.E., his temple was not built there until the mid-fifth century, almost 350 years later. Interestingly, the earliest temple on the most sacred site at Olympia was for the goddess Hera (begun ca. 650). In fact, the oldest and most important

Greek temples were for Hera at Argos and Samos. Sixth-century temples for both Hera and Artemis were the largest and served as prototypes for other temple buildings. The later Temple of Artemis at Ephesos was considered one of the seven wonders of the ancient world.

That the earliest temples were built for goddesses reflects another common phenomenon: that most sites were originally sanctuaries for female deities, including those that later became major sites for the worship of gods, such as Zeus at Olympia and Apollo at Delphi and Delos. Stories reveal this shift, including the *Homeric Hymn to Apollo*, one of the earliest hymns (possibly eighth century), which relates Apollo's birth on Delos and violent takeover at Delphi. These changes may represent what occurred when the Greeks with their patriarchal ideas settled among and conquered the goddess-worshipping peoples living there. While many of the stories about the gods depict gender hostility and antagonism among the deities, especially between Zeus and Hera, the king and queen of the Olympic pantheon, other evidence shows the importance of the worship of both female and male deities. Temples were built, hymns composed, and religious rites developed to honor all deities. Sanctuaries and rites for both gods and goddesses were central to Greek life, and both served to mark important religious, personal, cultural, civic, and agricultural occasions. Heroic cult sites, created at a hero's death to commemorate achievements in that hero's life, honored a hero and heroine together; the earliest is the shrine for Helen and her husband Menelaos at Therapne near Sparta.

Two important rites established in the Archaic period—which drew participants from all over the Greek world and which represent in distinctive ways the importance of both male and female deities—were the games for Zeus at Olympia in the western Peloponnesos, held every four years, and the Eleusinian Mysteries, the annual rites for Demeter and Persephone at Eleusis about thirteen miles northwest of Athens. Both epitomized a type of religious practice: the Olympic Games, then, as now, represented the highest test of athletic skill. Fulfilling a different spiritual need, the Eleusinian Mysteries, the most important of the mystery rites, offered initiates supreme blessings in this life and the next. And both provided the only occasions for a Panhellenic truce, so that participants could safely travel to the sanctuaries.

Two stories attribute the founding of the Olympic Games for Zeus to an illustrious forebear: the Panhellenic hero Herakles, or Pelops, for whom the Peloponnesos ("Pelops' island") is named. Opening with sacrifices and prayers to Zeus, the games initially consisted of only a 200-meter sprint (just over a third of a mile). In time, the competitions included separate boys' races, men's running, horse and chariot races, boxing, wrestling, a fierce combination of the two that also included kicking and strangling, and the *pentathlon*, "a contest of five events": running, long-jump, wrestling, and discus and javelin throws. The Greeks reckoned time by the Olympic Games, using their four-year cycle as a common standard of dating for all Greek communities.

The cherished prize of the Olympic Games was a wreath of wild olive leaves, and the victors set up valuable trophies to Zeus in appreciation for their victory. Numerous victory odes by the fifth-century poets Pindar and Bakkhylides praise the victors, comparing them to culture heroes and often relating mythological stories of the victor's homeland or gods. Due most likely to the origins of the games in men's rituals for Zeus, women were not allowed at the Olympic Games, under penalty of death, but women could compete in horse races and receive the prize if the horses they owned won. Women, however, celebrated their own, older rites for Hera at Olympia. The fifth-century temple for Zeus became a standard of the classical style, and the colossal (over forty feet high) gold-and-ivory cultic statue of the god seated on his throne was also considered one of the seven wonders of the ancient world. It was created by Pheidias, who also sculpted the colossal gold-and-ivory standing statue of Athena for her temple in Athens, the Parthenon. Recording of victors in the Games ceased in 217 C.E., and after almost 1200 years the Roman Emperor Theodosius abolished the Olympic Games in 393 C.E.

While the Olympic Games for Zeus illustrate one type of civic ritual activity, one that elicits and honors physical excellence as divinely endowed qualities, the worship of Demeter and Persephone in the Eleusinian Mysteries fulfilled a need for personal, spiritual expression, providing personal blessings in this world and salvation in the next. Since initiates vowed not to reveal the secrets of the rites, little is known about them. Unlike most forms of Demeter worship, which were for women only, these rites also welcomed men. Athens's domination of Eleusis from the eighth century B.C.E. enhanced the city's increasingly powerful position.

Preliminary rites for the Mysteries were held in Athens and included a ritual procession in which sacred objects were carried to Eleusis. For the next several days, initiates celebrated the gifts of the two goddesses in hymns, dances, and possibly enactments of their stories. The height of their experience was the *epopteia* ("the sacred viewing"), which secured for the initiate the goddesses' blessings. Though mystery rites for other deities existed, the Eleusinian rites developed into the most important religious practice in the ancient Greek and Roman worlds, celebrated by

Greek and Roman poets. Like Olympia, Eleusis was ultimately destroyed by Christian zealots in the late fourth century C.E.

The range of religious practices seen in these very different rites for Zeus and for Demeter and Persephone illustrates the varied and important ways religion imbued all aspects of Greek life.

INTERPRETIVE ESSAY
Jennifer Larson

In mainstream modern Western culture, religion is something to be kept separate and apart from public life. Prayer in schools or at public events like baseball games can be controversial, especially if it seems to be sponsored by those in authority. We think of religion as a private matter, a question of personal belief. Nothing could be further from the way the ancient Greeks experienced religion. As polytheists, the Greeks worshipped a large number of different gods and heroes, and people in different cities and towns gave more emphasis to some gods than others. In Athens, people conferred special honors on their city goddess Athena, and in Korinth people especially worshipped Aphrodite, goddess of love. But the system of gods and heroes, the stories about them, and the basic modes of worship like prayer and sacrifice were common to all the Greeks. Far from attempting to keep religion out of the public life of their cities, they never came to think of prayers or sacrifices as a special category of activity that could be separated from other aspects of daily life. Ancient peoples, including the Greeks, wanted the gods to favor them and help them in their daily struggles, large and small. Therefore, ancient individuals, families, and cities sacrificed to the gods and consulted their oracles (forms of prophecy) before undertaking any important or dangerous task.

Ancient Greek religion also differed from most modern ones in its focus on acts not beliefs. No one but a few philosophers ever questioned that the gods existed; the proof of their power was easy to see in the way Zeus sent the rains every year, Poseidon made the earth shake, and Aphrodite caused people to feel sexual desire. In an age before science and modern technology, people had little control over their lives or understanding of what caused illnesses or crop failures. They assumed that powers stronger than themselves dispensed good and bad fortune. Therefore, one should try to gain the favor of these powers through prayers, gifts, and festivals celebrating the gods. The gods and heroes desired this recognition from humans, and they became angry if the proper acts were not performed in their honor. While individuals and families might pray privately in their homes, the most important religious acts were performed in public, by the community as a whole, and coordinated by the *polis*. Each had its own unique religious calendar, with festivals for nearly every month of the year. These festivals were an integral part of daily life, and it is often difficult to separate "religious" activities from what we would consider profane or secular ones. For example, comedies and tragedies were performed as part of the Lenaia (January–February) and the Great Dionysia (late March), city festivals in honor of the god Dionysos. This combination of public entertainment (which could be quite crude and boisterous in the case of comedy) with religion is one that many today would find odd.

GAMES AND GREEK CITIES

Another such combination is religion and sports. The Greeks loved to compete, and they held contests in everything from music, poetry, physical beauty, and handicrafts to athletics—again, in the context of festivals for the gods. The best known of the sports competitions took place at the Panhellenic sanctuaries of Delphi, Nemea, Isthmia, and above all, Olympia. (Panhellenic means they were open to all Greeks.) In addition to the competitions at the Olympic festival, there were numerous sacrifices. Pausanias, who visited the site of Olympia in the second century C.E., gives a list of more than fifty altars in the sanctuary (Pausanias 5.13.8–15.10). On the third day of the festival, there were no competitions; instead a sacred procession and great sacrifice to Zeus, the patron god of the sanctuary, were held. Zeus's altar was a huge mound of ashes built up over time from the thousands of sacrificial offerings burnt there since the traditional founding date of 776 B.C.E.

The festival at Olympia, then, goes back to the eighth century B.C.E., a time before the great cities and temples were built, before Greek culture as we now picture it had come to exist. Modern historians see an important relationship between the rise of Panhellenic sanctuaries like Olympia and the development of the *polis*, the characteristic form of political organization in Archaic and Classical Greece. In the eighth century, people began to leave expensive offerings at sites like Olympia: bronze figurines, jewelry, and tripods, three-legged cooking vessels like those Homer says the heroes possessed. All of these objects were showy and valuable, much more impressive than the usual gifts of pottery and clay figurines. What might explain the new popularity of Olympia?

Around this same time, exciting changes were taking place. The Greeks were becoming more prosperous and their population was growing. They traded extensively with other peoples in the Mediterranean and gradually became aware that, in spite of all their differences from one another, all Greeks spoke the same language, worshipped the same gods, and told stories about the same heroes of the past. They began to recognize that they shared a common culture and to see non-Greek peoples as different (and inferior) to themselves. At the same time, different groups of Greeks, and, especially at this period, aristocratic families, were highly competitive with each other. They needed neutral places where they could come together to express their cultural pride and unity as Greeks, but at the same time advertise their prestige, wealth, and power to each other.

Panhellenic sanctuaries like Olympia, located outside the political boundaries of any one city, proved to be ideal for these purposes. The athletic competitions themselves, especially the chariot races, recalled the great achievements of individual heroes; there were no team events. But an athlete's victory brought great glory to his hometown. As cities became wealthier, they paid for monuments to be erected at Olympia to hold and display their offerings to the gods and to commemorate their victories. These projects, too, were competitive, and each city tried to outdo the others in its offerings. In this way, cities gained a sense of identity, even of "team spirit," that might otherwise have taken much longer to achieve.

Just as the privileges of citizenship were limited to males in the new city-states, so the Greek athletic festivals were largely restricted to men. At Olympia especially, married women were not only barred from competing, but were kept out of the sanctuary on pain of death during the athletic events. According to Pausanias (6.20.9), an exception was made for the priestess of Demeter, who was given a special seat at the Games. In addition, the important rites of Hera at Olympia seem to have stimulated the development of a separate athletic event for girls, a footrace. This was organized by a committee of sixteen adult women, who were also responsible for weaving a robe for Hera's cult statue. On the day of their competition, the girls were permitted into the Olympic stadium, where they ran a 500-foot footrace. Winners were given an olive-leaf crown, a portion of the cow sacrificed to Hera, and the right to set up inscribed statues in the sanctuary to record their victories—all privileges similar to those enjoyed by male victors (Pausanias 5.16.1–4). On the other hand, the girls' race was deliberately set apart in conspicuous ways. Unlike the boys and men who competed in the nude, girls wore knee-length tunics to protect their modesty, and their race was 500 feet in contrast to the males' 600, thus discouraging any comparison between male and female performances. Pausanias, moreover, is the only ancient author to mention the Heraia, or women's games, at Olympia, which suggests that the female victors never achieved fame, as the men and boys did, and that the girls' race was considered a minor event, perhaps of only local importance.

RELIGIOUS INSTITUTIONS

Most of today's religious denominations have some type of central authority, a group of clergy who guide believers and decide how resources should be used. There also tends to be a hierarchy in religious matters: priests, rabbis, or other clergy are often specially educated for their positions, devote their entire lives to religion, and have more authority than laypersons. In ancient Greece, religion was much less organized and systematic. Priests, both male and female, presided over sacrifices, prayers, and festivals to the gods, but generally they received no special training for this role. Most priests and priestesses filled this role only "part-time," not as a lifelong occupation. There was no organized "church" hierarchy, no creed, and no sacred scriptures. Instead, there were traditions, passed down through hundreds of years in families and villages. Tradition itself was a powerful authority, which discouraged change in the rituals, even in the absence of written instructions such as prayer books. Where people believed that the welfare of their community depended on pleasing the gods through their ritual activities, they also tended to believe that any change in the established ritual might be dangerous.

Historians have suggested that some rituals, such as the widespread festival of female fertility, the Thesmophoria, have roots in the Neolithic period (see following discussion). At the same time, some change was inevitable, and religious rituals adapted with the needs of the community. We can confirm these changes by looking at the differences in the Thesmophoria practices in geographically separated communities in the Greek world. Everywhere the festival honors the agricultural goddess Demeter, and everywhere it involves the sacrifice of pigs and a temporary seclusion of the community's women, who gather in the sanctuary and exclude all men. But while the Athenians celebrated their Thesmophoria in the month when grain was sowed, the Thebans held theirs as much as two months earlier. Some places, such as Paros, had a complementary men's group that worshipped Demeter separately from the women.

TEMPLE AND IMAGE

Given the lack of a central religious authority, we might well ask who made the important decisions when it came to religion, especially when these decisions involved a large investment of wealth. For example, who paid for the monumental stone temples to the gods that began to be constructed in the seventh century B.C.E.? In early Archaic times, Greek religious observances were primarily the concern of individuals, families, and "clans." Since major religious occasions required a heavy investment of resources (for example, a sacrifice of 100 oxen), they were generally controlled by elite, aristocratic families such as the Bakkhiads who ruled Korinth. As the Greek city-state developed, however, and began to reduce the power of these aristocrats in favor of the citizen body as a whole, it also took over the responsibility and prestige of the major religious festivals. The festival calendars mentioned above were created by cities as they reorganized the rites that had previously "belonged" to separate villages, clans, and outlying districts. In this way, political power and religious authority went hand in hand.

Temples were not required for the worship of the gods and goddesses. Prayer and sacrifice were conducted at outdoor altars placed within special sacred areas marked by boundary stones. Early Greek temples were small buildings of wood and mud-brick with thatched roofs, constructed in a variety of shapes and sizes. By the seventh century B.C.E., a common idea of what a temple "ought to" look like began to spread. The early temples of Poseidon at Isthmia, and of Hera at Argos and Samos, were rectangular buildings 100 feet long, with stone steps and a row of wooden columns running all the way around. Soon these wooden structures were replaced by stone, as thatched roofs gave way to heavier terra-cotta tiles. The Greeks probably learned the basic plan of the colonnaded temple and the methods of cutting and working stone from the Egyptians, who also built temples in which to house the images of their gods. Temples were the largest and most expensive, labor-intensive building projects in Greek society. But if the gods did not demand temples for their worship, why did the Greeks spend so much time and money on them?

It is no coincidence that these massive temples began to be built at the same time the *polis* was becoming the characteristic form of Greek urban life and gaining control over public religious expression. Cities could advertise their power and prosperity by building one of these grand temples, a project that took many years to complete but provided the citizens with an impressive, permanent symbol of their city. Today we recognize certain cities by famous landmarks: Paris has the Eiffel Tower and Sydney its opera house, but even now Athens is best known for the Parthenon, the grand temple of Athena atop the Akropolis (see Figure 5). As cities today build stadiums, convention centers, and museums in competition with one another, Greek cities keenly competed to build the best temples.

Building projects were begun in prosperous times, often with the spoils taken from rival cities defeated in war. This was the case with the temple of Zeus at Olympia, which the Eleans built during the fifth century B.C.E. after their war with Pisa. If all this sounds rather far removed from religion, keep in mind that the Greeks did not clearly distinguish "religion" from other aspects of their lives. Temples served many functions, some of which we would call religious and others political. An example of this political use comes from the second century C.E. biographer Plutarch's *Life of Perikles*, the principal leader of Athens in the second half of the fifth century B.C.E. (see Chapters 6 and 7), in his account of Perikles' building program in Athens, which used monies from the cities held subject under Athens's empire. Plutarch says that Perikles proposed the building projects so that those who were not serving in the military might also have an opportunity for public service and be able to share in the city's wealth. Virtually every Athenian laborer and businessperson could benefit from the massive influx of wealth into the economy provided by these projects (*Perikles* 12.1–4). Yet Plutarch also tells a story to illustrate the goddess Athena's interest in the projects undertaken in her honor. During the building of the Propylaia, or gates to the Akropolis, one of the best workers fell and was seriously injured. The goddess appeared to Perikles in a dream and prescribed a course of treatment for the worker, who was quickly healed. To commemorate this event, Perikles set up a bronze image of Athena Hygeia (of Health) on the Akropolis (*Perikles* 13.8).

The temple's utilitarian purpose was to house an image of the god or goddess, and as temples became more elaborate, so did the images. By the time Zeus's temple at Olympia and Athena's Parthenon in Athens were built, the sculptor Pheidias had brought the art of the cult image to its climax (see Figure 3). Known as the "maker of gods," Pheidias created monumental statues for these temples using ivory and gold over a wooden core. The statue of Athena, like the Parthenon itself, was as much a political statement of Athenian imperial power as a religious one. It was adorned with such a large amount of gold that Perikles considered it part of the Athenian treasury. In spite of the admiration aroused by this statue, the Athenians reserved their greatest respect and reverence for the ancient wooden image of Athena, which was kept in the Erechtheion. This statue, thought to have fallen from the sky, possessed its own clothing and ornaments. These were removed in a special festival every year and the statue was dressed in a new gown woven by the women and girls of the city. The contrast between these two images is striking: one was a recent, sumptuous work by human hands that expressed the Athenians' gratitude to their city goddess for their prosperity, and at the same time advertised their power to all onlookers. The other image had little intrinsic value, but its age and supposed divine origin established it as the focal point of the Athenians' relationship with their goddess. Both images are crucial to our understanding of this relationship.

ORACLES AND DIVINATION

The Panhellenic sanctuary at Delphi, established early in the eighth century B.C.E., has already been mentioned as part of the circuit for athletic contests honoring the gods. But at Delphi this function was secondary to that of the famous oracle of Apollo. The term "oracle" refers both to places like the Delphic sanctuary, where humans could ask advice of a god, and to the messages thus received. The Greeks believed that certain gods, such as Zeus and, above all, Apollo, could be consulted for help with human dilemmas. Many methods were used to determine the will of the gods. At the oracle of Zeus in Dodona (northern Greece), priests interpreted the rustling of leaves in the oak tree grove or the behavior of sacred doves. Other oracles operated through the dreams of the person consulting them, who must sleep in the sanctuary in order to obtain an answer. The method used in Delphi was the most spectacular: questions were addressed to a female medium known as the Pythia, who was inspired by Apollo and transmitted his answers during an ecstatic trance.

The Delphic oracle became the most prestigious in the Greek world, partly because in the early period its responses were limited to important matters of state (later we find more individuals asking about their private problems). As city-states developed, they experienced many internal and external conflicts. In particular, there was tension between the small land-owning elites and the rest of the growing population, who needed to earn a living. Therefore, *poleis* found it useful to submit their planned courses of action to the oracle to find out whether they had divine approval. Usually those consulting the oracle approached it with a detailed proposal, such as a plan for colonization, or the draft of a new law code. The oracle then indicated whether or not it would be better for the city to proceed. In this way the religious authority of Apollo could help developing cities to reach a consensus by putting a divine "seal of approval" on their plans. For example, in the seventh century B.C.E., the Spartans submitted their reformed constitution to the oracle and received the answer: "it is better in every respect to obey these laws." And when the Athenians consulted Delphi about their plans to colonize Thrace (ca. 560), they were told to appoint the aristocrat Miltiades as leader of the expedition.

The importance and prestige of the oracle grew as more cities found its aid useful. Eventually, however, cities reached a point in their development when they no longer needed the support of the god for political decision making. While the prestige of the oracle remained very high, the questions addressed to it became less overtly political. Apollo was viewed as the final authority on questions pertaining to religious practice: could a sanctuary rent out its lands if the proceeds were used to repair the temple? (No.) Should the holy dress and ornaments of Artemis's statue be made larger and finer? (Yes).

This description of the Delphic oracle does not correspond very closely to literary and mythic accounts such as the Oedipus saga. In Sophocles' *Oedipus the King*, the oracle is said to have predicted the future, that Oedipus was fated to marry his mother and kill his own father. In Herodotos's writings, the Lydian king Kroisos consults the oracle on whether he should invade the Persians and receives a deceptively ambiguous answer: if Kroisos attacks, he will destroy a great realm. Of course the hapless king misunderstands Apollo and brings about the fall of his own kingdom (Herodotos 1.53). These stories about the oracle demonstrate the widespread awe and respect in which it was held, and the related view that the Pythia usually spoke in enigmatic riddles. In fact, very few of the recorded responses of the "enigmatic" or predictive type are considered authentic by scholars.

MYSTERIES

The Greek polytheistic system permitted a great deal of personal choice within certain limits. One must not neglect the gods of one's own family, tribe, or city, but once these obligations were upheld, people could pick and choose deities to whom they wished to give special attention. Those who were ill might visit the healing god Asklepios, those who wished to conceive might bring gifts to the nymphs (female nature deities), and so on. The so-called Mystery rites, which offered secret knowledge to the believer and required initiation, were another example of this optional religious activity. They began in early Archaic times as local or family rites, but gradually spread and increased in popularity. Most focused on "salvation," which could refer either to immunity from illness, shipwreck, and other dangers of earthly life, or to an escape from the ultimate fate of death.

The Greeks held many conflicting views about what happened to a person after death. The most common was that the "shade" of the dead person left the body and traveled to the underworld, a gloomy place where the shade, a mere remnant of the former personality, must remain indefinitely. Many of the Mystery rites offered the hope of a blessed afterlife in contrast to this sorrowful one. The Homeric *Hymn to Demeter* (ca. 7th century), which tells the founding myth of the Mysteries at Eleusis, says, "Whoever on this earth has seen these is blessed, but he who has no part in the holy rites has another lot as he wastes away in dank darkness." Nobody knows what the initiates at Eleusis were shown in the climax of the ritual, but the experience was a deeply meaningful one. The Roman orator Cicero, who was himself an initiate, said that the Eleusinian Mysteries showed one "how to live in joy and die with better hopes" (*On the Laws* 2.36).

At an early period, Athens, Eleusis' neighbor, took control of the rites, once the province of prominent local families. Each member of this partnership benefited the other, for the prestige of the Mysteries drew Greeks from far and wide to visit Athens, and Athens, in turn, financed improvements to the sanctuary to accommodate the growing number of initiates. Eleusis achieved a fame equal to that of the great Panhellenic sanctuaries, and it was similar to these in that its rites were open to all who spoke Greek. In contrast to the great athletic festivals like the Olympic Games, however, eligibility for participation at Eleusis did not follow the model of male citizenship; both women and slaves could become initiates.

The Bakkhic or Dionysiac Mysteries were other important rites with varied membership. Unlike the Mysteries of Demeter and Persephone, which were anchored at the town and sanctuary of Eleusis (and had lesser counterparts in certain other places), the Bakkhic mysteries were attached to no specific sanctuary. In the Archaic and Classical periods they were conducted by traveling priests and priestesses, who offered initiation in the towns and cities they visited. Because of the lack of external control, the Bakkhic rites varied over time and in different areas, but they seem to have shared the concepts of ecstatic communion with the god Dionysos through joyous dancing, consumption of wine, and, in some cases, sexual activity and symbolism.

The goal of initiation, as at Eleusis, was salvation from death, in this case on the model of Dionysos. Secret teachings about the god told that he had been killed and devoured by the Titans, who were then struck by Zeus's thunderbolt. From their ashes the human race was formed, mortal yet containing the divine spark of the god. Meanwhile, Dionysos himself was raised from the dead. Initiates apparently did not expect a bodily resurrection of the kind recounted in the myth, but instead relied on their newfound knowledge to give them a privileged place in a blessed afterlife. In the tombs of Dionysiac initiates from Crete, Thessaly, and Italy, amulets of inscribed gold foil have been discovered that provide the deceased with special instructions for navigating the underworld. The soul is to drink from the spring of Memory (Mnemosyne), not that of Forgetfulness (Lethe), as most souls do. When asked its identity, the soul must answer: "I am a child of Earth and starry Heaven, but my race is of Heaven alone." Thus the initiate reveals his or her knowledge that the human soul partakes of the heavenly nature of Dionysos. Through this recognition, a different experience of the afterlife awaits.

WOMEN AND GREEK RELIGION

The development of the *polis* and other forms of Greek political self-definition in the eighth century B.C.E. gave rise to the concept of the citizen, one who exercises political rights such as voting, speaking in the assembly, or holding office. But who counted as a citizen? For the most part, the category excluded immigrants, slaves, and women, all of whom were thus cut off from participation in public life. Especially for elite women, who were discouraged from meeting with strangers, or even being seen by them, in line with Greek concepts of female sexual honor, roles in public life were extremely rare. The one exception lay in sacred traditions, which could not easily be changed and which often predated the concept of the citizen and the restrictive mores of the Archaic and Classical periods. One example is the ancient custom that gods be served by priests and goddesses by priestesses, just as male animals were sacrificed to gods and female ones to goddesses.

In Athens the priestess of Athena Polias held an important public position. The historian Herodotos (5.72) tells an interesting story of events in 508 B.C.E., when the Spartan Kleomenes, who was interfering in Athenian politics, attempted to enter Athena's sanctuary on the Akropolis. He was confronted by the priestess of Athena, who warned him that as a stranger he must not set foot in the holy place. He ignored the priestess, but after attempting to hold the Akropolis with his men, he was expelled from the city. For Herodotos, the priestess acted as the conduit through whom Athena made known her wishes. In this role, but not as a woman per se, her participation in the incident was appropriate. As if to underscore this attitude, Herodotos does not record the priestess' name.

During the course of their lives, even girls and women who were not priestesses had the opportunity to participate in many public activities honoring the gods. These were often correlated with the stages of life: young Athenian girls could honor the virgin goddess Artemis by traveling to the coastal sanctuary at Brauron to participate in footraces around the goddess' altar. All over the Greek world, adolescent girls danced and sang as members of choruses during festivals for Artemis, Apollo, Hera, and other deities. For the most part, only adult women participated in festivals for the grain goddess Demeter and the wine god Dionysos. In certain festivals for Demeter, such as the Thesmophoria, men were excluded from the ritual. Some scholars believe that the roots of these festivals go back to the Neolithic advent of agriculture, a period when the fertility of the natural world and that of women were believed to be closely linked and interdependent.

Our most important sources for these rituals are postclassical, but they report that the women of the Athenian Thesmophoria, primarily matrons, camped for three days by Demeter's temple, living a "primitive" lifestyle. After this period of purification, they gathered at a pit where certain objects (the remains of sacrificed pigs, along with models of male genitals made from dough) had been thrown down to rot in a sort of sacred compost heap. These objects were retrieved from the pit and placed on the altar; they would be mixed with the seed grain for that year in order to make it fertile. The ritual symbolically reenacts human sexual intercourse by placing together the pigs (a symbol of the female genitals) and the dough models of male genitals. By excluding men, it also reaffirms the idea that the women have a special, mysterious role to play in maintaining prosperity for the community.

HEROIC RELIGION

We usually think of Greek religion as being focused on the twelve Olympian gods: Zeus, Hera, Athena, Apollo, and so on. In fact, the picture was a good deal more complicated than that. Greek polytheism was an "open system" that could admit new gods and allow the worship of others to atrophy over time. The pantheon included a large number of lesser, local, or foreign deities, such as the birth goddess Eileithyia, the triple-formed witch goddess Hekate, whose worship was imported from Asia Minor, and the goat-footed Arkadian god Pan, who watched over flocks. It also included the heroes and heroines, a class of powerful beings who were closely associated with the mythic heroes of Greek epic.

The practice of worshipping heroes seems to have arisen in the eighth century B.C.E., when (as we have seen) the Greeks were realizing that they shared a distinct culture, and the concept of the city-state was being developed. An important part of the process of self-definition for these Archaic Greeks was discovering links between themselves and the legendary men and women who had lived in the heroic age. Modern scholars associate this Age of Heroes with the civilization of the Mycenaeans, the Bronze Age inhabitants of Greece who built great palaces and monumental stone tombs (see Chapter 1). Although the Mycenaean culture was destroyed in a series of earthquakes and wars beginning around 1200 B.C.E., the eighth-century Greeks were surrounded by its ruins, and they possessed a rich tradition of epic poetry about the men and women of old, their close relations with the gods, and their deeds in the Trojan War and other famous conflicts.

Each district of Greece had its own native heroes; for example, Odysseus was from Ithaka, Achilles from Thessaly, Theseus from Athens, Helen and Menelaos from Sparta. Aristocratic families traced their descent from these heroic men and women, and cities too could claim heroes as their symbolic ancestors. Because the heroes had been so powerful in life and had belonged to a generation close to the gods (many of them had a god or goddess as a parent), the Greeks concluded that they were still powerful in death, able to exert influence from the site of their tombs. In this sense, the heroes' power emanated from their remains, so the worship of the heroes was similar to the medieval European veneration of saints. Many ancient tombs were singled out as the resting places of heroes or heroines, who received offerings and sacrifices adapted from those given to the dead and the gods of the underworld.

Sometimes a given tomb or burial mound became a focus of worship even though its occupant was unknown. In this case, offerings were simply made to "the hero." In other cases, a hero became so popular that his worship was no longer tied to a tomb, but spread throughout the Greek world. This happened with Herakles, the mighty Dorian hero, and the healer Asklepios, both of whom were eventually considered gods.

The worship of the heroine Ino likewise spread far, although the city of Megara claimed to possess her tomb. Ino supposedly met her death by leaping into the sea, where she was transformed into a sort of sea-nymph or mermaid. Already in Homer we hear of her, "Ino-Leukothea of the fair ankles, daughter of Kadmos, who was once a mortal speaking with the tongue of men, but now in the salt-sea waters has received honors from the gods" (*The Odyssey* 5.333–35).

In spite of these special cases, however, the most important function of these heroic cults was to help the Greeks in each individual city-state and town to construct a narrative about their own past, much as today in the United States we teach children stories about George Washington, Paul Revere, or Betsy Ross in order to illustrate the unique identity and values traditionally attached to American citizenship.

CONCLUSION

This discussion of Greek religion emphasizes two basic points: first, that Greek religion differed from the major monotheistic religions of the modern world in ways that make it seem quite alien. It had no creed, scriptures, or clerical hierarchy; it focused on acts (prayer, sacrifice, and festivals) rather than beliefs; and it evolved over time without planning by a central authority. Second, what authority did exist was connected with the developing political systems of the early Archaic period, especially the *polis*. The religion of the Classical period, with its grand temples, Panhellenic sanctuaries, festival calendars and heroic worship, resulted from a process of co-development, during which each city shaped its religious customs to reflect its own identity, so that an inhabitant of Thebes had different traditions from someone living in Korinth. At the same time, Greeks settled all over the Mediterranean recognized a common religious heritage.

SUGGESTIONS FOR FURTHER READING

Bremmer, Jan. 1994. *Greek Religion*. Oxford: Oxford University Press. An excellent, concise introduction to Greek religion.

Calame, Claude. 1997. *Choruses of Young Women in Ancient Greece: Their Morphology, Religious Role, and Social Function*. Translated by Derek Collins and Janice Orion. Lanham, MD: Rowman & Littlefield. A classic study of the ways in which dances by groups of girls contributed to ancient Greek religious worship, and the role these "choruses" played in the girls' transition to adult status.

Fantham, Elaine et al. 1994. *Women in the Classical World*. Oxford and New York:

Oxford University Press. A fine, well-illustrated introduction to women's lives in Greece and Rome, including discussion of their roles in religion.

Golden, Mark. 1998. *Sport and Society in Ancient Greece*. Cambridge: Cambridge University Press. Detailed discussion of Greek sport as depicted in poetry, art, and archaeology. More advanced than Swaddling (below).

Kraemer, Ross. 1992. *Her Share of the Blessings: Women's Religions Among Pagans, Jews, and Christians in the Greco-Roman World*. New York and London: Oxford University Press. A widely used introduction to women's religious roles in the ancient Western world.

Larson, Jennifer. 1995. *Greek Heroine Cults*. Madison: University of Wisconsin Press. An exploration of heroine worship among the classical and Hellenistic Greeks, for advanced students.

Meyer, Marvin W., ed. 1987. *The Ancient Mysteries: A Sourcebook*. San Francisco: HarperCollins. A collection of primary texts describing the mystery religions of Greco-Roman antiquity.

Morgan, Catherine. 1990. *Athletes and Oracles: The Transformation of Olympia and Delphi in the Eighth Century BC*. Cambridge: Cambridge University Press. Detailed study from an archaeological perspective of the origins of these Panhellenic sanctuaries, for advanced students.

Pausanias. *Guide to Greece 1: Central Greece*. Translated by Peter Levi. 1971. London and New York: Penguin Books. A translation of Pausanias's description of his travels in Greece.

Plutarch. "Pericles." In *The Rise and Fall of Anthens: Nine Greek Lives*. Translated by Ian Scott-Kilvert. 1960. London and New York: Penguin Books. A translation of Plutarch's life of the popular fifth century B.C.E. Athenian leader.

Swaddling, Judith. 1999. *The Ancient Olympic Games*, 2d ed. Austin: University of Texas Press. A revised edition of the standard introduction.

Zaidman, Louise Bruit, and Pauline Schmitt Pantel. 1992. *Religion in the Ancient Greek City*. Translated by Paul Cartledge. Cambridge: Cambridge University Press. The social role of Greek religion, with special emphasis on theoretical approaches to its study.

4

Sparta and Athens: Political Conservatism and Political Experimentation

INTRODUCTION

As seen in Chapter 2, Sparta's and Athens's political and historical experiences of the early Archaic period differed vastly. Both *poleis* responded to internal unrest by distributing governance more broadly among a greater but still restricted number of newly defined "citizen men." These new citizens expressed their views in popular assemblies that had varying power relations with the traditional royal and aristocratic rulers. The Spartans established a complex system of dual kingship, five *ephors*, city magistrates who dominated community affairs, and the *homoioi* ("equals"), the elite group of citizen men granted a voice in governance. This system worked in Sparta and over time provided a strong foundation for social cohesiveness among elite Spartans. By contrast, Athens fully experienced the political turmoil characterizing many Greek *poleis*, ranging from tyrannies to radical political reforms.

During the sixth century B.C.E., the Spartan social and political system, attributed to the legendary lawgiver Lykourgos, took definitive shape. Its society centered on its military, Sparta concentrated on controlling its enslaved helots and on expanding its hegemony over the rest of the Peloponnesos. Although they failed to impose their rule, awe of Spartan military might have enabled Sparta to dominate the alliances they

Figure 4. Athenian coin, early fifth century B.C.E. Head of Athena, obverse, Owl and Olive, reverse. Silver. © Copyright The British Museum.

formed with other cities of the Peloponnesian League and to control their political affairs. As *the* Greek superpower of the day, the Spartans were sometimes called on to oust tyrants, winning the title of "defenders against tyranny," a factor ultimately important for events in Athens.

Until the end of the sixth century B.C.E., Sparta's cultural life continued strong, though its focus became increasingly split. Except for participation in the Olympic and other games, its external cultural activity waned: poetry, pottery, bronzework all declined. Internally, Spartan ritual and cultural life remained strong, expressed largely through its choruses, separate and sometimes combined groups of young and adult women and men who sang and danced at festivals, in rituals, and as part of their educational system. However, we know of the importance of Sparta's internal cultural life only from references by other authors not from any Spartan records.

Sparta's increasing isolationist focus is well exemplified by its response to coinage, which was introduced by Lydia, whose coins were made of electrum, an alloy of gold and silver, naturally found there. The earliest evidence of Greek coins, made of silver, was found at the Temple of Artemis at Ephesos (ca. 600 B.C.E.). By mid-sixth century, Athens, Korinth, and Aigina acquired coins, their use spreading quickly throughout Greece. Coinage transformed *polis* economies, boosting trade and commercial activities, enabling mercantile powers like Athens and Korinth to prosper. In contrast to the economically expansive and cosmopolitan thinking of these commercial powers, Sparta forbade coinage, depending rather on older forms of barter exchange and its slave-based economy, which further fueled its idiosyncratic reputation.

As Sparta's distinctive identity became more firmly entrenched, Athens experienced a more turbulent sequence of events. In 594 B.C.E., Solon was elected principal *archon*, and he was granted extraordinary power to address the tensions caused by continued clan fighting and growing discontent by an increasingly indebted and indentured peasantry. Though many specifics are unknown, Solon may have outlawed debt servitude and affirmed peasant ownership of their small land-holdings. He created a four-tier system of wealth, which determined a male citizen's participation in *polis* affairs, and a new council of 400 (the *boulê*, later expanded to 500) to decide important matters. A statesman, who was called one of the seven sages of ancient Greece, Solon also recorded in several poems his thoughts about Athens's political situation and the legislation he enacted, providing a rare glimpse into an ancient politician's thinking.

Although late fifth century B.C.E. Athenians and subsequent observers credited Solon for preparing the ground for the development of democracy, initially his reforms were highly controversial, and aristocratic wrangling for political leadership in Athens continued. After three tries in fourteen years and with changing aristocratic alliances, in 546 Peisistratos established a tyranny that lasted with his sons until 510. Considered a capable ruler, who allowed traditional governance of *polis* affairs to continue, Peisistratos expanded Athenian hegemony, built or refurbished numerous public works, buildings, and temples, and solidified Athenian control over the Eleusinian Mysteries (see Chapter 3). He promoted the poetry festivals for Athena and drama festivals for Dionysos as Panhellenic celebrations that attracted international visitors to Athens, thereby transforming Athens into Greece's cultural center.

These activities continued in the first years after Peisistratos's death (527 B.C.E.), under the rule of his two sons, Hippias and Hipparkhos, who pursued a vigorous building program, including construction of the Temple to Olympian Zeus in Athens and the altars to the Twelve Gods, and further enhanced Athens's cultural prominence by bringing well-known poets to Athens. The traditional Athenian aristocratic clans, however, were chafing under tyranny, wanting a greater share in governance. Allegedly inspired by a jealous love triangle between the two principal conspirators and Hipparkhos, a group of conspirators plotted to kill Hippias at the Panatheneia, when men in the processions customarily wore arms. The plot went awry, but the chief conspirators—Harmodios and Aristogeiton—killed Hipparkhos (514). Although Harmodios was killed on the spot, and Aristogeiton died later under torture, the two became celebrated as heroes who overthrew the tyranny, and statues were erected and poems composed in their honor. At the time, however, the assassination of Hipparkhos resulted in increasing severity and suspicion under Hippias's rule.

Kleisthenes, a member of the traditionally powerful Alkmaionid family, had served as an *archon* in the early days of Hippias's rule (525–524), and emerged to challenge Hippias. When later in exile in Sparta, he urged Sparta's help in ousting Hippias, appealing to Sparta's reputation as the enemy of tyrants and relying on the support of Delphic pronouncements (that were no doubt influenced by Alkmaionid contributions to Delphi). In 510, the Spartan king Kleomenes helped the Athenians remove Hippias. The political uncertainty following the tyranny's overthrow became the fertile soil for the development of what would prove in time to be a radical political institution, the beginnings of *dêmokratia* ("democracy," "rule by the people"), the distinctive Athenian governmental experiment.

Kleisthenes was instrumental in designing and establishing these major political innovations. Like Peisistratos, he rallied popular support with proposals aimed at weakening his aristocratic rivals for rule in Athens. After defeating his Spartan-backed political rival, he instituted what came to be known as the "Kleisthenic reforms." These enactments reorganized the older clan affiliation of four aristocratic tribes and their control of governance into a system of ten new tribes composed of many *demes* ("counties") in which every male citizen in Attika was registered, and which formed the basis for their political and military activity. The reforms did not initially modify the assembly or the offices of the nine *archons*, but it did expand the *boulê*, the council, to 500, with fifty representatives from each of the newly established tribes. And Kleisthenes instituted ostracism, a way of voting out of office, and temporarily exiling from Athens, any leader by a majority of voting citizens, a strategy invoked periodically in Athenian history. While women, foreigners, and slaves were excluded from formal political participation, a larger base of citizen men now experienced a direct and active role in their own governance. Although he did not use the term *dêmokratia*, Kleisthenes is credited as the founder of "democracy" for the Athenian *polis*.

While Kleisthenes may have been seeking only to introduce ideas that would gain him support and secure the place of the Alkmaionids in ruling Athens, the result of his reforms had far-reaching effects. Over the next two decades, additional reforms increasingly strengthened Athens's democratic political system: command of the army and navy transferred from a single commander to a board of ten generals elected by the citizens, and the nine *archons* were selected by lot from a pre-elected slate—rather than by general election—a practice designed to ensure a fairer outcome. Further expansion of both the democratic system and the Athenian ideological adherence to their unique and radical democratic ideas took place over the course of the fifth century. Yet the foundation for both was established at the end of the sixth, by the overthrow of tyranny and the institution of Kleisthenes's major political reforms.

At the dawn of the fifth century B.C.E., which historians call the Classical period, Sparta and Athens stood at the crossroads of evolving definitions in their roles and in their relationships to one another. Sparta stood solidly in its unique political and cultural identity and was unquestioningly the major military power in the Peloponnesos and in much of Greece. Athens, buoyed now by its increased cultural prominence and its newly instituted and apparently effective overthrow of tyranny and reforms to the political system, looked to expand its own political hegemony and to further advance its culturally central role. Events in the fifth century would afford the Athenians many opportunities to do so.

INTERPRETIVE ESSAY
Donald Lateiner

As has been seen in earlier chapters, the Hellenes, who have never called themselves "Greeks," constructed identities based on ethnic perceptions (Dorians, Ionians), regional associations (Argives, Boiotians, "Athenians" throughout Attika), and city-states (Megarians, Syracusans). The Hellenic world contained hundreds of self-governing communities tied together by a common language, common gods and rituals, and a shared way of life. They were, however, separated by geography and competing claims for land and markets. Although we often focus on the dynamic Athenians and Spartans and their pervasive influence (as our sources force us to do), most Greeks never dreamed of networking alliances and led the lives of farmers and fishermen. This placid continuity characterized most decades of ancient Greek history.

The Greeks liked to associate major changes and even trends with specific events and heroic persons. Current historians tend to diminish the moment and the person in favor of faceless economic, social, and even environmental pressures. In the cases of Sparta and Athens (and their unusually large city-state territories and transboundary influence), for events that happened before political archives and law codes were inscribed and history written (that is, before the middle of the fifth century B.C.E.), Hellenic poets, philosophers, and historians, as well as fruit sellers in the *agora*, generally explained their truly peculiar institutions as great men's responses to great crises. Spartan Lykourgos responds to the Messenian wars and the need for adequate troops; Athenian Solon responds to aristocratic factionalism and exploitation of the peasantry; and Athenian Kleisthenes responds to factional civil war and threats of foreign (Spartan) invasion. This tendency of Greek historical explanation complicates modern reconstructions of political, social, and economic causes, issues, and solutions.

COLONIZATION

External colonization, especially to the west, continued through the sixth century B.C.E., but less intensively than before. To the east, contacts with Kroisos the Lydian and then with the Achaemenids of Persia limited Greek land-grabs but promoted luxury trade in two directions. To the west, the Greek colonies expanded their territories' hinterlands—sometimes in the face of native opposition—and declared their Hellenism through temple and sanctuary displays, monumental sculpture, purchase of Attic pots, minting of their own coins, and participation at the Panhellenic sanctuaries like Olympia and Delphi. Parian colonists on Thasos in the northern Aegean developed a lively and profitable metallurgical industry on their island and on the Thracian mainland opposite. In Italy and Sicily, on the western margin of the Greek world, local inhabitants were sometimes assimilated, sometimes chased away or eradicated, as newcomers divided city land on a grid, and agricultural lands were parceled out to the new Hellenic settlers.

Sanctuaries were built throughout *polis* territory to affirm colonial incorporation and extend control from the *polis* center. The architectural monumentalizing of political and religious life in temples and meetinghouses differentiated the Greeks from other nations in the less civilized western Mediterranean. The Greek Selinuntines of western Sicily appreciated this and built more temples in the sixth century B.C.E. than any other city, a course that the Akragantines, nearby to the east, also followed. The Athenians played catch-up under Peisistratos, but maintained their often parochial regional style and touted their local mythological subjects such as Theseus. These archaeologically significant cities had large territories, extensive trade, and plenty of local limestone, sometimes marble, to build with.

Many cities contributed to the permanent architecture and sculpture of the festival sanctuaries. Here *kudos* (reputation) was gained in athletic and musical competitions between aristocratic individuals and symbolic capital amassed among cities vying to erect prestigious structures. The small "treasuries" that cities erected in Panhellenic shrines became more standardized. At the same time, painted Attic pottery became the ostentatious luxury of choice among the rich in Greek, Etruscan, and other display-driven cultures. The standardization of form of the large Doric temple and the *kouroi* and *korai* (adolescent boys and girls) statues demonstrated increasing familiarity with other cities' architectural progress and acceptance of canonical forms.

On the other hand, every city quickly developed its own coinage and images—such as Aiginetan turtles, Athenian owls, and Ephesian bees. The electrum, silver, and gold coins were struck on a variety of weight-standards and metals and in small denominations. These facts suggest that the new medium was developed for internal needs, such as wages,

taxation, and payments of debt, in order to keep wealth local in mone-
tarized exchanges and not to employ it for distant trading. The cities of
the regions of Boiotia and Ionia fitfully entered into monetary unions,
but coinage was regarded as proof of local *polis* autonomy.

Internal colonization might be a more fruitful term for Spartan and
Athenian responses to population pressures and social developments.
Their political and geographical reorganizations in the sixth century
B.C.E. made them the leading powers in the next. Sparta emerged as the
most powerful single city at the end of the century, but not so powerful
that it could command Athenian obedience. The remarkable cooperation
of the two cities in the face of the aggressive expansion and attacks of
the Persian Empire in the early fifth century fired Herodotos to write his
monumental history, one distant progenitor of the book that you read
today.

SPARTA

The Spartan revolution provided a very small group with a very great
advantage: the Dorian *homoioi* or "equals" were freed from the otherwise
universal Hellenic need to farm for their sustenance and for a tradable
surplus, that is for their living. The helots or "captives," native peoples
(Messenians) conquered and enslaved by the Spartans, were tied to the
land and subject to execution without trial; they had to produce food,
drink, textiles, and so forth for the Spartan ruling class. The *perioikoi* or
"dwellers around" guarded the borders and engaged in some trading
activities—a better but still apolitical and subordinate existence. The
three groups with their families constituted the peoples of Lakonia or
Lakedaimon, a large and fertile valley in the Peloponessos. The Spartans
also controlled the next valleys east and west.

The gross inequality of this arrangement, however, forced the restricted ruling class to be forever on guard against possible revolt. The
Spartan military machine required lifelong training and a "ready-alert"
preparedness of all the full citizens and, thereby, a diminution of ordinary Greek joys and freedoms. While aristocrats and theorists in other
cities, including and especially Athens, might wistfully admire the effi-
ciency and rationality of Spartan life, they did not try to emulate it.
Herodotos, the first historian and the first anthropologist, writes with
both awe and scorn of the values and acts inculcated by the Spartan
rhetra (law code) and the rest of their "constitution," most of which was
not a written document, but one very stringent in its demands on the
hoplite (heavily armored) troops both on or after campaigns.

The consequences on family life, political options, and social institutions can barely be calculated, since the Spartans had little time or desire to write for a local audience. The distant admirers or critics often had to speculate about the exact origin and nature of unique Spartan institutions such as the dual kingship, the limited "up or down," "yes or no" options of the Spartan Assembly (*apella*), the partibility of Spartan property (inheritance rules), the secret police (*krypteia*) in the vast territory under Lakonian control, the role of Spartan women, and the nature of Spartan marriage and male "eating clubs" (*syssitia*).

Sparta's huge territory and subject population required her to lead aggressively in networking defensive arrangements against internal and external threats to her status quo. The Peloponnesian League was a painstakingly constructed series of bilateral alliances with Sparta as *hegemon* (leader). Argos may have been the original enemy; Athens became the menace in the fifth century.

Spartans attributed their *eunomia* ("good order") to Lykourgos and his *rhetra*, which distributed power among two kings (commanders in war like Kleomenes and Demaratos), a Council of Elders (30 men in the *Gerousia*), and an Assembly (*apella*). The five powerful *ephors* (annually elected overseers, who chaired the Assembly) probably were a later innovation (ca. 700?) among a people who usually denied any changes to their supposedly original law code. The constitutional settlement (like all Spartan history) is poorly known, because the Spartans did not write about it, and those who did write elsewhere described it for their own tendentious purposes (e.g., Plato). It may have been one radical moment or a series of changes (ca. 750–600 B.C.E.). Spartans divided their youth into age classes, both boys (from age seven) and girls. Another arbitrary grid imposed on the population of the southern Peloponnese (besides the legal statuses and military units), the Spartans used these age divisions to organize and train future soldiers, to promote their competition and their bonding, and to ration privileges.

Spartan aggression against neighbors and their permanent oppression of Messenia in part justified Spartan society—to Spartans. Some aggressive wars and helot-terrorizing may have been motivated so that the leadership could explain and justify harsh Spartan internal disciplines to their own people. Spartan self-definition had as its reverse the "othering" of dogskin hat–wearing Messenian helots and scorn for "effeminate" foreigners, such as "perverted" barbarians, Ionians, Athenians, and others.

Nevertheless, Sparta was precocious and forward-looking in constitutional change, foreign affairs, and even, for a time, in art. Its poetry, pottery, and ivory work were exceptional in the seventh and sixth centuries. The Spartan "mirage" of perfect obedience and stability, of little talk, less trade, and big sticks is largely a later and foreign invention, hard to distinguish from genuine historical traditions. Nevertheless, Spartan cultural and commercial eminence wanes in the sixth century. For instance, Lakonian authorities consciously rejected coinage. Modern students of ancient history argue about the motives for such decisions.

EXPERIMENTAL POLITICS

Americans assume that a written constitution is "natural." It is aberrant in world history, as is democracy, and neither the Lakedaimonians nor the Athenians had one. But the Athenians did write down and inscribe many laws—among the oldest surviving is one fragment of Drakon's severe penalties for murder and vendetta and arrangements for peaceful compensation.

Many Hellenic communities faced difficult jockeying for power among merciless Mafia-like elite clans and temporary groupings. In the sixth century, power conflicts often arose out of pre-existing, self-declared empowerments. Blood was often spilled deciding what governing bodies and officers (often many) would run a *polis*. What limits could be established on powerful individuals and on magistrates' and councils' authority? The majority of the people were not regarded as the ultimate authority by anyone, but they were a possible source of support for competing factions. Political parties did not exist, nor did platforms or ideologies.

Politics—the art of convincing the community that you know best what is in its own interest—occupied the energies and assets of many Greek families. Justice and wisdom were useful slogans, but the elite poets Theognis of Megara and Alkaios of Lesbos proudly assert a higher loyalty to clan or class. In a world of violence, the laws preserved or described for us slowly replaced disintegrating clan control and sometimes obsolete customs. Written rules emerged over time to protect property and contracts more equitably. Greek writers on the past—historians and also dramatists, philosophers, orators, and moralists—attributed most archaic law codes to inspired "individuals." History, the present recording of the useful past for future inquirers, occupied friends of the political winners, once it had been invented. It explained and justified as it selected and recorded.

TYRANTS

Not all elite-group conflicts found peaceful solutions. The Greeks' name (but a borrowed Lydian word) for the unexpected successful power grab of an individual was *tyranny*. The tyrants' successful coups and *modi operandi* varied greatly but they share certain characteristics. The new phenomenon has a bad reputation in Greek literature, modern discussion, and current political discourse because (1) men who came to power irregularly caused understandable resentment in their literate, defeated competitors; (2) the tyrants themselves did not have time to write memoirs or sufficient security to retire from "service"; (3) their defeated adversaries did have unwanted leisure and motive; (4) the tyrants rarely lasted more than two generations and were not locally replicated; and (5) their considerable achievements were usually buried in complaints about their unconventional—but often "legal" by contemporary standards—methods.

The defeated competitors abused the tyrants' parentage, lawless methods, bizarre sex lives, tricky treachery toward former allies, and all around arrogant insolence—in other words, the spectacular success of someone smarter, or at least "luckier," than they. But most Greek cities experienced tyranny, so we must discover what were the tyrants' attractions and their functionality. What did they do right, to attain power and to keep it? In Korinth, Mytilene, Athens, and Samos, for instance, in the sixth century, Periander, Pittakos, charismatic Peisistratos, and Polykrates promoted judicial access instead of the selfish interests of local *padrone* (men of authority whose will was enforced); they furnished jobs for essential programs of infrastructure such as water supply, roads, and docks; and they promoted *polis*-wide community identity and jobs by building cutting-edge, lavish temples, holding festivals that brought in drachmas—silver and gold coins. The tyrants redistributed elite wealth, sometimes introducing coinage or establishing a citywide emblem, and they raised their home-cities' profiles by making them centers for commerce and tourism. Peisistratos, for example, revamped the Panathenaia, the major festival to Athena in Athens, with athletic, music, dance, and poetry competitions; he established Athenian control over the Eleusinian Mysteries, and under his tyranny the dramatic festival to Dionysos began and the Homeric poems were probably written down in the form that we have them today. All of these accomplishments served to build Athens into the cultural center it would become for many generations.

For the tyrants, the personal was the political; their success marked the breakdown of aristocratic self-regulation in city management. Their ultimate failure, however, reflected their lack of a consensual political solution and the Greek drive for institutional rather than personal forms of policing and government, which were not democratic, however, except in Athens.

ATHENS

Athens was never typical but always relatively well recorded because of its later widespread literacy. We next consider the power elites' struggles that brought in, first, the surprise tyrant—his three reigns, two sons, and eventual overthrow. Later, a new kind of conflict-containing government emerged, one that the Greeks came to call "democracy," or government by the people. While Spartans systematically excluded from political participation all but the full warrior-landholder class, Athenians colonized their own *khora* (countryside) and networked their fellow citizens into the government and the army. Thus, they included the farming smallholders, the little people of Attika who grew olives, grapes, and wheat as much as thirty miles from the actual urban area of Athens.

Attika possesses some geographical unity, a triangular peninsula ringed by ridges of low mountains, but the area could have developed into several *poleis*. A "national Attic identity" was equally fostered by different regimes—oligarchy, tyranny, and democracy—and took well over a century to become fully realized. A generation before Solon, Kylon, an aristocratic Olympic victor, had tried and failed to establish a tyranny (632). Drakon, if he was a historical person in fact, attempted to control local competitive violence and persuaded the Athenians to pass laws (621?) that exacted severe penalties for murder and vendetta, at least. Solon was appointed *archon* (ruler for one year) in 594 to respond to various crises. We cannot identify precisely what problems he faced or what solutions he introduced, but his program of reform can be partly reconstructed from fragments of his reflective poetry.

The elite clans, such as the Alkmaionids and the Philaids, and their allies were feuding among themselves, ruling their fellow Athenians as permanent inferiors with favoritism to their dependents and little mercy for others. Solon tried to establish procedures for moderating political conflict among the leading families. He wanted the poorer Athenians to have access to land ownership and recourse to stable court procedures. He did not abolish debts (and currency did not yet exist in Attika), but he may have redistributed some land from the very powerful to the tenants farming it; these were otherwise landless peasantry, perhaps even sharecroppers (*hektemoroi*). Solon protected property by allowing the disadvantaged sectors of the population some ownership of it. He provided some reduction of existing burdens (*seisachtheia*). Perhaps he canceled agricultural labor obligations of a seasonal sort. Solon promoted the Attic export of wine and olive oil as well as the manufacture of fine decorated pottery. And he created a Council of 400 (the *boulê*), but the new institutions did not adequately quell systemic political instability.

Peisistratos, a former Polemarch or General, needed three tries (561–556, 555?, 546–527) before he succeeded in installing himself indefinitely as Athenian tyrant. Once established, Peisistratos secured his position by cutting deals with fellow kin-group leaders. He married the Alkmaionid Megakles's daughter, and he sent the Philaid Miltiades out to govern colonists in the north Aegean Chersonese. He did not ignore existing institutions or familial power webs, but he encouraged them to serve and share in his administration, and he networked with foreign powers (for instance, Eretria, Argos, Naxos, Thessaly, and Thebes), as well as with other tyrants.

Revenues were based on silver mined in Thrace and on a tithe tax, later reduced to a twentieth. Peisistratos or his sons replaced local family symbols on the silver with the head of Athena and her familiar owl (see Figure 4), and he manipulated real and symbolic capital successfully. Throughout Attika Peisistratos co-opted local *padrones* by respecting their land-holdings and giving them administrative responsibilities. He encouraged cultivation of poorer land in Attika, and he sent out circuit judges to the people for swifter conflict resolution. Peisistratos and his sons Hippias and Hipparkhos (527–514) encouraged connectedness to Athens by promoting the Panathenaic festival. This support included temple building, holiday drinking and meat-eating, and poetic, musical, and athletic contests. This ideological extension of "Athenian-ness" throughout Attika created a larger pool of raw materials, military manpower, technological know-how, and artistic talent. Economically, it enlarged both markets and resources, adding at least Salamis and Eleusis to the territory of Attika. Under Peisistratos, an ancient Greek superpower in embryo arose, which first expanded with acquisitions overseas (e.g., Thrace and Lemnos) and eventually built the largest Greek empire before Philip of Makedon.

Peisistratos laid the economic and social foundations for national prosperity and domestic tranquillity, and, a generation later, innovative Kleisthenes provided a viable and enduring political superstructure. When Peisistratos died in 527, his sons inherited an amorphous collection of powers, precedents, and friends (which is what tyranny is). Hippias succeeded in maintaining family power for seventeen years and may have initiated some reforms that later tradition credited to his father. Athenian legend touts Harmodios and Aristogeiton as a homosexual, tyrant-slaying team who killed Peisistratos's younger son Hipparkhos in 514–513 and thereby "restored" an equality that had yet to exist. Hippias, in fact, was only expelled as tyrant several years later by a Spartan expedition under King Kleomenes, which was strategically brilliant but politically unsuccessful. The Spartans had finally decided that the Athenian tyrant's elder son might no longer provide an Athenian government suited to them. Their alleged enduring ideological hatred of tyranny conveniently and attractively masked their fear of potential mainland competitors. The resulting rogue Athenian state, however, from the Spartan viewpoint, was even less satisfactory than the tyranny.

The power vacuum that came about after the dismantling of the tyranny left Kleisthenes, Isagoras, and any other faction leaders looking for allies. The tyrant and his supporters—"party" would be an anachronistic label—had just been removed from Attika. Some of Kleisthenes' competitors distrusted his Alkmaionid family more than they disapproved of the Spartan foreign forces backing Isagoras's bid. The calculating partisan Kleisthenes took the bizarre and unprecedented step of bringing the common folks into his faction (hetaireia) by promising their increased participation in the government of Attika.

The popular ancient view that Kleisthenes intended to establish real democracy, even the Athenian democracy lauded by later Athenian generations, founders on two objections. First, he did not create most of the later democratic institutions such as popular courts, and, second, no Greek had yet imagined direct government, such as office-holding and assembly decisions, by peasant farmers. Even the phrase "government of the people" probably did not yet exist; it is first attested to after 480. Already Herodotos (ca. 430) suggests that partisan politics rather than any not-yet-existent ideological attachments impelled the Alkmaionid underdog in the political free-for-all.

Kleisthenes divided the people of Attika into three geographical sectors: the plain around Athens, the coastal region, and the inland (and poorer, hilly) region. Every man belonged to a deme. These "wards" were sometimes a neighborhood of Athens, sometimes a major town in Attika (e.g., Akharnai, center of the charcoal industry, crucial to smelting, ceramic firing, and other technology-based industries), and sometimes only a tiny hamlet—perhaps a cluster of houses near a crossroads. The meanings of the word dêmos include: the whole people, the village, and the voting borough-unit. These approximately 140 demes (exact numbers varied over time)—real agglomerations of people on the ground—were allotted to the thirty artificial *trittyeis* ("thirds") in such a way that originally each *trittys* had approximately the same number of men. Some of them had one deme, some had several. These thirty *trittys* divisions (approximately equal subgroups of the native free and male population) were then combined by threes (one each from each region) into ten new tribes (where there had been four traditional tribes previously), named for newly important Attic heroes such as Akamas and Hippothon. The system was intentionally complicated, and not all the consequences could have been foreseen.

Older practices and customs (religious and social) were not abolished, but a new grid was laid on the citizenry that diminished the power of the elite factions based on big land-holders and encouraged pride in community units and the greater Athenian *polis*. Kleisthenes enlarged the annually elected Council to 500, with fifty members from each tribe and at least one from each deme. He instituted formal self-determination on the local deme and *polis* level in a way that permanently weakened the elite's grasp on power. The Assembly soon became the dominant organ of the government, because there was no longer any powerful executive. The Council of 500 discussed and prepared the agenda but did not control it in the Assembly. The magistrates were many in number and possessed only severely circumscribed powers.

Although all male freeborn inhabitants of Attika were equally Athenian citizens, before and after Kleisthenes, one's relative proximity to Athens continued to affect one's realistic political options and opportunities. The Marathon run of twenty-six miles may not seem much to people accustomed to automobile travel, but these are twenty-six up-and-down, hill-country miles. Few demesmen ("members of the village") of distant Oinoë, Sounion, or Marathon had the time or even a horse to speed the journey for the perceived pleasure or need to vote. In contrast to modern proponents of democracy, Kleisthenes probably did not intend to provide all freemen with equal power in the political process. *Isonomia* ("equal administration of laws") was his carefully chosen catch word. The phrase refers to equal protection under the law—without specifying exactly who designs, passes, or amends the law.

In 508–507, Kleisthenes cleverly directed a civil riot by channeling popular feeling against Spartan interference into support for his faction and by introducing a series of new institutions that came to seem natural to Athenians. These new demes and tribes were the political and military units that formed the basic divisions for his political revolution.

What Kleisthenes did is reasonably clear; what he intended or expected, or what motivated him can only be conjectured. Was he manip-

ulating his friends and confusing his enemies to secure his own power?
The result belies this intention. We hear nothing more of him in subsequent history, unless the institution of ostracism (civil exile for ten years)
was also his idea. Even his prominent family, the Alkmaionids, who
should have reaped credit from their proponent's achievement, soon dis-
appear from prominence.

Whether Kleisthenes' motive was to increase his own stature, to destroy the power of local bigwigs, or to unite the heretofore feuding communities and classes of Attika is a subject of speculation. The result,
however, of Kleisthenes' complex reorganization of the population is not.
The people of Attika transferred or cemented their larger loyalties to the
nascent Athenian state. This large population and area quickly became
a major power. Herodotos credits *isegorie* ("equal right to political participation") with the sudden prosperity and successes of Athens, against
Sparta, Boiotia, and Euboia, and soon against the great Persian Empire.
The role of newly discovered (ca. 483) silver resources at Laureion near
Thorikos in southern Attika certainly promoted this growth in Attic activity, industry, the naval fleet, and personal wealth.

In the early fifth century, power blocs were realigning in the (Athens)
Assembly (*ekklêsia*), but the Council of the Areopagos remained both an
influential law court and a source of ex-magistrates' wisdom. The *boulê*
was elected for a year, by sortition (lot), after examination for suitability
(proper parentage, lack of state debts or criminal past, etc.) and delib-
erated most issues (*probouleusis*) before they came to the *ekklêsia*, but this
council could not prevent popular legislation from advancing there.
Magistrates (*archontes*), chosen for a one-year term by sortition, had many
ceremonial and religious duties, and presided over the courts, but no
one man had extended military or political authority. The generalship
emerged (501; 490) as the only office for which election was required and
to which repeated re-election was possible. The "tyrannical" example of
the Peisistratid family was too fresh for other resolutions that entrusted
one man with serious power. Furthermore, the threat of ostracism annually faced individuals whose loyalty to the new government was ques-
tionable.

The new Athenian government was an oddity and remained so—"an
acknowledged folly" in the traitor Alkibiades' famous phrase delivered
to Spartans in the later Peloponnesian War. This government energized
the Athenians for two centuries to try all sorts of new ideas and practices,
some admirable and some foolish, many successful and many cata-
strophic. Very soon, their new political arrangements led them into war
with the Near Eastern superpower Persia. This long series of conflicts

(498–479) cemented their pride in their peculiar institutions and their loyalty to them, as the next chapter will show.

SUGGESTIONS FOR FURTHER READING

Boardman, John. 1999. *The Greeks Overseas*. 4th ed. London: Thames and Hudson. A study of Archaic Greek commerce and colonization emphasizing archaeological evidence.

Boardman, John, and G.L. Hammond, eds. 1982. *The Expansion of the Greek World, Eighth to Sixth Centuries BC. The Cambridge Ancient History*. Vol. 3.3, 2d ed. Cambridge: Cambridge University Press. A standard handbook with extensive bibliographies.

Cartledge, Paul. 1979. *Sparta and Laconia. A Regional History*. London: Routledge. A study of a limited area and its uniquely important development.

Dillon, Matthew, and Lynda Garland, eds. 1999. *Ancient Greece. Social and Historical Documents*. Rev. ed. New York: Routledge. Inscriptions, historical documents, and literature in translation.

Donlan, Walter. 1999. *The Aristocratic Ideal and Selected Papers*. Wauconda, Ill.: Bolchazy-Carducci. Papers examining the role of class and status in the Archaic period.

Dougherty, Carol, and Leslie Kurke, eds. 1993. *Cultural Poetics in Archaic Greece*. New York: Oxford University Press. Various specialists in art, social history, and literature examine the creation and questioning of Greek values and ideals.

Forrest, W.G. 1966. *The Emergence of Greek Democracy*. New York: McGraw-Hill. A brief but stimulating revision of the Herodotus-dominated traditions of Archaic history.

Graham, A.J. 1983. *Colony and Mother City in Ancient Greece*. Rev. ed. Chicago: Ares. A history of relations between founding cities and their overseas outposts.

Herodotos. *The Histories*. Translated Robin Waterfield. 1998. Oxford and New York: Oxford University Press. The essential ancient text for the period that this chapter covers and one of the most interesting books ever written. Good translation, superior introduction and notes.

Jeffery, Lilian. 1976. *Archaic Greece*. London: Benn. This study surveys regional developments in politics and material culture.

Korres, Manolis. 1995. *From Pentelicon to the Parthenon*. Athens: Melissa. An archaeologist examines how Athenians quarried and built monumental structures. Superior illustrations.

Kraay, Colin, and Max Hirmer. 1966. *Greek Coins*. New York: Abrams. A photographic introduction to a potent economic tool and the most beautiful products of that idea.

Lateiner, Donald. 1991. *The Historical Method of Herodotus*. Rev. ed. Toronto: University of Toronto Press. A guide for comprehending the first historian's peculiar presentation.

Osborne, Robin. 1987. *Classical Landscape with Figures*. Dobbs Ferry, N.Y.: Sheridan House. The farmer and the countryside are shown to be essential to ancient *polis* histories.

————. 1996. *Greece in the Making: 1200–479 BC*. New York: Routledge. A refreshing re-evaluation of the epigraphic, archaeological, and historical sources; richly illustrated.

Polignac, François de. 1995. *Cults, Territory and the Origin of the Greek City State*. Chicago: University of Chicago Press. Revised dissertation examines how land, gods, and political development dovetail with one another.

Powell, Anton, ed. 1988. *Classical Sparta: Techniques Behind her Success*. Norman: University of Oklahoma Press. Essays examine the infrastructure of Spartan political history.

Richter, Gisela. 1968. *Korai*. London: Phaidon. The development of dedications of draped female freestanding sculpture, in or near sanctuaries.

————. 1970. *Kouroi*. 3rd ed. London: Phaidon. The parallel development of Archaic Greek nude male sculptural dedications.

Salmon, John B. 1984. *Wealthy Corinth: A History of the City to 338 BC*. Oxford: Oxford University Press. Study of a crucial commercial and colonizing city rich in archaeological data.

Travlos, John. 1971. *Pictorial Dictionary of Ancient Athens*. New York: Praeger. Alphabetic survey of the topography and stone remains of the city that reached prominence circa 500 B.C.E.

Part III

The Rise of Political and Cultural Imperialism (5th century B.C.E.)

Figure 5. Statuette of a Hoplite warrior with spear and Boiotian shield. Bronze. Courtesy of Staatliche Museen zu Berlin—Preussischer Kulturbesitz Antikensammlung.

5

The Persian Wars

INTRODUCTION

Unlike earlier events, whose details are pieced together from different evidence, the events precipitating and comprising the two Persian invasions of Greece in the early fifth century B.C.E., the "Persian Wars," became the source for something new: a near contemporary history written by Herodotos of Halikarnassos, on the south Ionian coast. Called the "father of history," Herodotos wrote his *Histories of the Persian Wars* from survivors' accounts possibly between 460 and 420 B.C.E. With no Persian evidence for these events, his history is invaluable, but his interpretation of the wars' causes and consequences has another purpose besides simply recording events. Like Homer's poems, Herodotos's history also seeks to define Greek identity, in deliberate contrast to a newly formulated "barbarian" East. (Initially referring to any non–Greek speaking foreigner, the word *barbarian* acquired its negative moral implications as the Greeks refined concepts of their own *civilized* identity in contrast to that of an inferior, *barbarian* foreigner, which the Persians came to represent.)

Settled during the Dark Age, the Greek *poleis* in Asia Minor—referred to as the Ionian cities—enjoyed mostly amicable trade and cultural relations with civilizations to the east. Circa 550 B.C.E., King Cyrus began a campaign of conquests that first established then enlarged the Persian Empire. By 500, the Persian Empire extended from northwest Pakistan in the east, to a double-pronged reach in the west: Thrace in northern Greece; Makedonia, a friendly, semidependent state; and Egypt and Kyrenaica (Greek colonies) in northern Africa.

After defeating Lydia (546), Cyrus tightened control over the Ionian Greek cities. His successor, King Darius, who had violently wrested the throne, continued Cyrus's imperial expansion. By 500 Ionian *poleis* were chafing under higher taxes and tighter Persian control, and mainland Greece appeared squeezed between Persia's encircling from the east and Carthage's attacks against western Greece in Sicily and Italy.

Greek *poleis* in Ionia and the mainland were divided about how to deal with Persian control. Many *poleis* advocated acquiescence to Persian authority, and many communities and powerful individuals relied on ties with Persia. Others supported resisting Persian rule, developing notions of "free Greek men" for whom serving an eastern, non-Greek despotic master would be abasing. In 499 Aristagoras, deputy tyrant at Miletos, the most powerful and prosperous of the Ionian *poleis*, led several cities and islands in the "Ionian Revolt" against Persian domination. The revolt involved many Greek cities and fierce battles, causing Persia much trouble. The Ionian cities deposed their tyrants friendly to Persia and burned Sardis, the former Lydian capital and now the Persian *satrapy* ("governmental outpost") for contact with the Ionian *poleis*. Though Sparta refused, Athens and Eretria contributed ships, but left after early defeats. The fragile coalition of Ionian *poleis* crumbled in a battle at Lade, near Miletos (494), where they were outnumbered two to one, and the few forces left fighting were crushed. Miletos was destroyed, the nearby Temple to Apollo at Didyma burned, and those captured were killed, enslaved, or relocated. In the end, the Ionian cities were severely crippled.

After quashing this Ionian Revolt, Persia removed its tyrants and allowed the Ionian *poleis* more democratic governance, but demanded ultimate allegiance to the Persian king. The Ionian cities generally complied. Darius now intended to punish Athens and Eretria, thus beginning the Persian invasions of Greece. From 492 to 490, Darius's forces violently dominated the Aegean islands and Thrace, with several Ionian cities fighting, willingly or by force, for Persia. In 492, much of the Persian fleet attacking Greece from the north was lost in storms, but another force led by Datis in 490 sailed directly across the Aegean (not commonly done). It destroyed Naxos and Eretria, deporting and enslaving their populations, then landed at Marathon on the northeast coast of Attika.

The Battle of Marathon (490) became a significant marker in Athenian history: an Athenian army of about 10,000 hoplite soldiers (see Figure 5), including a small contingent from Athens's Boiotian ally, Plataia, routed Persian troops twice their number. Spartan forces never arrived, delayed by their religious celebrations, which they could not leave. Although the Athenian defense strategy at Marathon may have been the momentary response to their situation, it was victorious. Stretching out their ranks opposite their attackers left the Athenian center thin and vulnerable. After Persian troops broke through the center, the wings encircled and drove them back to the sea. According to Herodotos, 6,400 Persians died, against fewer than 200 Athenians (not counting Plataians and slaves). After a brief faceoff at Phaleron, Athens's coastal harbor, the Persian fleet retreated. This victory significantly boosted Athens's growing military power, almost rivaling Sparta's powerful military force.

Persian revenge for this defeat was delayed first by a revolt in Egypt, then by Darius's death; his son, King Xerxes, first reclaimed Egypt. By 480, Xerxes had gathered a massive land and naval force numbering perhaps 150,000 men to invade Greece. Athens found other Greek communities largely unwilling to resist this invasion, as they intensely debated every aspect of Greek defensive tactics. The oracle of Apollo at Delphi twice suggested cooperation with Persia. Eventually, Sparta agreed to lead the allied Greek land and sea forces. Not wishing to leave the Peloponnesos, the Spartans proposed fighting at the Isthmos, which was opposed by the Athenians, for it left Attika undefended. But as the Persians quickly advanced through Thessaly, the Greeks positioned their defense at the narrow pass at Thermopylai ("Hot Gates," that is, "springs"), while the navy amassed at nearby Artemision (August 480).

Greek forces were again aided by natural events, many of Xerxes' ships being lost at sea. Three days of sea battle proved inconclusive, both sides enduring much damage, and for two days Xerxes' army could not break the Greek position at Thermopylai until someone told the Persians of a path around the pass. Once aware of the betrayal, the Spartan commander, King Leonidas, dismissed most of the Greek troops, remaining against the advancing Persian army with 300 Spartan *homoioi* and a few allies. The Spartan and Thespian soldiers inflicted heavy casualties as they fought to their deaths, enabling the Greek forces to retreat, and their memories were honored for preserving Greece. The results of these two battles—the sea battle at Artemision, where many Persian ships were lost in storms at sea and much of the Athenian fleet was damaged, and the defeat at Thermopylai—were mixed. Some Greek states capitulated, while the Athenians strengthened their resolve to resist the Persians.

With the continuing Persian advance, Greek forces regrouped at the Isthmos, abandoning Attika and allowing the Athenian Akropolis to be burned. Commanding the fleet at Artemision and again at Salamis was Themistokles, a leading Athenian politician whose foresight and influence helped save Athens by advocating reliance on her fleet. As an *archon* (492), he began developing the Piraios as Athens's port city. He later urged using Athens's silver surplus from its mines at Laureion to build up the Athenian navy from 70 to 200 ships, which proved crucial for Greece's defense in 480.

Although the city of Athens was not saved, the Athenians were. Themistokles interpreted a Delphic oracle advising the Athenians to take to their "wooden walls" as suggesting that they rely on their fleet for defense. After having evacuated the residents of Attika by ship, Themistokles arranged the 380-ship allied Greek navy in the narrow channel between Salamis and the Attic coast. Luring the thousand-ship Persian fleet into these narrows, rather than fighting them on open waters, the Greeks successfully outmaneuvered the closely ranked Persian ships, whose large numbers hindered mobility and escape in the narrow straits. The surviving Persian ships retreated, and the Athenians could once again boast of their leading role in the Greeks' victory over the Persians at the Battle of Salamis (September 480).

Although Xerxes, his fleet, and many of his troops withdrew, the king left an imposing force commanded by his general, Mardonios, who urged Athens to accept Persian hegemony. However, in the next year, 479, the largest Greek force yet assembled, 38,000 soldiers, almost half of whom were Spartans and Athenians, engaged the Persian army at Plataia. Initially the two Greek flanks became separated when the center troops retreated and Mardonios led his troops in. But the two flanks successfully encircled the Persian army; they defeated the Persian cavalry, Mardonios was killed, and the Persians retreated, ending their invasions into mainland Greece.

Deepening the significance of these last two victories were two others, reputedly coinciding with the former: Syracuse's defeat of Carthage on the same day as the Battle of Salamis, and another Greek defeat of the Persian navy at Mykale on the same day as the Battle of Plataia. All these victories were seen as important milestones for securing the independence of Greek *poleis* from east to west. Athenian and Spartan actions in the Persian Wars forged their historical development. While Sparta was still regarded as Greece's leading military power, Athens would imperiously exploit its claim as champion of the Greek defense against Persian domination.

INTERPRETIVE ESSAY
Steven Hirsch

For a very long time, the Greeks were fortunate to be situated beyond the reach of great powers, such as the Neo-Assyrian Empire which dominated western Asia from the ninth to seventh centuries B.C.E. and might have posed a threat to the Greeks' political and cultural development. During most of the Archaic period (eighth to sixth centuries), the Greeks were both independent in their burgeoning city-states and kinship groups and free to develop culturally along their own trajectory. They were, indeed, influenced by ideas and technologies derived from neighboring peoples, but they adopted these by their own choice and folded them into their own cultural fabric.

All this changed in the sixth century. First, some of the Greek cities on the seaboard of western Anatolia became subject to Kroisos, the king of nearby Lydia. Other than paying a certain amount of money each year (*tribute*, as it is often called), however, the Greek cities were not much burdened by Lydian rule, and there was a comfortable flow of people and culture between the Lydian capital, Sardis, and the Greek coast. When Kroisos challenged the Persians in 546 and was ultimately defeated, he inadvertently brought his Greek subjects into contact with the new great power from the East. This is why Herodotos chose to begin his account of the conflicts of Persians and Greeks with Kroisos. The era of relative isolation was over for the Greeks, and for the next two centuries the shadow of the mighty Persian Empire—the largest empire the world had yet seen—loomed over the affairs of the Greek cities of Ionia, the Aegean, and the mainland. How did the Greeks react to this threat and how did it help to shape the political and cultural landscape of the late Archaic Greek world?

Our primary source of information for the early encounters of Greeks and Persians is the sprawling account given by Herodotos, from the Greek city of Halikarnassos in southwest Anatolia. A child at the time of Xerxes' invasion, Herodotos apparently devoted his adult life to traveling and gathering information about the known world—*historia* as the

Greeks then called such research—which he eventually published half a century after the defining event of his age. The earlier sections range widely in space and time and encompass a wide variety of materials, including the geography of foreign lands and customs of other peoples as well as folk tales, religious wonders, scientific curiosities, and tourist attractions. The later stages of the work narrowed the focus to the several clashes of Greeks and Persians in the early fifth century, and for this accomplishment Herodotos has come to be known as "the father of history."

As the first historian in our sense of the word, Herodotos had to develop new techniques for evaluating, organizing, and reporting the information he gathered, and he has often been regarded as naive and gullible. However, recent scholarship has moved toward a greater appreciation of Herodotos's achievement, given his lack of precedents, dependence on oral testimony, and difficulties in verifying reports about occurrences that happened long before his time. We must also remind ourselves that Herodotos was writing, not for the Greeks who experienced the Persian Wars but rather for their children and grandchildren, at a time when the former allies in the defense of the homeland, Athens and Sparta and their various dependencies, were plunging into the bitter, internecine struggles of the Peloponnesian War. Surely Herodotos and his audience were deeply aware of the irony of that conflict, whose seeds had been laid in the great victory half a century before.

There is little else of a contemporary nature besides Herodotos. We have a few epigrams, poems composed to commemorate the heroes and dead of the war, and a few public inscriptions carved in stone. The most interesting of these—the so-called "Themistokles Decree," which gives detailed prescriptions for the evacuation of Athens before the arrival of Xerxes' forces in 480—was actually carved in the third century. While some have argued that it is a modified copy of an authentic original, most experts regard it as a later forgery. And there is an anomalous play, *The Persians*, composed and staged by the Athenian Aeschylus less than a decade after the invasion, in which a messenger arrives at the Persian court with a report of the Persian naval debacle at Salamis. While this is manifestly tragic drama rather than history, we should not forget that playwright, actors, and audience had been witnesses to that event.

Because of the scarcity of Persian records, we know nothing about how these events appeared to the Persians. However, we can infer that the Greeks posed unique problems to the Persian administration. The Greeks of Ionia and the offshore islands were, for all practical purposes, the first seafaring peoples to come under Persian control. Herodotos's peculiar story of the first meeting of Greeks and Persians illuminates this issue. Cyrus, the great conqueror and founder of the empire (reigned ca. 558– 530), was angry with the Ionian Greeks for not joining his side before the battle with Kroisos. He told them the parable of a flute-player who tried to entice some fish to land by playing his instrument. When this failed, he dragged the fish in with a net and as they were flopping around on the beach, he chastized them, "It's too late to dance now!" While many have doubted the truthfulness of this story, it is at least plausible that Cyrus, who was almost certainly not literate, would use the oral form of an animal fable to make his point. And this story reflects an awareness of the difficulties faced by a land-based military power like Persia in dealing with peoples who lived by or on the sea and could take to their ships to escape domination. This story sets up a contrast between the seafaring Greeks and landlubber Persians, which operates throughout Herodotos's account of their rivalry.

Cyrus left the conquest of the Greek cities of western Anatolia to a subordinate, since this appeared to be little more than a mopping-up operation after the conquest of Lydia. Here, for the first time, Greek states tried but failed to unite in their resistance and were reduced one by one. Unity did not come easily to small, independent communities habituated to quarreling with one another, even in the face of the threat posed by Persia.

We know little about the nature of Persian domination of their Greek subjects in the nearly half-century after the conquest. At a later time we find local individuals or groups with Persian backing in control of the Greek cities. The Persians, who had risen rather suddenly from a relatively simple tribal society to masters of a vast empire, were a practical people. They normally were willing to grant considerable autonomy to local elites willing to collaborate with them. This spared the Persians the necessity of creating a large administrative bureaucracy and stationing military forces in many places. While the details can no longer be recovered and must have varied depending on local circumstances, we can presume that particular individuals and groups in the Greek cities were able to maintain or seize power with Persian support.

In the early days, subject communities were expected to periodically contribute "gifts" to the king. In the reign of Darius, the third Persian king (reigned 522–486), the empire was divided into twenty or so administrative districts, called *satrapies*, with fixed amounts of annual tribute demanded from each region. The Greeks of the coast would have had to deal with one or the other of two Persian *satraps* (governors) stationed at the former Lydian capital, Sardis, and Daskylion in the northwest. Given the slowness of communications in the ancient world, governors in provinces so distant from the center of the empire had considerable freedom of action. Few Greeks would have made the journey of many months to the court of the king, though there is strong evidence of Greek artists and craftsmen working at the Persian capitals, and other professionals (military officers, doctors, political advisers, etc.) also joined the Persian king's entourage. Precisely because so few Greeks had really been there and returned, the splendor of the palaces of the "Great King" and the scandalous behavior of the royal family were the subject of much gossip and rumor in the Greek world.

All things considered, the Greeks of Anatolia seem to have tolerated Persian rule without much difficulty for half a century. Why, then, did they rise up in revolt at the turn of the fifth century? We have already seen that Darius imposed a more regular system of tribute, which may have increased the financial burden on Greek subjects. Darius also extended the bounds of empire in the west, crossing into Europe to secure Thrace, receive the submission of Makedonia, and attack the Skythian nomads north of the Danube. During his reign a Persian fleet, composed primarily of ships manned by the Phoenicians (a Semitic people from the coast of modern Lebanon who had a long history of rivalry with the Greeks), first sailed into the Aegean. And in a number of instances Darius installed his favorites in power in Greek communities. Thus, Persia's Greek subjects may have been feeling increasingly squeezed by a more overt Persian presence when they revolted between 499 and 494.

It is hard to accept Herodotos's explanation for this uprising—that it was due to the selfish and reckless ambition of two "tyrants" from Miletos, the greatest of the Greek cities. The Ionian Revolt, as it has come to be called, raged for five years and spread not only through the Greek cities of western Anatolia but also to non-Greek Anatolians and even as far as the island of Cyprus. The Persians had to expend many lives and much money to put it down. We must assume that the rebels had strong grudges. Our best evidence for the nature of the problems comes from the surprisingly enlightened arrangements made by the Persians after they had crushed the revolt, which included improvements in the system for allocating tribute obligations and support for democracies in the Greek cities. First, however, a brutal example was made of Miletos. After it was captured and sacked, the surviving population was carried off to a place of exile near the head of the Persian Gulf.

Some scholars have seen the failure of the Ionian Revolt as the main cause of both the apparent poverty of Ionia in the subsequent period, as reflected in the archaeological record, and the end of Ionia's cultural primacy in the Greek world. After all, the Ionian cities, and Miletos above all, had constituted the most populous and prosperous part of the Greek world in the later Archaic period and was the source of many of the great poets and scientific thinkers of that age. In all fairness, while the widespread destruction resulting from the Persian reconquest of Ionia undoubtedly contributed to its decline in the subsequent period, so, too, did the rise of the Athenian Empire after the Persian Wars, which cut off the Greek cities of Anatolia from commerce with the Persian-controlled east and put them in a weak position vis-à-vis dominant and commercially aggressive Athens. The underlying question—whether Persian political domination of Greek communities inevitably restricted economic and cultural progress—assumes particular significance because, as we shall see, the Persians soon launched several attacks against Athens. While historical "what if" questions can never yield definitive answers, one cannot help but wonder whether the great cultural achievements of the Greek Classical period—much of which was centered on Athens—ever would have happened if the Persians had succeeded in conquering mainland Greece in the early fifth century.

The Ionian rebels had received a little assistance from the western side of the Aegean. After a Persian fleet was destroyed by storms in the northern Aegean in 492, Darius dispatched another armada across the central Aegean in 490. Given the relatively small size of the expedition and the fact that it was commanded by subordinates (whereas it was customary for the early Persian kings to personally lead the armies on major new conquests, unless prevented by age or illness), the aims must have been limited to punishing Athens and Eretria, two states that had aided the Ionian rebels, and to giving the other mainland Greeks a demonstration of Persian power. After a stubborn siege, Eretria was betrayed to the Persians by some of its leading citizens, who must have expected to be put in charge of their home city by the Persians, as had often been the case in Ionia. But Darius had determined to make an example of the Eretrians and had given explicit orders that the population be carried off into captivity.

The Persians made occasional use of this ultimate punishment of *mass deportation*—the physical removal of an entire population from their home and transplantation to a distant location—which they had taken over from the Assyrians and earlier imperial predecessors in the ancient Near East. Not only did it break the spirit of a troublesome community and render the survivors utterly dependent on the imperial power for protection in an unfamiliar and inhospitable new home, but it delivered a terrifying message to others about the cost of rebellion. In addition, deportees were often used as forced labor on construction projects and agricultural estates. The Greeks were also painfully aware of one other consequence of deportation—cultural death. Perhaps half a century after the Eretrians had been deported to the vicinity of Susa in western Iran, Herodotos claims to have knowledge of their descendants, who were clinging to their Greek language and heritage. Almost a hundred years after the deportation, a Greek doctor named Ktesias, serving at the Persian court, claimed that the descendants of the original deportees no longer spoke Greek, though they still inscribed Greek characters on their tombstones. And it is even possible that their distant offspring, now entirely assimilated to the surrounding indigenous population, fought on the Persian side against Alexander the Great in 334 B.C.E.

No doubt the Persians had a similar fate in store for Athens, and Western history would have been greatly altered had the Athenians not prevailed at the plain of Marathon, twenty-six miles northeast of Athens. The Athenians chose to march out and meet the enemy away from the city, perhaps fearing a betrayal from inside the walls, as happened at Eretria. The two armies faced each other across the plain for a number of days until the Athenian armored infantry charged, perhaps because the Persian cavalry was away for the moment. This first pitched battle between mainland Greek hoplites and Persian forces previewed the superiority of Greek armament and tactics for centuries to come. The Athenians who fought at Marathon bragged about their achievement for the rest of their lives (according to tradition, the tomb inscription of the great tragedian Aeschylus mentioned only his service at Marathon), and Athens gained new respect in the eyes of other Greeks.

Darius did not live to take vengeance on Athens, and his son and successor Xerxes initially had to deal with a matter of higher priority, the suppression of a revolt in the wealthy and strategically important province of Egypt. In 480, however, Xerxes crossed into Europe with a huge army that was clearly directed at the conquest of Greece. Herodotos attempts to explain the motives behind this invasion through a detailed account of events at the Persian court. The confused sequence of events probably mirrors Herodotos's struggle to blend multiple traditions. Xerxes is pressed by various self-interested parties, including his ambitious cousin Mardonios and the exiled family of the former tyrant of Athens. After changing his mind several times, he is stampeded into attacking Greece by terrifying dreams sent by the gods. It is not very likely that Herodotos had access to accurate accounts of deliberations at the Persian court half a century earlier (though the families of leading Persians at court could, perhaps, have passed on traditions about such events), and it is inconceivable that he would have known what transpired in the royal bedchamber.

Presumably Herodotos or his sources have imaginatively fleshed out whatever skeletal information was available. In Herodotos's rendition, Xerxes gives a number of plausible explanations that may reflect real motives: that he has an obligation to complete his father's campaign of vengeance and that, in order to be a worthy successor to Cyrus, Kambyses, and Darius, he needs to engineer a new great conquest for the Persian Empire. To this we might add a geopolitical consideration that must have occurred to the Persian high command in the wake of the Ionian Revolt. The Aegean Sea did not provide a secure western boundary for the empire. To the contrary, with seagoing Greeks living on either side of it, the waters served to connect rather than divide. With the Greeks of the eastern Aegean already under Persian control, the conquest of their mainland cousins was a strategic necessity.

Xerxes' forces were preceded by envoys dispatched to many Greek states to demand "earth and water"—the symbolic tokens by which a community acknowledged the Persian king's rights over their resources. Most in northern and central Greece made the "sensible" choice and submitted to Persia. We should not be surprised by this decision. First, we must remember that there was no Greek nation. Greeks were divided into hundreds of fully independent political entities. Second, while there was a general recognition of a cultural affinity among *Hellenes* (as the Greeks called themselves)—widely scattered peoples who shared a roughly common language, religious beliefs, social practices, and fundamental values—this had never stopped the Greeks from fighting one another. There had been occasional groupings of Greek communities, often based on shared maintenance of a religious shrine and joint participation in worship of a deity at a communal festival, such as among the Ionian and Dorian communities of western Anatolia. Sparta was the leader of a "Peloponnesian League," based on its military supremacy and a web of relationships between Sparta and other states in southern Greece, which was used to maintain a stable political situation in the Peloponnese.

But there was no tradition on the mainland of Greeks putting aside their local rivalries and coming together in a military alliance to resist a non-Greek aggressor. The Greek cities of western Anatolia had failed to do so at the time of the initial Persian conquest, and money, promises, and threats had been effectively used by the Persians to pry apart the Ionian rebel alliance. Faced with the prospect of a huge army of invasion, and, perhaps, also recognizing that Persian interference in the internal affairs of its Greek subjects had normally been minimal, the many Greek communities which *medized*, that is, they took the Persian side, were simply making a seemingly safe and logical choice. (It is instructive to note that the Greeks, unable to distinguish the linguistic and cultural differences between the Persians and neighboring Medes, used these ethnic designations synonymously.) Even the highly respected Oracle at Delphi—a shrine of the god Apollo, managed by a group of priests who were extremely well informed about Greek and foreign geography and peoples and political affairs—appears to have expected a Persian victory, since it gave out discouraging predictions to Greek states determined to resist Xerxes.

Only in southern Greece did a group of states come together to form the Hellenic League, as modern historians call it, a military alliance bent on resisting the Persian advance. Sparta and Athens, the two leading states in the alliance, really had no alternative. The Athenians knew what fate Darius had in mind for them before Marathon, and the Spartans had killed a set of Persian envoys. Herodotos tells of bickering among the larger states as to who would have the command of allied military forces, but Sparta, the foremost military power in Greece, was the inevitable choice, and the other Peloponnesian states followed its lead. Some communities in central Greece initially collaborated with the alliance, but fell away after allied forces were overwhelmed at Thermopylai (summer 480) and the Persians moved south. Other Greek states, more distant from the line of invasion, sat back and awaited the outcome.

Allied forces regrouped at Salamis, an island off the west coast of Attika (the region controlled by Athens). Herodotos depicts an alliance deeply divided over interests and policy. Even though the Athenians had abandoned their city to destruction by the Persians, they were determined to stand and fight at sea, and they provided fully half the allied fleet. Many of the Peloponnesians wanted to retreat and defend the Isthmos. In the council of commanders, the Athenians threatened to desert the alliance, and their leader, Themistokles, secretly sent a message to the Persian king, claiming that the Athenians were prepared to defect from the fragmenting alliance if the Persians blocked the escape routes. By this brilliant deception he both forced the allies to remain at Salamis and drew the Persian ships into the narrow straits between the island and the mainland, where their advantage in numbers and maneuverability was nullified and the Greeks won a great naval victory.

A number of challenges can be raised to Herodotos's picture of near fatal dissension in the allied camp. Our most contemporary portrait of the battle is found in the tragic play *The Persians*, written by the Athenian

Aeschylus, himself an eyewitness and participant at Salamis, and presented to an audience that included many Athenian participants just eight years after the event. Aeschylus represents Themistokles' message as a trick that all the allies were in on and plausibly explains the successful outcome of the battle as due to close cooperation and a shared purpose among the allied combatants. How, then, do we explain away Herodotos's picture of an alliance nearly destroyed by internal squabbling and stumbling into victory by virtue of luck and the exceptional deviousness of one individual? It could have resulted from versions of these events given the historian half a century later by bitterly partisan members of Greek states then engaged in the hostilities leading up to the Peloponnesian War who, consciously or otherwise, reflected back into the earlier period the later divisions in Greece. But one could equally well argue that Aeschylus, in the atmosphere of euphoria and good will following the alliance's victory, and as part of the process of inventing a myth of Greek unity at a time when Athens had taken over leadership of the anti-Persian alliance, has downplayed the dissension within the alliance.

After the defeat of his navy at Salamis, Xerxes returned to Asia. However, he left behind his cousin Mardonios with a huge and, as yet, undefeated land army. The smart money was still on Persia. Passing the winter with his troops in Thessaly, Mardonios also resorted to the generally successful tactic of employing promises, threats, and bribes to try to pry the Athenians from the Greek alliance. Herodotos himself goes on record with his belief that the Athenians were the key to the outcome of the war. Herodotos gives a stirring account of the meeting at Athens at which Mardonios's representative, the Makedonian king Alexander, promised the Athenians amnesty for past offenses, reconstruction of damaged religious shrines, and additional territory if they should take the Persian side. The Spartans, alerted to the event, had dispatched envoys who urged the Athenians not to desert their fellow Greeks. The Athenians made a show of being annoyed that the Spartans would even consider that they might sell out, and assured their allies that they would never desert the cause of Greece and freedom.

Here we see one of the series of dichotomies used by Herodotos to distinguish between Greeks and Persians and to crystallize what was at stake in this war. In part, this probably reflects some of the propaganda created by the Greek alliance during the war; in part, justifications developed afterward. The Greeks see themselves as fighting for freedom, willing to risk their lives and die rather than be subject to barbarian despotism. The most vivid exposition of this dichotomy in Herodotos's pages comes out of the mouth of the Spartan king-in-exile Demaratos, who warns an overconfident Xerxes before the encounter at Thermopylai that the Spartans will fight to the death regardless of the numbers set against them. Why? Because the master they serve is their own law. Xerxes, who is convinced that his own soldiers have a superior capacity to face danger because of their fear of him as they are driven by the lash into battle, shows his utter inability to understand the mentality of free men.

This contrast between Greeks and non-Greeks, between courageous, free men who live in accordance with the laws and customs of their community and fearful, slavish men who serve an arbitrary master, is established geographically by the division between West and East. Xerxes, by seeking to extend his power from Asia into Europe, is crossing a natural, divinely ordained boundary, and for his impiety he is severely punished by the gods. We must remember that this is a Greek perspective, and that Persians would have understood these events differently.

The last act of the invasion is played out the following spring at Plataia in Boiotia. Despite the fact that Mardonios attacks at a moment when the allied Greek force is repositioning itself and therefore is vulnerable, the strong discipline of the Spartans and general superiority of Greek hoplites proves decisive. The Persian land army is shattered, Mardonios killed, and the immediate threat to the Greek mainland banished.

If we ask ourselves why the Persians failed in Greece in 480—for all practical purposes the first major setback to Persian arms in seventy years—and how a fragile coalition of fractious Greek states managed to defeat the superpower of that time, a number of factors are paramount. First, the Persians were fighting far from home, in an unknown land, with the necessity of finding supplies of food and water for a large army. Second, the Persian navy was severely damaged by storms, then fell victim to a major tactical error by being drawn into the straits at Salamis. Third, in pitched battle heavily armed Greek hoplite forces could prevail against larger numbers of lighter-armed non-Greek troops. Finally, the Greek alliance was able, despite the stresses and strains, to forge a common policy and strategy, and the Greeks were fighting for the protection of their homes, families, and communities.

It does not take too much imagination to picture the relief and exhilaration that must have swept through Greece in the aftermath of Plataia. In an earlier time, while the Greeks distinguished between *Hellenes* and *barbaroi*—those who spoke Greek and shared a Greek lifestyle and those who did not—they recognized the antiquity and advanced culture of their eastern neighbors. In the giddy decades after the repulse of Xerxes' invasion, the Greeks came to regard themselves as superior to all others and the term "barbarian" came to have the connotations of backwardness and savagery that it still holds.

It is important to keep in mind that the war was not over in 479. There was neither treaty nor truce, and for a long time to come the Greeks lived in fear of another invasion. The Spartans, impressed by the energy shown by the Athenians and perhaps already fearful of Athenian ambitions, tried to persuade the Athenians not to rebuild the walls of their city, making the argument that it might be used as a fortress by the Persians should they invade again. The cagey Athenian leader Themistokles stalled for time while the Athenians used all available materials to rebuild their walls to a defensible level. Two years later, against a backdrop of strange actions and intrigue on the part of certain Spartans and Athenians that is hard for us to make sense of, the Athenians supplanted the Spartans as leaders of a new alliance—the Delian League in modern parlance—constituted to prosecute the continuing war against Persia.

Herodotos, presumably reflecting the hostility between Sparta and Athens in his own day, may be exaggerating the suspicions and rivalries of the immediate post-invasion period. The new phase of the war would primarily involve naval activities as the anti-Persian alliance set about sweeping the Persians out of the Aegean and liberating the Greeks of the islands and the Thracian and Anatolian coastline. Sparta was not a naval power and the Spartans were famously reluctant to keep their men away from home for long periods of time. Athens was the foremost naval power in Greece and, as an Ionian state, more closely connected to the Ionian peoples of the Aegean islands and coasts. It must have made sense to all parties for the Athenians to take the initiative in the next stage of the war against Persia.

Thus, it can be seen that Xerxes' great invasion of 480–479 altered the equation of power among the Greek communities of the mainland. Sparta, the foremost military power and leader of the alliance, had lived up to expectations by the heroism of its soldiers at Thermopylai and Plataia and continued to be feared and respected by all. However, the Athenians, who had twice sacrificed their city to destruction, had provided half the allied navy, and had shown energy, courage, and perseverance at every step, had emerged to join Sparta in the first rank of Greek states.

The next chapters will show how the Athenians exploited the opportunities provided by the war to become masters of their own empire, and how the confidence and resources derived from these victories contributed to the towering political and cultural achievements of fifth-century B.C.E. Athens. Other leading states were embarrassed and lost prestige—Argos by its neutrality and Thebes by its medism. And the Oracle at Delphi, which had frequently played an important political role throughout the Greek world in the Archaic period, had been compromised by its pro-Persian stance. The Delphic priests labored to do damage control after the war by putting out stories of how the god himself had wreaked havoc on the Persian force sent to take the sanctuary. Nevertheless, while continuing to be an important source of pronouncements from the gods for individuals and communities, Delphi was never again politically influential in the Greek city-states.

We cannot say how the Persians viewed the two failed invasions of Greece in the early fifth century, since no Persian source makes any mention of these events. But from the vantage point of the imperial capitals in Mesopotamia and western Iran, this must have appeared as little more than a temporary setback on a distant frontier. The fact that no subsequent Persian king ever led troops to the west probably reflects the priority of other interests. Surely no one in Persia or Greece at that time could have suspected that within a century and a half the tables would be turned.

SUGGESTIONS FOR FURTHER READING

Burn, A.R. 1962. *Persia and the Greeks: The Defense of the West c. 546–478 B.C.* New York: St. Martin's Press. A classic study of the historical encounter of Greece and Persia, valuable because of its in-depth approach.

Cook, J.M. 1983. *The Persian Empire.* New York: Schocken Books. A solid general survey of the history and institutions of the Achaemenid Persian Empire.

Fornara, Charles W. 1971. *Herodotus: An Interpretative Essay.* Oxford: Clarendon Press. A stimulating discussion of Herodotos's achievement, emphasizing the meaning of his work for a Greek audience at the outbreak of the Peloponnesian War.

Green, Peter. 1996. *The Greco-Persian Wars.* Berkeley: University of California Press. More up-to-date than Burn on the struggles of Greece and Persia.

Grene, David, trans. 1987. *Herodotus: The History.* Chicago: University of Chicago Press. Our fundamental source for late Archaic Greece, the rise of Persia, and Greek-Persian interactions and conflicts through the invasion of Xerxes. Grene's translation captures much of the flavor of Herodotos's Greek.

Hall, Edith, ed. and trans. 1996. *Aeschylus' Persians.* Warminster, England: Aris and Phillips. Translation and discussion of Aeschylus's tragedy, a contemporary but problematic source for the battle of Salamis.

Herodotus and the Invention of History, special issue of *Arethusa*. Vol. 20. nos. 1/2. (1987). A diverse collection of papers, including a valuable annotated bibliography of Herodotean scholarship.

Podlecki, Anthony J. 1975. *The Life of Themistocles: A Critical Survey of the Literary and Archaeological Evidence*. Montreal: McGill-Queen's University Press. A detailed analysis of the evidence for the career of the most important Greek military and political figure at the time of Xerxes' invasion.

Romm, James S. 1998. *Herodotus*. New Haven: Yale University Press. An up-to-date discussion of knowledge and controversies concerning "the father of history."

Sekunda, Nick. 1992. *The Persian Army, 560–330 b.c.* London: Osprey. A well-illustrated introduction for those interested in military history.

Usher, Stephen. 1988. *Herodotus, The Persian Wars: A Companion to the Penguin Translation of Books 5–9 from Herodotus: The Histories*. Bristol: Bristol Classical Press. A brief historical commentary providing background and interpretation of the sections of Herodotos's text pertaining to the wars of Greeks and Persians.

Warry, John. 1995. *Warfare in the Classical World*. Norman: University of Oklahoma Press. A superbly illustrated, excellent description of all aspects of warfare in the ancient Greek and Roman world; see Chapter 2 on the Persian Wars.

Wiesehoefer, Josef. 1996. *Ancient Persia: From 550 b.c. to 650 a.d.* London and New York: I.B. Tauris. A recent survey by a specialist in Iranian history, it covers not only the Achaemenid Empire but its Parthian and Sassanian successors.

Figure 6. The Parthenon, Temple to Athena Parthenos, 448–432 B.C.E. Marble. Courtesy Alinari/Art Resource, N.Y.

6

Athenian Imperialism and Cultural Expansion: The Delian League, the Parthenon, and Drama

INTRODUCTION

Although the Greeks decisively defeated the Persians in several battles in 480 and 479, the threat of Persian attacks remained, while skirmishes between Greeks and Persians continued until mid-century in Ionian cities and on Cyprus. Expecting that Sparta, the strongest of the Greek *poleis*, would lead it, the Greek cities formed a defensive alliance. But the misconduct and recall of Sparta's king and general led to Athens's selection as alliance leader. The league was based on the island of Delos, home to a major festival for Apollo, Ionian in origin and open to all Greeks; hence, later historians have called this defensive alliance the Delian League.

Initially, like other member states, Athens had only one vote in league affairs, which successfully pursued a policy of freeing Greek cities from Persian rule, and the league's number reached 200 in its early years. But from the outset Athens established a leading control: it determined each city's contribution, whether ships and navy or tribute money, and it appointed the all-Athenian treasurers who controlled the tribute payments. Athens increasingly tightened control by forcing communities to join, or preventing those wishing to withdraw from the league to do so; instead of "allies," Athens openly asserted that league cities were "subject" to Athenian rule; and it enforced its own policies, supporting or imposing

Athens-friendly governments in subject cities. In 454 Athens moved the league's treasury from Delos to Athens, thereby solidifying its control of league finances and affairs. The harsh treatment by Athens of league cities wishing to pursue their own political course, and hence branded as "recalcitrant" by Athens, provided the reasons for the outbreak of both Peloponnesian Wars and the breaking of the truce intended to end the first (see Chapter 7).

As Athens was expanding its imperial power throughout Greece, further reforms at home led to increased political democratization. Shortly after the political reforms instituted by Kleisthenes, the ten *strategoi*, "generals," began to be elected, one from each tribe. Their responsibilities expanded beyond command of the military. By 487, their authority extended to political affairs, supplanting many of the governing powers of the nine *archons*, who were chosen by lot. Successful generals could be elected repeatedly and thus exercise considerable influence over Athenian policies. In the 470s and 460s, the general Kimon led the Delian League's successes in freeing Ionian cities from Persian domination. He advocated severe Athenian treatment of league cities, and he successfully rebuffed prosecution by his political rival Perikles in the annual review of an official's term of office. However, Sparta summarily dismissed him when he arrived to help quell a helot revolt, and Kimon was formally ostracized from Athens in 461.

In the vying for political power, Kimon's opponents enacted democratizing measures. In a move perhaps intended to ensure Kimon's ouster from office, Ephialtes, Perikles' political ally, spearheaded changes that transferred many of the civil powers of the Areopagos, a traditional overseeing body composed of former *archons*, to the Council of 500 (the *boulê*), other courts, and the Assembly (*ekklêsia*). These changes left to the Areopagos only its authority to judge trials of homicide, a feature significant in Aeschylus's play *Eumenides* (458).

About the same time, Perikles, who would lead Athens for the next quarter of a century, sponsored two proposals that both increased citizen participation and tightened the definition of an Athenian citizen. First, he proposed pay for participating in the courts and the *boulê*, which enabled poor citizens to become more active in the political process. Second, he proposed defining an Athenian citizen as the offspring of both an Athenian mother and father. Though a popular restriction in the mid–fifth century by excluding offspring of one non-Athenian parent, when citizen rolls declined later in the century due to high war casualties, this citizenship decree was relaxed. Moreover, by the latter half of the fifth century, most decisions were debated and determined in the Assembly, in which every male citizen could speak and influence policy, regardless of property class.

Coming to prominence with these political moves, and apparently a charismatic leader, Perikles was repeatedly elected general from about 443 B.C.E. until his death in 429. Like Kimon, he supported strong Athenian control of the Delian League with harsh treatment of disaffected cities, and he encouraged Athenian imperial expansion both to the east and the west. In contrast to Kimon's Sparta-friendly policies, however, Perikles saw Sparta principally as a rival to Athenian power, and he opposed any peaceful accommodations with Sparta. Instead, he directed the Athenian policies that resulted in the outbreak of the second Peloponnesian War.

While much of Perikles' foreign policy seems today to be at variance with the goals of modern democratic states, his pro-Athenian activities gave another major boost to Athens's cultural prominence. Like the cultural expansion under Peisistratos and Hipparkhos, Perikles' policies expanded Athens' role as a center of Greek culture. With the tribute monies kept in Athens, Perikles supported an ambitious building and arts program, which included a new Temple of Athena on the Akropolis, the Parthenon, and temples to Zeus and Hephaistos in the plain below, each one adorned with complex relief sculptures. Pheidias sculpted the colossal forty-foot-high, gold-and-ivory cult statue of Athena for her temple, outdone, according to ancient sources, only by his even larger cult statue of Zeus for his temple in Olympia. Athenian pottery making, especially as an important export item, continued strong.

Athenian drama represents a major cultural achievement. The performances were occasions for Athens to display both its cultural excellence and its political and military hegemony. Begun in the sixth century under Peisistratos, the dramatic festivals were closely connected with the developing Athenian democratic *polis* and with its image both at home and abroad. The principal dramatic festival, which occurred in March, was called the City or the Great Dionysia, and its Panhellenic significance increased through the fifth century. Originating as part of sacred rites for Dionysos, the opening procession included a display of giant *phalloi*, celebrating Dionysos as the god of vegetation, the vine—hence wine—and male fertility.

By mid-fifth century, the opening ceremonies included commemorations of the previous year's war dead, official recognition of sons of the war dead as the city's charges, and public presentation of the tribute collected from subject Delian League states, whose participation in these public displays Athens required. These activities opening a festival dedicated to Dionysos—its highpoint being the three days of dramatic competitions—emphasize the close interaction among religious, cultural, political, and military affairs to the Greeks. Important city political and military events are marked in a public ritual, which, in turn, serves as a prelude to a display of poetic, musical, and dramatic excellence in a festival competition important for Athens's increasing cultural centrality.

Athenian drama was another forum, in some ways like the assembly, council and law courts, where political views could be aired, as the plays expressed the concerns of Athenian citizen men within the democratic *polis*. Except for some plays earlier in the fifth century—Aeschylus's *Persians* is an example—the tragedies did not deal with contemporary concerns directly but through traditional mythological stories, which provided distance in both time and place. Some plays seem to openly glorify Athenian democratic institutions, such as Aeschylus's trilogy, the *Oresteia* (458), with *Eumenides* as its final play. Many more seem to call into question some aspect of Athenian rule or domestic or foreign policy. The plot lines of Sophocles's two plays culled from the Oedipus cycle of stories, *Antigone* (442) and *Oedipus the King* (ca. 427), deal with events in the royal family of Thebes centuries before. But their themes of ruling power and its abuse may well reflect contemporary Athenian concerns with their leaders' policies.

This questioning increased during the Peloponnesian War, when dramas highly critical of Athenian policies were produced; most of the extant tragedies by Euripides and the comedies by Aristophanes voice strong antiwar sentiments. As examples: *The Trojan Women* by Euripides (415) explores war's devastation through its effect on its vulnerable victims, the conquered women. The Athenian female heroine in Aristophanes' comedy *Lysistrata* (411), whose name means "Releaser of armies," secures peace with Sparta by organizing a sex strike by both Athenian and Spartan women against their men. Although the comedic aspects are in tune with the fantasy world of Greek Old Comedy, the message may derive from an actual, influential priestess of Athena named Lysimakhe, "Releaser of battle."

Thus, by the end of the 430s, just before and leading up to the outbreak of the second Peloponnesian War, through his influence over domestic and foreign policies, and his promoting continued Athenian cultural expansion, Perikles directed the course of Athenian affairs. His policies demonstrate the close interaction of political, military, religious, and cultural activities. However, the particular course Perikles charted led the Athenians into devastating war.

INTERPRETIVE ESSAY
Robert Garland

The period covered by this chapter is often regarded as one of the most remarkable—if not *the* most remarkable—in the history of Western civilization, owing to its extraordinary political, cultural, and artistic achievements. Indeed, the only period that properly stands comparison with it is Renaissance Italy, which was itself based on a rediscovery of many of those same achievements, albeit received through the medium of Roman culture. And just as the explosive outpouring of creative energy that we call the Renaissance had its ultimate origin in a single Italian community—fourteenth-century Florence—so, too, almost all the important developments of the Classical era radiated from Athens, a community with a population of perhaps 30,000 adult male citizens and 150,000 noncitizens including women, children, foreigners, and slaves.

It is a period framed by two events of fundamental importance: at the beginning, the wars against Persia, which a coalition of Greeks, largely due to the enterprise of the Athenians, won, and, at the end, the Peloponnesian War, an intra-Hellenic struggle that the Athenians and their allies lost. Counterfactual history—history, that is, that seeks to answer questions that are contrary to what we know to be the truth—has limited value as a tool of historical inquiry. Nevertheless, there is little doubt that the world would be a very different place today if the Persians had won the Battle of Marathon against the Athenians in 490 B.C.E. and subsequently gone on to subjugate the entire Greek world—as they might well have done but for the courage and resourcefulness of their opponents, who managed temporarily to bury their endemic rivalries. The continuing significance of the Greek victory in these wars can be seen 2,500 years later. When the Greeks rebelled against the Ottoman Turks in 1821, the memory of the Persian Wars was invoked by Philhellenes, that is to say, those who fervently admired classical Greek civilization. Most prominent among the Philhellenes was the English Romantic poet Lord Byron, who saw Greece's war of liberation as a reenactment of the ancient conflict between East and West.

The fact that the Athenians defeated the Persians at Marathon and ten years later at Salamis and Plataia, with forces vastly inferior in size to that of their enemies, is sometimes seen as the "explanation" behind the enormous rise in self-confidence characterizing Athenian society in the following half-century. Whatever its precise explanation, we can at least acknowledge that in the aftermath of that struggle, the Athenians came to believe that there was nothing they could not master. And when historians speak of Western civilization's "debt" to Greek culture, what they primarily mean is its debt to the two generations of Athenians who converted their state into a naval power of first-rank importance within the space of two years; invented participatory democracy; introduced trial by jury; built the Parthenon and other outstanding architectural works; produced magnificent works of sculpture in bronze and marble; painted graphic scenes on pottery; wrote comedies and tragedies that are now performed in theaters all over the world; made historiography subject to strict rules of evidence; saw the birth of a scientific tradition in medical inquiry; formulated the theory that all matter is composed of atoms; and established the enduring principle that ethics is a central concern of philosophical inquiry.

Yet at the heart of this achievement lies a historical paradox, which no amount of special pleading can evade; namely, that although the Athenians of the fifth century B.C.E. unquestionably changed the Greek world and shaped the future course of Western civilization, they were also a people who considered women, slaves, and non-Greeks to be biologically and intellectually inferior, committed brutal acts of barbarism against noncombatants in time of war, and selfishly exploited their fellow-Greeks in the furtherance of their aggressive imperialistic aims. And they did this while at the same time providing invaluable insights into the human condition and by establishing a sense of egalitarianism that was based on an intense hostility to autocracy. It is this central paradox relating to the achievements and failures of fifth-century Athens that this essay will seek to explore.

RISE OF THE ATHENIAN EMPIRE

Athens's power from 478 on derived from the controlling influence that the *polis* exercised over a maritime alliance known as the Delian Confederacy, so named because its council and treasury were centered on the sacred island of Delos, the birthplace of Apollo and Artemis, in the Cyclades. Formed in the wake of the devastating Persian Wars, which all but succeeded in reducing the entire Greek world to a vassal of the Persian Empire, the confederacy at its inception exemplified what the Greeks themselves regarded as their most distinctive political hallmark, namely an ideological and practical commitment to the ideals of freedom and equality. It represented one of those rare phenomena in the history of international relations—the attempt to harness the resources of its member states in an arrangement that was consistent with a democratic system of government. Thus each of the 200-odd member states exercised a single vote, irrespective of their size, military strength, and political importance, an arrangement similar to the voting system of the United Nations, which also operates on the principle of one state one vote. In theory, therefore, the Delian Confederacy constituted a free association of states linked together by a common aim, which, in principle, overrode the interests of its individual members.

Yet over the course of time the Delian Confederacy also demonstrates other, less admirable tendencies that are perhaps inherent in all human societies. The most notable of these is the tendency of the strong to dominate the weak. This is indicated by the fact that within a generation, if not sooner, Athens transformed the confederacy into an instrument of its imperialistic ambitions. In so doing, it succeeded in converting the Aegean Sea into an extension of Athenian territory and was even beginning to have designs on the Adriatic to the west. To be sure, this development could hardly have come about without the compliance of the other member states, particularly the weaker and less energetic ones, who from the start voluntarily ceded all pretensions of military muscle to Athens.

By the terms of membership any state that elected to do so was permitted the softer option of paying money into a common fund rather than providing ships to the common fleet. Before long, many larger cities, too, found that paying the annual tribute was less of a burden than providing ships, and in time only the islands of Lesbos, Chios, and Samos, situated off the western Anatolian coast, continued to do so. In this way the majority of the membership deprived itself both morally and politically of the ability to speak with a strong voice in the council. As Athens increasingly found itself shouldering the main military burden, it gained the power to dictate the decisions taken in the council, which in this way became subservient to Athenian policy making. There is no evidence suggesting that the conversion of the Delian Confederacy into an Athenian empire was a deliberate act on Athens's part, though there may well have been individuals who calculated early on that, since it was Athenian sailors who were primarily being put in harm's way, the state deserved some material reward for its disproportionate commitment of manpower.

It is impossible to determine at what precise moment the changeover from free alliance to empire occurred, though several events seem to mark the transition. The first was in 470 when the island of Naxos tried to secede and was forced back into membership. Another occurred in 454 when the league treasury was transferred from Delos to Athens, following a disastrous expedition to Egypt. The justification for the transfer, which gave Athens exclusive access to the funds contributed by the allies, was that it was undertaken in the interests of security.

As the century progressed, Athens's subjugation of its allies became more and more overt, although as late as 430 the statesman Perikles could, according to the historian Thucydides, still claim before an Athenian audience that the state made it its policy "to protect the weak." Perikles, however, made this remark at a service over the ashes of the war dead, an extremely patriotic occasion; whether many Athenians would have believed him is another matter altogether. The ultimate proof of Athens's tyrannical control over its allies and of the nakedness of its will to grab power was demonstrated in 415, when the citizen body took the decision to execute the entire male population of the tiny island of Melos and enslave its women and children, merely for professing neutrality and refusing to join the alliance.

The history of the Delian Confederacy thus exemplifies the best and the worst in the history of international relations. If one were to seek a modern institutional analogy, the closest would probably be NATO, a free alliance that was similarly formed in the wake of a victory against foreign aggression. Though NATO has never become an instrument of American imperialism, it is nonetheless subject to the same kind of tensions that invariably exist between a militarily superior power and its weaker allies, such as characterized the early days of the Delian Confederacy.

ATHENIAN DEMOCRACY

Athens's increasing stranglehold over its allies abroad went hand in hand with the establishment of a radical democracy at home. By the late 460s or the early 450s Athens had introduced a system of direct participatory democracy that gave every male citizen influence over the political decision-making process. It is a system without parallel in history. Never before or since has so much confidence and authority been invested in the common man. There is also some evidence to suggest that the state fostered democratic institutions within the Delian Confederacy, though it is unlikely that all the member states were as "advanced" democratically as Athens.

The Athenian *dêmos*, or citizen body, wielded its political power through the *ekklêsia*, or Assembly, which met regularly four times a month. Magistrates and all lesser officials were its servants and subject to investigation both before and after assuming office. Each citizen exercised one vote and had the right to address the *ekklêsia* on whatever subject was under debate. The agenda presented to the *ekklêsia* was prepared by the *boulê*, Council of 500, whose members were elected by lot, fifty from each of the ten tribes. Allotment was further proof of the egalitarian nature of the citizen body, since it assumed that all Athenians were equal in intelligence. The only magistrates who were not elected by lot were the board of ten generals known as *stratêgoi*, who were chosen by popular vote, one from each tribe. Even so, their authority was severely limited. Like ordinary citizens, they had to propose measures before the assembly and even when campaigning they were dependent on the wishes of the *dêmos*, which had the power to recall them whenever it wished. Finally, the *dêmos*, sitting as the *hêliaia* or law court, exercised supreme judicial authority. The jurors, who received a modest wage for their services, largely comprised elderly citizens no longer fit for more active work.

Though our word democracy derives from two Greek words, *dêmos*, meaning "people," and *kratos*, meaning "power," *dêmokratia* itself was not in common usage in the fifth century. Instead, the terms most closely expressing what today we describe as the democratic ideal were *isêgoria* ("equality of speech") and *isonomia* ("equality before the law"). What these signify is that Athenian democracy was both a legal and a political ideal. In other words, it was as much the establishment of a people's court as equal access to the political decision-making process that constituted the cornerstone of Athenian democracy. This is further suggested by the famous trial scene in Aeschylus's *Eumenides*, the third play in the *Oresteia* trilogy, in which a jury of Athenian citizens—the first such jury ever appointed according to legend—vote to acquit Orestes, the son of Agamemnon, who had been accused of murdering his mother Klytaimnestra.

The reason why Athens was able to practice radical democracy at home while subjugating fellow-Greeks abroad is due in part to the fact that the Greek world lacked any concept of what we would call today civil rights or civil liberties. Athenians were quite prepared to share their privileges with those whom they identified as members of their citizen body but they never made the imaginative leap of extending those privileges to other groups, such as women or foreigners—let alone slaves.

The disenfrachisement of women, which is often regarded as one of the most unpalatable aspects of Athenian democracy, was predicated on a strong conviction in their inferiority.

In fact, exactly at the moment when political rights and privileges were being extended to the citizen body, the qualifications for citizenship itself were being tightened. In 451 the *dêmos* voted to restrict the citizenship to those of citizen birth on both sides of their family. It is for this reason that, although Athens may justifiably be said to have "invented" democracy, our own modern Western democratic systems of government owe little to the fifth-century model. In fact, for more than a thousand years democracy completely died out, not only in Greece, but throughout Europe. It is abundantly clear, therefore, that the enlightened words of the American Declaration of Independence, "We hold these truths to be self-evident, that all men are created equal . . ." were in no way anticipated by the elitist Athenian reforms of 462, however much we may applaud the general leveling principle upon which they were based.

Some Athenians were, however, extremely hostile to the democracy, though not perhaps for the reasons that we would give today. One of its most distinguished critics was Plato, who put into the mouth of Sokrates statements such as, "The city is full of liberty and free speech and everyone is allowed to do what he likes" (*Republic* 8.557b). Similarly Xenophon attributed to Sokrates the observation, "No one would be prepared to employ a pilot or carpenter or flautist chosen by lot, but when you want anyone to run your city, you go to any common amateur to do the job" (*Memorabilia* 1.2.9).

It was the Peloponnesian War that constituted the most serious challenge to the effectiveness of Athenian democracy. Since there was no allegiance to party, no government and opposition, and no elected head of state who exercised political authority, it was inevitable that the *dêmos* should have been subject to sudden and occasionally violent changes of policy. One such violent change of policy took place in 427 when, having voted to execute all the male citizens of Mytilene on the island of Lesbos for insurrection, it rescinded its decision the very next day.

Probably the worst decision that the *dêmos* ever took was to launch an expedition against Sicily in 415. Even after the failure of this expedition, and the resumption three years later of hostilities with Sparta, Athens carried on the war against increased odds for nearly ten more years. It is often forgotten how much self-discipline and determination this must have required on the part of a "fickle mob." Only for a brief interlude—in 411—was the franchise reduced in size and never, until the final months of the war, was democracy actually suspended. This in itself is a remarkable achievement, given that even representative democracies such as those that exist in the free world today are put under enormous strain whenever warfare becomes protracted.

The most celebrated "crime" that is laid at the door of Athenian democracy was the trial and execution of Sokrates, in 399 B.C.E. Some historians see the trial as proof that the Athenian *dêmos*, far from being liberal and tolerant, was both repressive and conservative. Whether this is true or not, there was clearly a political dimension to the charges brought against him, even though Sokrates himself conspicuously played no part in politics. However, he numbered among his pupils several conservative hard-liners, most prominent among whom were Alkibiades, who betrayed Athens, and Kallias, one of the Thirty Tyrants, both judged to have played a leading role in Athens's defeat. Sokrates' trial occurred in the immediate aftermath of the war, and it seems to have functioned very much as a show trial. Hence, rather than being a mark of repressiveness as such, we should perhaps view the trial as an attempt by the newly restored democracy to heal political wounds by making a scapegoat of its most prominent and outspoken critic. With the exception of Sokrates and the Thirty Tyrants, the *dêmos* proclaimed a general amnesty to all political dissidents at the end of the war.

CULTURAL ACHIEVEMENTS

The coincidence between Athens's democratic coming of age on the one hand, and its imperialistic ambitions on the other, is embodied in the Parthenon, the Temple of Athena Parthenos ("Maiden"), which was built on the south side of the Akropolis over the rubble of a previous temple to the same goddess (see Figure 6). The Akropolis is a high rock that rises sharply out of the level plain of Attika. The previous temple had been destroyed by the Persians in 480 and for thirty years the Athenians had left the Akropolis in ruins as a memorial to Persian savagery, in much the same way as the Temple Mount in Jerusalem remains a memorial to the destruction of the city by the Romans in 70 C.E. On the recommendation of Perikles, however, the *dêmos* took the decision in 448 B.C.E. to build a magnificent new temple on a majestic scale that was consistent with the grandiose political aspirations of the city and the claims to preeminence of its protective deity Athena. Curiously, however, though Athena Polias ("Of the city") was worshipped on the Akropolis, there do not seem to have been any rites to Athena Parthenos there before the temple was built.

The Parthenon is the crowning achievement of classical Greek architecture. Yet it was paid for out of the surplus money that was accruing to Athens's coffers from the allied tribute. This is a significant fact, because, although the Parthenon is often cited with justification as the quintessential expression of Athenian democracy, we should also bear in mind that it was paid for from tribute money reaped by a repressive imperialistic power.

The architects were Iktinos and Kallikrates, but the guiding spirit behind the sculptural decoration was Pheidias, perhaps the greatest sculptor of his day, who was also responsible for the colossal forty-foot-high statue of Athena, which stood inside the temple. It was covered in gold, ivory, and other costly materials, which, however, all disappeared in antiquity; hence, we know of it only from descriptions and small-scale copies. The architectural sculpture, which is one of the chief glories of Greek art, is redolent with allusions to Greek and, specifically, Athenian cultural supremacy. It demonstrates the fact that the Athenians were fully aware of how to exploit art—even what we today would call religious art—for propagandistic effect. Thus the scenes on the metopes, or rectangular slabs, which surmount the outer colonnade of the Parthenon, were intended to present the Persian Wars to the spectator as a simple case of good versus evil. Since the Parthenon was a sacred building dedicated to the goddess Athena, however, this message could only be conveyed obliquely. Pheidias therefore clothed this message in the language of mythology by depicting the battle between the Lapiths and Centaurs, mythological creatures with the bodies and legs of horses and the torsos and heads of men. The battle was intended to symbolize the Persian Wars, which similarly involved a struggle between a higher and lower order of civilization, as viewed from a Greek perspective. The choice of myth was doubly appropriate, however, in that it presented the higher order of civilization as innocent victims, since the ensuing struggle resulted from the abduction of a Lapith bride by drunken and debauched Centaurs at a wedding feast to which they, the Centaurs, had been invited as guests.

The sculpture that fills the triangular pediments that crown the east and west side of the building proclaims no less loudly the special favor that Athens enjoyed from the gods. The west pediment depicts the contest for the guardianship of the land of Athens, which took place between Athena and her rival, the sea god Poseidon. According to the charter myth of the Athenian state, both deities were so enamoured of Attika that they bestowed gifts on the land. In the contest that followed, Athena's olive tree was judged superior to Poseidon's salt spray, and Athena was appointed tutelary deity.

Finally, the great frieze that runs around the outer wall of the building depicting the Athenians celebrating the festival of Athena known as the Panathenaia perfectly exemplifies the spirit of a democratic and free society. This is particularly evident in the famous cavalcade of horsemen, all of whom are rendered in strikingly different and highly naturalistic poses, some straining forward, others reining back, all in ceaseless motion yet all yoked together in the service of a single ideal. The frieze is state-sponsored art at its most ideological, in that it celebrates Athenian democracy as a hallowed and sanctified institution that enjoyed the favor and protection of the gods. It thus embodies everything that many artists and non-artists alike today regard with horror. Even so, by the variety and vigor of the sculptural poses Pheidias brilliantly succeeded in evoking the spirit of unfettered freedom upon which Athenian democracy was ideally based.

Probably the most influential cultural development of fifth-century Athens was the establishment of a vibrant dramatic tradition, excelling in the the two theatrical genres still vital today—tragedy and comedy. The sixth-century Athenian tyrant Peisistratos promoted drama to a first-rank Athenian endeavor by giving it a prominent place in the City Dionysia, a festival held in honor of Dionysos, patron god of drama, at which tragedies and some 486 comedies were performed. The City Dionysia was not devoted only to drama, however. Since it coincided with the beginning of the sailing season, many foreigners and tourists attended, including Athens's allies. The tribute they were required to give Athens was displayed in the theater—compelling evidence of the intermingling of the secular with the divine so characteristic of Greek culture. It was also the custom to parade the orphans of the war dead in the theater so they could receive the blessings of the *dêmos*. In circa 440, the Athenians established a separate festival devoted exclusively to comedy, the Lenaia.

In the fifth century, drama achieved its fullest potential through the tragedies of Aeschylus, Sophocles, and Euripides, and the comedies of Aristophanes. There are 32 extant tragedies in all, 7 by Aeschylus and Sophocles apiece and 19 by Euripides. Of Attic comedy, we have 11 plays by Aristophanes. This represents but a small fraction of their entire output—and an infinitessimal fraction of all the plays that were written and performed. Aeschylus produced at least 73 plays, Sophocles 123, Euripides 92, and Aristophanes about 30.

Staging a play was truly a civic undertaking. Each tragedian submitted a trilogy and a satyr play. (Satyrs were half-human and half-animal creatures whose drunken antics provided a lighthearted antidote to the seriousness of tragedy.) Comic playwrights submitted only one play. Only three dramatists received public funding in each category. Once the magistrate in charge had selected the plays to be performed, he allocated to each production a *chorêgos* or chorus master, whose responsibility was to pay all the expenses. *Chorêgoi* were wealthy Athenians or resident aliens, who were expected to spare no expense in the undertaking. In fact, they competed with one another as much as did the playwrights, and, if victorious, were permitted to erect a monument commemorating the fact. A conservative estimate puts the size of the Athenian audience that attended the Theater of Dionysos on the south slope of the Akropolis at somewhere between 14,000 to 17,000—possibly the largest number of citizens that gathered together on a regular basis anywhere in the Greek world, except for the Olympic Games. When the plays had been performed, ten judges, appointed by lot, cast their votes in a secret ballot in order to determine which playwright was the winner. It is estimated that no fewer than 1,500 Athenians were involved in the staging of the plays that were performed at the City Dionysia each year. The second-century-c.e. Greek writer Plutarch claimed that the Athenians actually spent more money on dramatic festivals than they did on their defense budget (*Moral Precepts* 349a).

Though the subject matter of tragedy is almost exclusively based on stories that are taken from the timeless world of myth, the playwrights were free to reinterpret and rework these stories in whatever way they saw fit. Thus, as we have seen, Aeschylus's *Eumenides* gives sanction to the democratic reforms of Perikles and Ephialtes. Only very occasionally, however, can we determine what event might have prompted a playwright to select a particular story as the vehicle for his ideas. Euripides' *Trojan Women*, for instance, which was once thought to have been inspired by the destruction of Melos, is now believed to have been composed prior to that event. If so, the play constitutes a generalized warning against acts of brutality committed in war, rather than a condemnation of a specific action. But whatever the degree or frequency of allusions to fifth-century politics in Attic tragedy, scholars agree that the genre played a major part in shaping civic identity and in exposing and exploring tensions within civic thought.

One of the most striking features of tragedy is the prominence of female characters, which is in stark contrast to women's marginalized and subordinate status in the society. Indeed fifth-century tragedy has bequeathed to us some of the most memorable female roles of any period, including Klytaimnestra, Antigone, Medea, Phaidra, and Hekabe. Klytaimnestra, who murdered her husband in revenge for his sacrifice of their daughter Iphigeneia; Phaidra, who falsely accused her stepson of trying to seduce her; and Medea, who murdered her own children to get back at her husband are among the most terrifying female characters in the entire Western dramatic repertoire. The explanation for this paradox between the virtual invisibility of Athenian women in real life and their prominence on the stage has been much debated. For many it demonstrates the tragedians' keen interest in and insight into the female psyche not manifested in any other aspect of Greek culture, where the drama itself offers an opportunity to explore what the society otherwise keeps hidden. However, it is highly unlikely that the dramatists would have thought to use the theater as a way to improve women's social or political status.

Attic comedy, by contrast, is highly topical in subject matter and contains abundant references to events and personalities in contemporary Athens, many of which, unfortunately, are lost on us. It is also ribald and scatalogical. Frequently the plot involves a solution to a contemporary problem, such as how to bring about an end to the Peloponnesian War. In *Acharnians*, for instance, the hero achieves his goal by making a private peace with the Spartans. In *Lysistrata*, the women of Athens decide to initiate peace negotiations by refusing to have sex with their husbands.

Attic drama is illustrative of several important trends within Athenian society. In the first place it provided a context in which matters of public concern could be literally aired in public. It was thus part of what has been called the culture of public display and played a similar function to that of the assembly and the law courts. Second, it was highly conventional. Though the playwrights were free to innovate in the interpretation of a myth, a prominent role was assigned to the chorus in every tragedy and comedy. And third, it was highly competitive. Though the criteria the judges used to make their choices are unknown to us, it is clear that the Athenians took winning very seriously, evidenced by the fact that they recorded the names of the victorious plays in an inscription they erected on the Akropolis.

From 387 B.C.E., Athenians began to revive fifth-century tragedies, and from the third century they became the inspiration for numerous plays by Roman tragedians, including Ennius, Accius, Livius Andronicus Pacuvius, and Seneca. Though fifth-century Attic comedy had no direct progeny, tragedy continues to play a major part in shaping the history of Western drama, both directly and indirectly. Its influence is apparent in the works of some of the most distinguished Western playwrights from the Renaissance to the present day, including Christopher Marlowe,

William Shakespeare, Jean Racine, Henrik Ibsen, August Strindberg, and Arthur Miller, even though each has his own distinct vision of what constitutes the tragic. It is a fair bet that without Greek tragedy we would not have *Hamlet*, which owes something—we do know how much—both to Aeschylus's *Libation-Bearers* and to Sophocles' *Electra*. However, Shakespeare, like most men of his time, probably received Greek tragedy through the lens of the Roman tragedian Seneca, since Latin was far more accessible than Greek to the reading public of the Renaissance. Greek tragedy inspired the creation and the subject of many operas, from Christoph Gluck (1714–1787) to Sir Harrison Birtwhistle (1934–). Indeed, Wagner's reading of J.G. Droysen's German translation of Aeschylus' *Prometheus Bound* and *Oresteia*, probably inspired him to undertake his celebrated musical tetralogy, the Ring of the Nibelungs.

The horrific carnage of World War I catapulted Attic tragedy to prominence in the commercial theater, particularly the plays of Euripides, which became an effective medium for expressing pacifist and antiwar sentiments—a role they have retained to this day. The popularity of Greek tragedy increased throughout the twentieth century, and by the 1980s Greek tragedies were being produced in countries as diverse as Kenya, India, China, Japan, Korea, Ethiopia, and South Africa. One of the liveliest traditions is maintained in Greece itself, whose touring companies regularly perform Greek tragedy in theaters throughout the world. Aeschylus's *Oresteia*, Sophocles' *Antigone* and *Oedipus the King*, and Euripides' *Bacchae, Medea,* and *Trojan Women* are among the most popularly staged plays.

Though the classical Athenian tradition of using drama as a way of articulating political concerns is no longer a prominent element in contemporary mainstream drama, these dramas are often selected by directors who wish to convey an overtly political message. They will surely continue to do so in the future, whenever protests are made against the conduct of war and those who wage it. And we can be equally confident that Greek tragedy will remain a part of Western civilization for as long as Western civilization itself endures.

It is difficult not to contemplate the achievements of fifth-century Athens without viewing it as a kind of Greek tragedy. Here, after all, was a society that expanded human potential to limits that have rarely been equaled since, yet one too that committed terrible political and military blunders. It was a society that pushed forward the frontiers of human achievement in so many fields, yet one that acted repressively and vindictively to its enemies and so-called allies alike. In short, it was a society founded on a principle of commonality, which also remained rooted in privilege and prejudice. The successes and failures of fifth-century Athens painfully remind us of the tragic gap that all too frequently exists between high culture on the one hand and a civil society on the other.

SUGGESTIONS FOR FURTHER READING

Barrow, R. 1992. *Athenian Democracy: The Triumph and the Folly*. Surrey, UK: Thomas Nelson. An evaluation of the achievements and failures of Athenian democracy.

Davies, J.K. 1986. *Democracy and Classical Greece*. London and Stanford, Calif.: Fontana and Stanford University Press. Standard and highly dependable introduction to the classical period.

Easterling, P.E., ed. 1997. *The Cambridge Companion to Greek Tragedy*. Cambridge: Cambridge University Press. A collection of essays covering various aspects of the reception of Greek tragedy.

Fantham, Elaine et al. 1994. *Women in the Classical World*. New York and Oxford: Oxford University Press. Chapter 3 provides an extensive discussion of women's roles in Classical Athens and Sparta.

Foley, Helene P. 1999. "Modern Performances and Adaptations of Greek Tragedy." *Transactions of the American Philological Association* 129:1–12. A brief account of tragedy on the contemporary commercial stage.

Goldhill, Simon, and Robin Osborne. 1999. *Performance Culture and Athenian Democracy*. Cambridge: Cambridge University Press. A collection of essays emphasizing the importance of performance in Athenian culture in contexts outside the theater.

Jenkins, Ian. 1994. *The Parthenon Frieze*. London and Austin: British Museum and University of Texas Press. A reconstruction of the Parthenon frieze in light of the most up-to-date imaging research.

Just, Roger. 1991. *Women in Athenian Law and Life*. London and New York: Routledge. A detailed examination of women's roles in Athenian society.

Knox, B.M.W. 1979. *Word and and Action: Essays on the Ancient Theatre*. Baltimore and London: The Johns Hopkins University Press. A collection of important essays on Greek tragedy.

Meiggs, Russell. 1979. *The Athenian Empire*. Oxford: Oxford University Press. The most authoritative examination of the evolution of the Athenian Confederacy into an Athenian Empire.

Ober, Josiah. 1997. *The Athenian Revolution: Essays on Ancient Greek Democracy and Political Theory*. Chicago: University of Chicago Press. Collection of essays evaluating the relationship between the masses and the elite.

Roberts, Jennifer. 1994. *Athens on Trial: The Antidemocratic Tradition in Western Thought*. Princeton, N.J.: Princeton University Press. An investigation of the degree to which Athens can claim to have constituted a genuine democracy.

Roberts, J.W. 1984. *City of Sokrates: An Introduction to Classical Athens*. London and Boston: Routledge and Kegan Paul. Basic handbook dealing with a variety of aspects of Athenian political life and culture.

Steiner, George. 1961. *The Death of Tragedy*. London: Faber and Faber. Investigation of the attempts by postclassical dramatists to write tragedies equal in quality to those of the Athenian tragedians.

———. 1984. *Antigones*. Oxford: Clarendon Press. The reception of Sophocles' *Antigone* and other plays based on the Antigone theme from antiquity to the present.

Taplin, Oliver. 1978. *Greek Tragedy in Action*. London: Methuen. Greek tragedy from the perspective of performance.

Woodford, Susan. 1981. *The Parthenon*. Cambridge: Cambridge University Press. Basic introduction to the Parthenon, including discussion of its construction and later history.

7

The Peloponnesian War: The Challenge to Athens and the Triumph of Sparta

INTRODUCTION

Athens's increasing self-aggrandizement in the years following the Persian Wars ultimately led to open hostilities between Athens and other Greek communities. This series of hostilities, battles, and open warfare was known as the Peloponnesian War. While Herodotos provided retrospective accounts of the Persian Wars, the Athenian historian Thucydides kept a chronicle of the year-by-year events of these intra-Greek hostilities. Himself a participant in the war he narrates, Thucydides' contemporary account provides our principal source for many details of that war. The major antagonists were Athens and its allies on the one side, and the principal cities of the Peloponnesian League on the other. Heading this defensive league, which predated the Persian Wars, were the only two other Greek *poleis* that could match the growing military and political might of Athens: Korinth, an important port city whose fleet rivaled the Athenian navy, and especially Sparta, still considered the most formidable military force of the Greeks and which had controlled the Peloponnesian League since its inception.

The First Peloponnesian War was precipitated by Korinth in 460 B.C.E. Korinth's strategic location on the Gulf of Korinth in the northern Peloponnesos gave it major control of the western trade routes with Sicily.

Figure 7. Attic grave stele of Philoxenos and Philomene, circa 400 B.C.E. Marble. Courtesy of The J. Paul Getty Museum, Malibu, California.

Fearing that Athens' growing mercantile interests would threaten their control of these trade routes, leaders in Korinth actively agitated for war and tried to convince Sparta to join them. At about the same time (461–456), Athens built what came to be known as "the Long Walls," with a third one added in 445, which connected Athens with its two harbors, Phaleron and Piraios, and which ensured Athenians' access to supplies by sea during the war.

When Korinth was unsuccessful in enlisting the isolationist-inclined Spartans to their cause against Athens, Korinth attacked the town of Megara (460). Megara, about midway between Athens and Korinth, was frequently beset by its more powerful neighbors, and its allegiances would shift depending on contemporary circumstances. Attacked by Korinth, Megara appealed to Athens for aid, and the resultant battles, principally between Korinth and Athens, became known as the First Peloponnesian War. When Sparta attacked Attika, the region around Athens (446), the Thirty Years Peace was negotiated in which Athens agreed to give up the lands it had gained during this war, and each side agreed to respect the other's autonomy, as well as that of other Greek commmunities.

However, the Thirty Years Peace did not slow Athens's empire-building activities, nor did it allay Korinth's or Sparta's discontent with these Athenian policies, and the peace lasted barely fifteen years. Megara was again a key factor in the subsequent outbreak of hostilities in 431. The city had begun cultivating sacred land on its border with Athens, and, in retaliation, Athens restricted Megarian access to Athenian markets both in Athens and throughout its empire. Sparta now openly entered into the fray, intending to liberate Greece from the tyrant city Athens, and the Peloponnesian War proper began. It lasted, with some intermittent periods of truce, until 404. According to Thucydides, the war consisted principally of a series of yearly raids by Athens or Sparta against the territory and allies of the other. These raids began in the spring and lasted through the summer, with the winter frequently a period of respite from hostilities. Spartan invasions of Attika often included burning of crops, resulting in greater hardship for the Athenians than for the Spartans, whose location in the southern Peloponnesos across difficult mountainous terrain insulated it somewhat from similar destruction of their food supply by the Athenians.

From the very beginning of the war, Athenians suffered terribly. One year after the war's outbreak, from 430 to 426, a plague ravaged Athens, which Sophocles recalls in the opening scene of his play *Oedipus the King*. Its cause unknown, the plague was especially devastating because inhabitants of the countryside and outlying areas, whose farms and crops were destroyed by the Spartans, were crammed into Athens's city walls. Perikles, the leader of Athens through the second half of the fifth century, who spearheaded and was lauded for the course he set for Athens, succumbed to the plague and died in 429.

Overcrowded, undergoing severe political upheaval, suffering from the ravages of war and disease, Athens engaged in a number of policies that starkly demonstrated its despotic notions of power. In 427, putting down a revolt in Mytilene, the principal city on the island of Lesbos, the Athenian assembly debated killing the men and enslaving the women and children. While they established an Athenian colony on Lesbos, at this time the Athenians decided against taking this extreme action. The island of Melos was not so fortunate. Athens could not abide the Melians' intention to remain neutral. After a failed attempt in 426, in 416–415, Athens overpowered the island, killing the men, enslaving the women and children, and establishing an Athenian colony on the island. In 425, Athenian forces occupied Pylos on the southeastern Peloponnese and isolated Spartan troops on the nearby island of Sphakteria. Concern for the fate of their soldiers captured by the Athenians encouraged the Spartans to agree to an armistice in 423 and to sign the Peace of Nikias in 421.

This peace treaty was fashioned by the principal leader in Athens since Perikles' death, Nikias, who advocated a more moderate course for Athens, which included making peace with Sparta as soon as Athens could do so honorably. And he engineered the peace treaty that bears his name. His arguments, however, could not sway the extreme democratic followers of Alkibiades, a charismatic and erratic political figure, who advocated active Athenian intervention in the Peloponnesos. In 416, the same year that the siege of Melos began, Alkibiades persuaded Athens to embark on another action that violated the 421 peace treaty—conquest of Sicily. Opposed to this imperialist policy, Nikias was nevertheless chosen one of three commanders to lead the Athenian forces, and he reluctantly accompanied Alkibiades and the third general, Lamakhos, on this mission.

Suffering from divided leadership, the expedition was fraught, in Athenian eyes, with bad omens from its outset. The night before the fleet sailed, numerous sacred stone icons called "herms" were desecrated throughout the city. Implicated in this "destruction of the herms" scandal, Alkibiades was recalled to Athens to stand trial. He fled instead to Sparta, where he urged the Spartans to send forces to Sicily to fight the

Athenians. When Lamakhos died shortly thereafter, the reluctant general Nikias was left alone in command. Despite some initial military success, when the Spartan forces arrived, the Athenian troops were overrun. The almost total destruction of the Athenian forces has been attributed to weak decisions by Nikias. Despite this devastation, known as "the Sicilian disaster," Athens recovered and continued the war effort.

In the last decade of the fifth century, Athens endured severe political and military turmoil, resulting largely from the violent actions of the antidemocratic, aristocratic young men's clubs. Prompted by Alkibiades, who had by now fled Sparta and was trying to enlist Persian aid for Athens, an oligarchic revolution overthrew the Athenian democracy in 411. Rebuffing Alkibiades and killing prominent democrats, a tyrannical council of 400 was established and canceled numerous democratic laws. Short-lived, this oligarchic revolution was itself overthrown and democracy restored in 410.

Although Athens won a few more battles, in 405, with Persian financial help, Sparta destroyed the Athenian fleet at Aigospotamoi at the Hellespont and cut off Athenian trade connections to the east. When Athens surrendered in 404, the Spartans destroyed the long walls to the accompaniment of flute music and established a Spartan-friendly oligarchy. Like the earlier one, this oligarchy too was soon ousted, as the Athenians restored their democracy in 403. But their defeat in the Peloponnesian War subdued Athenian imperialism for a time.

By contrast, buoyed by their victory over Athens and support from wealthy Persia, Sparta embarked in the next few years on its own imperialist course, engaging in wars with Thebes, Korinth and other Greek cities on the mainland and in Asia Minor, and, within a decade, with Persia as well. Decisively defeated by the Thebans in 371, Spartan might was reduced and the Peloponnesian League itself was disbanded in 366.

Athens's glorious century, from its prominent role in repelling the Persian invasions, through its political expansions and cultural achievements in drama, temple architecture, and the arts, came to an end. In the fourth century, Athens would continue as an intellectual center with the emergence of noteworthy orators and the development of the philosophic schools of Plato and Aristotle. But the fourth-century conquests of Philip II of Makedon and of his son Alexander the Great ended the attempted political hegemonies of these individual Greek city-states, submerging them into the large-scale Makedonian and Hellenistic empires that were to rule Greece until their eventual conquest by the Romans in the second century B.C.E.

INTERPRETIVE ESSAY
John W. I. Lee

Imagine this: you're born a citizen of a prosperous and powerful democracy. With its mighty navy, your city rules a far-flung maritime empire. From a thousand different places, tribute, grain, and exotic goods flow into its bustling ports. Culture and the arts flourish: each year, playwrights offer new and provocative dramas, while marble temples adorn the heights. Since you were a teenager, the same skillful politician has guided your city, moderating the passions of its assembly and checking the ambitions of foreign rivals. As a propertied citizen with good family connections, you have a promising political career to look forward to. And then, everything changes. For almost thirty years, the last half of your life, your city wars with its greatest rival. Early on you are elected a general, but botch your assigned mission. Exiled for this failure, you become a wandering observer, a chronicler of the war rather than a participant.

The man in whose sandals you are standing was an Athenian named Thucydides, son of Oloros, who composed an eight-book history of the twenty-seven-year struggle between Athens and Sparta, which we call the Peloponnesian War. Although later writers, such as the Athenian Xenophon (ca. 427–355 B.C.E.) and the biographer Plutarch (ca. 50–120 C.E.), as well as inscriptions and archaeology, provide much information about the war and its participants, Thucydides' account remains our main narrative source. Indeed, the Peloponnesian War as we know it is in a sense Thucydides' war, colored by his own experiences, beliefs, and methods.

Of Thucydides himself, little is known. He was born about 460 B.C.E. into a prominent Athenian family; Kimon, the aristocratic rival of his hero Perikles, was one of his relatives. Thucydides' father's name was Thracian, indicating marriage ties with the royal family of Thrace. Thucydides, like Perikles, caught the plague that swept Athens at the beginning of the war, but survived to be elected general in 424. Because of his connections with Thrace, Thucydides was dispatched to defend Athenian possessions there against Spartan attack. He failed, however, to prevent the Spartan general Brasidas from seizing the key city of Amphipolis. For this the Athenians tried Thucydides, stripped him of his generalship, and banished him. He would not return to Athens until after the end of the war, more than two decades later.

Already from the outset of hostilities, Thucydides had been recording the course of a conflict he judged the greatest disturbance in human history. But, as he tells us, it was "my fate to be an exile for twenty years after my command at Amphipolis; and being present with both parties, and more especially with the Peloponnesians by reason of my exile, I had leisure to observe affairs more closely" (Thucydides, 5.26.5). Perhaps we should be grateful that Thucydides was not a successful commander, for had he defeated Brasidas and gone on to a political career in Athens, he might never have turned his energies to writing history. Instead, exile allowed him to devote himself to this project. Moreover, exile gave Thucydides a certain freedom of movement, an opportunity to see what was happening from both sides rather than solely from the Athenian perspective, and thereby to arrive at a fuller picture of events.

As raw material for his history, Thucydides used his own observations combined with interviews of participants and eyewitnesses. He did sometimes consult documents, but in a world where information was, for the most part, transmitted orally rather than in writing, it was only natural for him to rely more on what he heard or saw than on what he read. Still, Thucydides did not accept oral accounts uncritically: he knew that different eyewitnesses could give drastically different versions of the same event, and he tried to correct for his informants' biases and sometimes faulty memories. He did not, he claims, even trust his own impressions of an event, without first checking them against the information he received from others.

Like his predecessor Herodotos, Thucydides combined narrative passages with speeches in direct discourse. Yet Thucydides far exceeded Herodotos in the use of speeches; his history contains more than 140 of them, often paired to illustrate opposing political views or battle strategies. However, the speeches in Thucydides are not word-for-word transcripts. The phrasing, and perhaps sometimes the views expressed, belong to Thucydides, not the actual speakers. Nevertheless, Thucydides did not fabricate these speeches; rather, he tried to make them adhere as closely as possible to what the speakers actually said. Each speech, then, has a genuine core.

Whether in narrative or speeches, Thucydides pursued accuracy. He implemented his own chronological system, dating events by year and season of the war, in order to avoid the confusion caused by the multiplicity of local calendars. For each year, he recounted events throughout Greece systematically, region by region. He described unfamiliar phenomena in exacting detail, for example, devoting more than eighty lines to the symptoms of the plague. He even went so far as to examine archaeological evidence, on occasion, including walls and graves.

Despite this preoccupation with accuracy, Thucydides did not write simply to record events, nor, he claimed, did he seek to entertain in the manner of Herodotos. Instead, Thucydides saw his history as a tool, as a "possession for all time" (1.22.4). "If it be judged useful," he writes, "by those inquirers who desire an exact knowledge of the past as an aid to the understanding of the future, which in the course of human things must resemble if it does not reflect it, I shall be content" (1.22.4). Specific events, therefore, were important, but more important were the eternal principles of human behavior underlying these events. In describing the spread of civil strife throughout the Hellenic world, Thucydides asserts: "The sufferings which revolution entailed upon the cities were many and terrible, such as have occurred and always will occur as long as the nature of mankind remains the same, though in a severer or milder form, and varying in their symptoms, according to the variety of the particular cases" (3.82). Unlike Herodotos, whose narrative of the Persian Wars shows the hands of the gods at work everywhere, Thucydides rejected divine will as a means of historical explanation. Luck and fate, to be sure, did have their place, but in the end human behavior, not the gods, set events in motion.

His concern for general principles and his view of history as a guide to the future led Thucydides to neglect certain topics considered essential by modern historians. He has generally little to say about social or economic affairs, focusing rather on political and military events. This focus also led him largely to ignore women and slaves; women, in particular, make only a handful of brief appearances. Conversely, Thucydides gave detailed treatment to some episodes that had scant bearing on the course of the war because they illustrated central themes of his work. The little island of Melos, for instance, receives a substantial digression in Book 5 not because Melos was a major belligerent, but because the dialogue over its fate helps reveal how empires behave. We might fault Thucydides for his omissions and preoccupations, yet within the framework of his world this focus on war and politics made sense. For a Greek citizen, these were the essentials of life, being a doer of deeds and speaker of words. Indeed, Thucydides may have placed such emphasis on war and politics precisely because, as an exile, he could no longer take part in either.

Although he lived to see the end of the war, dying after 400, Thucydides did not complete his history. Book 8 stops abruptly midsentence, in 411. Unlike the preceding books, Book 8 lacks speeches, further indicating that Thucydides never revised it. Incomplete as it is, Thucydides' work remains arguably the greatest ancient Greek historical text. It was recognized as such in his own time; Xenophon paid Thucydides the supreme compliment of starting his own history of Greek affairs exactly where Thucydides left off. Ultimately, the best way to comprehend Thucydides is to read him for oneself, carefully and repeatedly. The effort is worth it, for his history recounts, in poetic, forceful, and sometimes jarring language, not only the words and deeds of famous orators and generals, but also the sufferings and endurance of ordinary people caught in the agony of a prolonged and brutal war.

GREEK WARFARE

The Peloponnesian War changed Thucydides: it cost him his political career, made him an exile, turned him into a spectator rather than an actor. And the war changed Greece. In particular, it upset centuries-old conventions of warfare, convulsed Athenian politics and society, and ultimately fostered the collapse of its victor, Sparta.

Since the rise of the *polis* in the eighth century B.C.E., Greek warfare had been dominated by the hoplite, or heavily armored foot soldier (see Figure 5). Protected by a large, round shield (*hoplon*) and a bronze helmet and breastplate, the hoplite carried an eight-foot spear and a short sword. Hoplites fought standing shoulder to shoulder in a phalanx formation four to eight men deep, stabbing with their spears over the wall of shields created by their dense arrangement. In a head-on fight on level ground, a phalanx was nearly impervious to cavalry or archers; only another phalanx might defeat it.

Under the agrarian conditions of the traditional *polis*, hoplites were middle-class citizens, mostly farmers, who furnished their own arms and armor. Hoplites were militia, not professionals; most got little formal training, and as farmers they could afford to leave their fields only for limited periods each summer. So hoplite battle tended to be ritualized and limited, if horrific. Invaders advanced onto enemy soil, expecting that their opponents would offer battle rather than see their fields and ancestral shrines desecrated. Phalanxes would line up against each other, speeches and sacrifices would be made, then the two sides would march forward and collide. Inevitably, one phalanx broke and ran. Rather than pursue the fleeing warriors, the victors more often stopped to put up a trophy before returning home to tend their crops.

The middling farmers liked traditional hoplite warfare, for it kept battle from intruding too much on their agricultural labors, limited the destructiveness of war, and gave them dominance in the conduct of military affairs. Furthermore, because military and political participation were closely linked in the early *polis*, and not everybody could afford the necessary equipment, hoplite warfare helped keep the landless and the poor out of politics.

Sparta was the exception to the hoplite rule. From early childhood, male Spartan citizens trained full-time for war, their helots taking care of the farming. In battle, Spartan troops advanced to the cadence of flutes; their red cloaks and long hair often terrified opponents into flight even before real fighting began. While other phalanxes could usually only advance or retreat, the Spartan phalanx could maneuver effectively on the battlefield, or detach segments of its line to outflank the enemy. Still, the Spartans adhered to the mindset of hoplite battle: when they invaded, they expected their enemy to meet them in open battle on level ground.

The Peloponnesian War toppled all these conventions. For the first ten years of the war, called the Archidamian War after the Spartan king Archidamos, the Peloponnesian League invaded and ravaged Attika each summer, hoping to goad the Athenians into pitched battle. At the outset of the conflict, however, Perikles had, with difficulty, convinced the Athenians not to meet the Spartan challenge. Athens, Perikles argued, could import food by sea; the Spartans would soon wear themselves out and propose peace. Agrarian Athenians were unhappy with this strategy. Reluctantly, they crowded into the city, thereby facilitating the spread of plague in 430–426. Rural Attika suffered under these repeated invasions, although olive trees and agricultural property were difficult to destroy, and the Athenians returned to repair the damage every autumn. Even so, Perikles' strategy had a demoralizing effect on Athenians accustomed to traditional warfare: they saw their fields violated and could do nothing about it.

The scope and duration of the war also meant that hoplites found themselves fighting far from home, not only head-on on level ground and not only in the summer. Brasidas, for example, took Amphipolis during a winter storm in 424. Two years later, when the Athenians attempted to recapture Amphipolis, Brasidas launched a surprise attack rather than conduct a traditional phalanx battle with his weaker army. During the course of the war, Athenians and Peloponnesians fought each other at night, in hilly terrain, and in and around fortifications. Between 431 and 404, there were only a handful of large-scale hoplite battles on open ground, notably at Delion in 424 and Mantinea in 418.

Furthermore, hoplites increasingly had to contend with new military challenges, particularly from light troops and cavalry. Four hundred twenty Spartan hoplites, trapped by Athenian troops equipped with bows, darts, stones and slings on the island of Sphakteria opposite Pylos in the southwest Peloponnesos, demonstrates the threat light troops posed even to a trained and disciplined army. The unarmored Athenians easily eluded Spartan attempts to pursue them across the rugged and rocky island, and the cornered Spartans were forced to surrender; only 292 survived to do so.

The Peloponnesian War accelerated changes in hoplite warfare, which had been brewing since the start of the fifth century, but at the outbreak of war in 431, the Spartan army was still superlative. With its Peloponnesian allies, Sparta could muster perhaps 40,000 hoplites, against about 30,000 of Athens and its allies. There was, however, another factor to consider: the Athenian navy.

According to Thucydides (1.13), the earliest sea battle in Greek history took place between Korinth and Kerkyra around 660. Korinth excelled in naval architecture, and is supposed to have built the first triremes—galleys with three banks of oars. But Athens took the lead in naval warfare. That the Athenians went to sea was somewhat fortuitous—a chance bonanza of silver had enabled them to construct a fleet just in time to ward off the second Persian invasion of Greece in 480–479—but once in the water they stayed there. In the fifth century, its powerful navy made possible Athens's maritime empire, and during the Peloponnesian War the city's very survival came to rest on the shoulders of its oarsmen.

The standard warship of all Greek navies during the Peloponnesian War was the trireme (*trieres*). Only about 120 feet long and 15 feet wide, the light and nimble trireme carried 170 oarsmen crammed into three levels one above the other, and about thirty other crewmen, including sailors, marines, and archers. The trireme mounted a bronze ram on its prow; at top ramming speed of about nine knots, this could smash opposing ships apart. The vessel was optimized for fighting only—the crew had to disembark to eat and sleep, while the ship itself needed to be drawn out of the water whenever possible. Otherwise its timbers would become waterlogged, reducing speed and maneuverability.

At the outbreak of war, a number of Greek states had fleets, including Korinth and Kerkyra, but Athens unquestionably possessed the best. The Athenian navy could muster some 200 first-class triremes, each outfitted and maintained by a wealthy citizen. The navy's strength lay in its trained professional crews. Where other navies turned sea battles into land battles by ramming and then boarding enemy ships, the Athenians were masters of naval maneuver. Their crews could attack quickly, then disengage in search of another target; they could even sail through a line of enemy ships before turning rapidly about to ram their opponents from astern. So superior were the Athenians at naval warfare that in 429, off Naupaktos in the Gulf of Korinth, they literally sailed circles around a Peloponnesian fleet before closing in for the kill.

The rowers on Athenian triremes were free men, not slaves, who received pay for their service. Being a rower was a way for poor men to break the middle-class hoplite monopoly on violence: a citizen oarsman could justly say that he too contributed to the defense of the city, and therefore deserved political power. In addition, many foreigners served as mercenary oarsmen. In the last decade of the war, the Peloponnesians built their own fleet in part by luring these mercenaries away from Athens with promises of better pay. Finally, on desperate occasions the Athenians also employed slaves as rowers.

So Athens was strong at sea, Sparta on land. Little wonder that the Peloponnesian War has been likened to a contest between a whale and an elephant. The respective strengths of the two belligerents explain the strategies they pursued during the war. The Peloponnesian League during the Archidamian War relied on annual invasions of Attika, both to ravage the countryside and to lure the Athenians into pitched battle. The Athenians, in turn, used the mobility of their fleet to launch amphibious assaults on the vulnerable shores of the Peloponnesos and elsewhere. The Spartans could not ignore the Athenian navy, as Pylos demonstrated. On the other hand, when Athens met Sparta or its allies in hoplite battle, as at Delion in 424, Athens lost.

Thus, neither side could force a decision unless it beat the other on its own terms. In the end, this is exactly what Sparta did. After 412, Persian financial subsidies enabled the Peloponnesian League to build and maintain a fleet, and therefore to challenge Athens at sea. Meantime, on the advice of Alkibiades, the Spartans changed their land strategy by fortifying the district of Dekeleia from which the Peloponnesian League maintained a year-round presence in Attika, using its superior cavalry to harass Athenians who ventured beyond the city walls. According to Thucydides, 20,000 slaves ran away from their masters to refuge at Dekeleia—a significant blow to the Athenian economy. Deprived of its countryside, Athens became increasingly reliant on imported Black Sea grain, successfully defending the grain routes against Spartan naval challenges for several years. When, however, nearly every remaining Athenian trireme was captured on the beach at Aigospotamoi in 404, for all practical purposes, the war was over.

Why did the Spartans with their powerful army not simply storm

Athens directly? The truth is that fifth-century Greeks were awful at taking walled cities. The Spartans tried to take Plataia in central Greece for several years (429–427), but the Plataians only surrendered when they ran out of food. Still, the Peloponnesian War witnessed several developments in siege technology. At Plataia, the Peloponnesian attackers built ramps and an encircling wall, while the defenders responded with countermines and counterwalls. At Delion in 424, the Boiotians used a sort of flamethrower to overcome Athenian defenders.

Perhaps more significant than the technological advances in siege warfare was the increased brutality fostered by combat in confined urban areas. No longer were battlefield and home separate places. Instead, cities became battlegrounds. Soldiers fought house to house at Plataia in 431; at Mykalessos in 413, Thracians in Athenian service killed everyone in sight, including all the students of a local school.

ATHENIAN WARTIME POLITICS

Just as the war shattered established conventions of battle, it convulsed Athenian politics and society. To begin with, Perikles, who had been elected general almost continuously from 443 B.C.E. onward, died from plague in 429. He was, asserts Thucydides, able to lead the citizenry rather than being led by them, and so incorruptible that he could afford to disagree with them. His strategy for the war, we have seen, was defensive: refuse hoplite battle, rely on the navy to protect the empire, wait for the Peloponnesians to give up. He told the Athenians that if they did not attempt to expand their empire, and did nothing risky, they would win.

Thucydides idolized Perikles—he had grown to adulthood knowing no other leader—so it is no surprise that he depicts the politicians who succeeded Perikles as inferior. The successors of Perikles were to Thucydides (2.65) "more on a level with one another, and each grasping at supremacy, they ended by committing even the conduct of state affairs to the whims of the multitude."

Thucydides' judgment of wartime politics in Athens is certainly skewed. Nonetheless, the character of Athenian leadership did change. Nobody during the war held a generalship for as long as Perikles had, so Athens lost a sense of continuity in its policies. Wartime politics roughly broke down into two camps: while aristocratic conservatives consistently pushed for peace and accommodation with Sparta, others advocated continued war and expansion of the empire.

Notorious among the prowar leaders was Kleon (d. 422). Not an aristocrat, Kleon's father had become rich in the leather business. Thucydides depicts Kleon as vulgar and unrestrained, someone who hitched up his robe uncouthly before speaking in the assembly. Since Kleon had helped send Thucydides into exile, it seems safe to say that Thucydides did not like Kleon and took every opportunity to slander him. Yet even Thucydides' slanted narrative reveals Kleon as an effective politician who enjoyed some success as a general—notably as one of the Athenian commanders at Pylos in 425.

After its unsuccessful revolt in 427, Kleon proposed that the adult male population of Mytilene be executed, and that its women and children be enslaved. Mytilene, he argued, deserved extreme punishment, for it had rebelled despite preferential Athenian treatment. Pity and compassion, he went on, had no place in the heart of an imperial power; the Athenians must make an example of Mytilene or face losing everything. The assembly at first agreed, but changed its mind after a second debate held the next day.

Thucydides makes much of Kleon's violence, and the near-destruction of Mytilene shocks modern readers. Yet the Athenians had never scrupled the use of force to maintain their empire; they spared Mytilene out of self-interest, not compassion. The common people (dêmos) of Mytilene had helped Athens suppress the revolt. To execute them, the assembly must have recognized, was to eliminate the very class that favored Athens's democracy. Furthermore, Mytilene was a populous city; it would have been no easy task to execute so many adult men. Tiny Skione in northern Greece was another matter. In 423, Kleon proposed that the rebellious Skioneans receive the same treatment he had wanted for Mytilene. When the Athenians retook the city in 421, they put the adult males to death and enslaved everyone else; Thucydides passes over the episode in a single sentence.

Not all the prowar leaders were political newcomers like Kleon. The aristocratic Alkibiades (451–404) grew up as a ward of Perikles, and had been an associate and lover of Sokrates. If Kleon favored maintaining the empire through frightfulness, Alkibiades advocated expanding it through audacity. After the Peace of Nikias in 421, Alkibiades set Athens back on course for war by engineering an alliance with Argos and other Spartan enemies in the Peloponnesos. Defeat at the battle of Mantinea (418) ended Alkibiades's Peloponnesian venture, but he pressed on undeterred; two years later, he convinced the Athenians to sail against Sicily even though, Thucydides claims, they were ignorant of the island's size and population.

Against new politicians like Alkibiades, the old leadership of Athens—

men like Nikias (ca. 470–413), renowned for his piety and moderation—struggled in vain. In the debates preceding the Sicilian expedition, Nikias tried to dissuade the assembly by stressing Sicily's resources and the still-precarious situation in Greece, where renewed war with Sparta threatened. Nikias even appealed to the older men in the assembly to help curb the expansionist dreams of young men like Alkibiades. Ironically, the younger Alkibiades successfully reached across this generation gap, convincing both young and old to support him. Sicily, he promised, would make easy pickings; even if the Athenians did not conquer the island, their powerful navy would prevent them from incurring serious losses. In the end, Alkibiades won by playing with the emotions of the assembly; Nikias appealed to common sense and lost. The Athenians went overconfidently to Sicily, and suffered a catastrophe (415–413). Athens lost thousands of irreplaceable men and hundreds of ships; by 413 Sparta was back in the war and had fortified Dekeleia.

Alkibiades never saw the end in Sicily. Implicated in the mutilation of the herms—an incident that revealed the growing presence in Athens of secret aristocratic clubs—he fled to Sparta, then Persia. By 411 he was back, helping convince the Athenians that Persia would retract support from Sparta if only Athens got rid of its democracy. Demoralized by the Sicilian disaster and renewed war with Sparta, cowed by well-organized agitators at home, the Athenians voted to overthrow their own government and turned power over to the Four Hundred, a narrow oligarchic council.

In some fashion the short-lived (May–September) oligarchy of 411 fed an Athenian need for stability and a return to earlier ways of doing things. Democratic mainstays, such as pay for jury service, would be abolished, and political power restricted to those who owned hoplite equipment. The oligarchic clubs that helped instigate the revolution were a new, disturbing development. Their members, usually young and aristocratic, often pro-Spartan, gathered ostensibly for social purposes but also to advance their own political careers and antidemocratic philosophies. They disliked the democracy's conduct of the war, which they considered incompetent and inconsistent. During spring 411, club members had intimidated the *boulê* and committed political murder. Like the mutilation of the herms a few years before, the oligarchy of 411 showed what the war had done to Athens: the great imperial power was now subject to the whims of men who plotted in secret. But the oligarchs could not settle on a coherent program; despite a bewildering variety of temporary regimes, Athens was a democracy again by 410.

Alkibiades flitted in and out of Athens during the last decade of the war, ultimately alighting in Asia Minor, where he was murdered in 403. The antidemocratic clubs, though, persisted. Their members formed a base of support for the Thirty Tyrants, the oligarchic junta appointed by the Spartans to rule Athens after its surrender in April 404. Backed by a Spartan garrison and by gangs of armed thugs, the Thirty terrorized Athens until September 403, during which time they are said to have executed some 1,500 people, including prominent resident aliens as well as citizens.

As much as the demagogues and oligarchic clubs, with their appeals to emotion and violence, reshaped wartime politics, the persistence of Athenian democratic values in the face of military disaster, internal dissent, and dictatorship remains striking. In 411 the fleet, then based at Samos in the eastern Aegean, recovered from its initial shock and opposed the Four Hundred. Indeed, for several months the fleet functioned as the legitimate democratic assembly. Numerous Athenians, joined by many slaves and foreigners, took up arms against the Thirty Tyrants in 404–403. After the restoration of democracy in 403, an amnesty was passed, prohibiting prosecution of those who had supported the Thirty, and Athenian democracy in the fourth century became, if anything, more vibrant and stable than before.

Thus the war shook Athenian politics; it also wrought basic societal changes. In Aristophanes' comedy *Ekklesiazousai* (Assemblywomen), produced in the 390s, three old women and a young girl fight to have sexual intercourse with a single young man. Behind the humor of the scene lies sobering demography: there were probably over 40,000 adult male Athenian citizens in 431; by 400 there were only 16,000—roughly a 60 percent drop. The poignancy of this loss is well represented in the relief images on grave stelai ("monuments") commemorating the dead (see Figure 7). How many of those men would have been famous orators, playwrights, or artists had not the war stripped them of life? If Athens in the fourth century seemed less exuberant, perhaps it was in part because so many had died. In other, less well-documented cities, the demographic shift may well have been similar.

Throughout Greece, those who survived found themselves in difficult circumstances. The Spartan occupation of Attika had cost many Athenians their farms and livelihoods; mercantile cities like Korinth suffered from disruption of trade. Elsewhere, others were exiles or had been soldiers for so long they could not readjust to civilian life. Thousands of impoverished or displaced Greeks took service as mercenaries in the western provinces of the Persian empire. In 401, 12,000 of these men backed the Persian prince Cyrus in his bid for the Achaemenid throne.

Cyrus failed, but the epic march of his mercenaries through the Persian empire, recounted in Xenophon's memoir *Anabasis* (The March Upcountry), indirectly inspired the conquests of Alexander.

SPARTA

Finally, what of Sparta, the victor? Although little fighting had occurred on its home territory, and although its oligarchy had avoided the upheavals that befell Athenian democracy, Sparta, too, suffered internally from the war. The war exacerbated the fifth-century decline of Sparta's citizen population, to the point that Sparta increasingly deployed helot rather than citizen hoplites to distant theaters such as Sicily and Thrace. That the Spartans were willing to make peace in 421, largely in order to recover the 292 prisoners from Sphakteria, says much about their manpower difficulties. What is more, Spartans who went abroad to fight were often corrupted by foreign influences. Gylippos, for example, commander of the army that defeated Athens in Sicily, fled ingloriously into exile after Aigospotamoi when it was discovered he had stolen a considerable sum of government money.

During the war, Sparta enjoyed some success as an international power. It held together a coalition, including Korinth and Thebes, powerful states that it could not readily compel by force, as Athens could its imperial subjects. Moreover, Sparta secured Persian financial support, enabling it to challenge Athens at sea. Yet, although Sparta's banner of liberation convinced some Athenian allies, Mytilene, for instance, to rebel, large-scale defections did not occur until after the Sicilian disaster. Even then, some states, like Samos, remained loyal to Athens until the bitter end.

The Spartans faced new challenges almost as soon as hostilities ceased. Having entered the war to liberate Greece from the tyrant city Athens, Sparta now found itself an imperial power, a role for which its isolationist way of life had not prepared it. Accustomed to unhesitating obedience at home, Spartan governors abroad alienated local populations with their harsh administration; wartime allies like Thebes and Korinth chafed under Sparta's overbearing manner. Within a decade, these states would be at war again—allied with Athens against Sparta.

Even Sparta's wartime accommodation with Persia soon backfired. Aiming to liberate the Greek cities of Asia Minor from Persian dominion, King Agesilaos (445–359) conducted a number of campaigns against the Persian satraps (governors) there, starting in 396. He was soon forced to withdraw, in order to confront the new alliance of Athens, Korinth, and

Thebes, and eventually agreed to the humiliating King's Peace (386), which recognized Persian authority over the Ionian coast. After this, Sparta could never be considered a liberator.

The Spartans clung grimly to their status as victors, but by 371 Sparta's imperial sun had set. Theban victory that year in a pitched hoplite battle at Leuktra destroyed the myth of Spartan invincibility; the Thebans followed up by invading the Peloponnesos and setting free the helots, thus kicking the legs out from under Sparta's economy. Sparta had brought this collapse on itself, for it was the installation of a Spartan garrison in Thebes (382) that led the Boiotians to war against Sparta. Theban hegemony lasted little longer than a decade. Its great leader Epaminondas died in battle in 362, after which, observed the historian Xenophon, Greece was even more confused and uncertain than it had been before.

CONCLUSION

Long and destructive as the Peloponnesian War was, it did not utterly ruin Greece. After 404, the olive trees of Attika grew fresh shoots; Athens rebounded from oligarchy and loss of empire, even reestablishing an Aegean naval confederacy (379). Significantly, the Athenians repudiated the exaction of tribute from, and the stationing of governors or garrisons in, the member states of this League. They had learned some lessons from the fall of their empire. At home, antidemocrats like Plato abandoned political life for the security of the Academy; meanwhile Athenian democracy recovered and flourished.

Despite this postwar recovery, the Peloponnesian War showed both Athenians and Spartans the limits on traditional ways of war and politics. Several major phalanx clashes lay ahead, but the old agrarian way of war was clearly ending. The armies of the future would be professional, combined forces, not hoplite militias. At Athens, the stresses of prolonged conflict had revealed societal rifts, which the long ascendancy of Perikles had papered over, and given voice to a generation of young, aristocratic antidemocrats. The *polis*, too, had shown itself incapable of meeting the demands of international politics. Neither the maritime empire of Athens nor the land domination of Sparta could effectively control Greece; the Spartans, in particular, could not adequately cope with an outside world so different from the closed barracks life of their homeland. In the end, repeated attempts at hegemony, from the Peloponnesian War on through Leuktra, only exhausted and demoralized the Greeks, opening the way for a new sort of power: the monarchy of Makedon.

SUGGESTIONS FOR FURTHER READING

Cartwright, David. 1997. *A Historical Commentary on Thucydides: A Companion to Rex Warner's Penguin Translation*. Ann Arbor: University of Michigan Press. A useful commentary, including introductory essays and notes.

Cawkwell, George. 1997. *Thucydides and the Peloponnesian War*. London: Routledge. Six concise and well-argued chapters examining various aspects of Thucydides' writing, including his attitudes toward Kleon, Perikles, and the empire.

Connor, W.R. 1984. *Thucydides*. Princeton, N.J.: Princeton University Press. A complex and fascinating study of Thucydides as literature.

Hanson, Victor Davis. 2000. *The Western Way of War: Infantry Battle in Classical Greece*, 2d ed. Berkeley: University of California Press. Examines hoplite equipment and tactics, and the battlefield experience of the Greek soldier.

Henderson, Jeffrey. 1996. *Three Plays by Aristophanes Staging Women*. New York: Routledge. Modern, colloquial translations of three Greek comedies including *Ekklesiazousai*; recommended for those interested in Athenian culture and in the lives of Athenian women.

Kagan, Donald. 1969. *The Outbreak of the Peloponnesian War*. Ithaca: Cornell University Press. The first of a four-volume history of the Peloponnesian War; the standard general treatment in English.

———. 1974. *The Archidamian War*. Ithaca: Cornell University Press.

———. 1981. *The Peace of Nikias and the Sicilian Expedition*. Ithaca: Cornell University Press.

———. 1987. *The Fall of the Athenian Empire*. Ithaca, N.Y.: Cornell University Press.

Meiggs, Russell. 1972. *The Athenian Empire*. Oxford: Oxford University Press. Exhaustive and detailed analysis of the empire's foundation and development; includes numerous appendices on the ancient sources.

Moore, J.M. 1975. *Aristotle and Xenophon on Democracy and Oligarchy*. Berkeley: University of California Press. Translations of several important ancient treatises on Athenian and Spartan government, each accompanied by a full commentary.

Morrison, John S., J.F. Coates, and N.B. Rankov. 2000. *The Athenian Trireme: The History and Reconstruction of an Ancient Greek Warship*, 2d ed. Cambridge: Cambridge University Press. Examines the ships and their crews, tactics and strategies; several chapters cover important naval battles.

Strassler, Robert B. 1996. *The Landmark Thucydides: A Comprehensive Guide to the Peloponnesian War*. New York: The Free Press. An excellent translation accompanied by maps, indexes, and supplementary essays; highly recommended.

Strauss, Barry S. 1986. *Athens After the Peloponnesian War*. Ithaca: Cornell University Press. Scholarly yet readable examination of Athenian politics and policies from 403 to 386 B.C.E.

Warry, John. 1995. *Warfare in the Classical World*. Norman: University of Oklahoma Press. A superbly illustrated, excellent description of all aspects of warfare in the ancient Greek and Roman world; see Chapters 3 and 4 on the Peloponnesian War and the years following.

Part IV

Transition and Expansion of Empire
(4th–1st century B.C.E.)

Figure 8. Bust of Sokrates, fourth century B.C.E. Marble.
Museo Archeologico Nazionale, Naples, Italy. Courtesy
Alinari/Art Resource, N.Y.

8

The Death of Sokrates and the Development of Greek Philosophy

INTRODUCTION

> The unexamined life is not worth living.
>
> —Sokrates

His life spanning 469–399 B.C.E., the Athenian philosopher Sokrates personally experienced key events in Athenian history: while he grew to manhood, Athens was expanding its military might, political dominance, and cultural importance. Since he did not write, we know of Sokrates' ideas mostly from two writers, both Sokrates' followers in the late fifth century: about twenty-five dialogues by Plato, in which "Sokrates" forms the central figure, and the histories, memorabilia, and dialogues of Xenophon.

Distinguishing between these writers' images of Sokrates and their own identities is sometimes difficult, but Plato's earlier works and the similarities in their portrayals paint a substantial picture of Sokrates, the man and the philosopher. They describe Sokrates as a leading figure in the philosophical discussions of the day, little concerned with political affairs, but actively attending religious and cultural festivals. They also concur on several distinguishing traits: going into instantaneous trances, one of which lasted for two days; easily withstanding temperature extremes; able to outlast drinking partners without getting drunk; and listening to an inner voice he called his *daimonion*, "little spirit," which he claimed never told him what to do but only warned him if he was embarking on a wrong action. By humorously ridiculing its main character "Sokrates," Aristophanes' comedy, *The Clouds*, produced at the City Dionysia (423), shows that Sokrates was a familiar and colorful figure in Athens.

Although he claimed to shun public life, Sokrates was married and had children, a civic duty in ancient Greece; he served as a hoplite in early battles of the Peloponnesian War, distinguishing himself with courage; and he represented his deme in the *boulê*, even presiding over a major trial against several generals (406), at which he apparently alone voted against the illegal decision to execute the generals. While their depictions differ in some respects, both Plato and Xenophon portray Sokrates as maintaining the highest standards of ethical behavior in all situations: he ignored an order by the Thirty Tyrants to arrest an innocent citizen rather than act unrighteously. Practicing right action formed the cornerstone of Sokrates' philosophy.

Sokrates' contributions to the development of Greek philosophy came a century after new modes of thinking were first being written down by sixth-century Ionian philosophers, who came mostly from Samos and Miletos, its "Milesian School" a center for intellectual speculations. These early, Presocratic thinkers investigated natural phenomena, exploring physics (even atomic), astronomy, geography, geology, and mathematics, without, however, the aid of modern technology to verify their theories. Influenced by ideas emerging from Near Eastern civilizations and Egypt, they developed naturalistic theories, which they considered an advance over traditional mythological stories to explain various phenomena. This shift to rational thinking transformed Greek ways of thought and set the foundation for the development of Western thinking.

Some of these Ionian philosophers, including the earliest known one, Thales (early sixth century) from Miletos, studied the movements of the sun, the planets, and the stars, predicting eclipses. Some developed practical geometrical applications: for examples, how to measure the height of a pyramid by comparing its shadow with that of a person's; or the Pythagorean theorem of Pythagoras (mid-sixth century), from Samos, who set up his religious, scientific, and mathematical order in Croton, southern Italy. And they theorized about the origins of the earth and the universe, postulating the existence of a primary material like water, fire, air, earth, wood, or (later) atoms.

Other philosophers expanded the reflections on origins by questioning the nature of reality: is it singular, fixed, and unchanging, or multiple, ever-moving, and changing? In theology, several Ionian philosophers, all transplants to southern Italy, clearly influenced Plato, and so may have Sokrates as well: Xenophanes (mid-sixth century), by rejecting the Homeric images of the gods as engaged in immoral misconduct and suggesting that the gods could only represent the best of human qualities; Pythagoras, with his views on the transmigration of souls; and Parmenides (early-fifth century, origin of the "Eleatic school"), who advanced the idea of a constant, unchanging, true reality. Expanding on these ideas, which form key elements in Plato's philosophy, Sokrates may well have propounded the idea that divinity is an unchanging, ultimate goodness, which serves as a model for human virtue.

Besides these two principal lines of rationalistic inquiry, other early philosophers claimed to study and teach "wisdom," *sophia*; hence, they were called Sophists. By debating issues of right conduct, their questions and methods of argumentation laid the groundwork for Sokrates's own questions and method. But unlike Sokrates, writers describe the Sophists as promoting successful argumentation in order to win, regardless of its rightness, criticizing them for "making the worse argument the better." In later centuries this idea developed into the notion of "sophistry," making a specious or fallacious argument. Sophists also charged fees for teaching rhetoric to aristocratic youth, preparing them for *polis* leadership roles, which Sokrates denied doing.

All these philosophical ideas were debated publicly by Sokrates and others in Athens's fifth-century marketplace and mall (*stoa*). Sokrates brought a new focus to these intellectual inquiries: interested neither in explaining natural phenomena nor in Sophistic rhetorical argumentation, Sokrates is shown exploring fundamental values, such as justice, goodness, love, or virtue, and what these values mean in one's life. Sokrates' emphasis on principles of behavior (ethics), called "ethical philosophy," became the model for the development of future philosophy, in Greece, in Rome, and, after the Renaissance, in modern Western European and American societies. Sokrates' method of inquiry, through questions and answers, called "dialectic" (from the same Greek root as *dialogue*, hence Plato's literary form), became known as the "Socratic method."

Basic to Sokrates' thinking is knowing what "the good" is, in the abstract and in particular situations. He believed that wisdom is virtue, and that once one knows the good, one will necessarily choose to act only virtuously. In Plato's *Apology* (not an "apology," but an *apologia*, Sokrates' "defense speech" at his trial), Sokrates claims that he never did wrong knowingly; those who choose wrong do so out of ignorance, for they are not aware of what the good action is. Contrary to popular Greek morality, Sokrates claimed one should never harm another because one is ultimately harming one's own soul, which he considered immortal. He therefore thought that care of one's soul should be everyone's main concern. When he investigated the meaning of a Delphic oracle that called him the wisest of men by questioning politicians, poets, and artisans on their wisdom, Sokrates drew an important conclusion: in contrast to others who pretended to know things they really did not, he did not claim to know what he did not. Hence, he could be called the wisest, since he was willing to acknowledge the limits of his knowledge.

In the *Apology*, Sokrates calls himself a gadfly, sent by the gods to remind the Athenians of what is most important, challenging them to live ethical lives. He also acknowledges that in doing so, by publicly questioning prominent figures in front of others, he won himself the enmity of powerful men. This practice may well have contributed to the charges for which he was tried, convicted, and sentenced to death in 399. The *Apology* gives two sets of charges: first that he practiced natural and Sophistic philosophy, and second, that he corrupted the young, did not believe in the city's gods but imported foreign gods. Most interpreters believe the charges were fabricated, reflecting the political hostilities after the Peloponnesian War, the influential Sokrates making a convenient target for his political rivals. The vote for conviction seems to have been close, and he was sentenced to death by drinking hemlock.

Although Plato and other supporters urged Sokrates to flee Athens into exile, he claimed that to do so would violate the city's laws and the principle of virtue that had guided his conduct throughout his life. Responding to the idea that he had received the worst punishment in the sentence of death, he claimed that the fear of death arises from ignorance and the pretense of knowing what one does not know. Since no one knows what really happens after death, Sokrates suggests it may actually be the greatest good, and he looks forward to the wisdom and bliss the world after death may offer him. Illustrating this view is Plato's *Phaedo*, which takes place around Sokrates' bedside before his death. After discoursing at length on the nature of the soul, at the end of the dialogue, Sokrates drinks the hemlock and describes the physical sensations as they begin to take effect.

Sokrates' ideas have had enormous impact. First, upon his follower Plato, who completely abandoned his obligations to the *polis*, virtually unheard of, and devoted himself to philosophical writing. His works both preserved the legacy of an influential thinker and used them to form the basis for subsequent philosophical discourse. Plato established a school, the Academy (which lasted for 900 years), a center for intellectual discussion, which attracted the young Aristotle and shaped the development of this next major ancient Greek philosopher. Many subsequent philosophical movements in Greece and in Rome claimed Sokrates as the inspiration for their views. And his inquiries into ethical meanings and the purpose of human life still form core questions that all people face.

INTERPRETIVE ESSAY
Walter G. Englert

PRESOCRATIC PHILOSOPHERS

The trial and death of Sokrates in Athens in 399 B.C.E. formed a turning point in the development of Greek philosophy. Before Sokrates, thinkers throughout the Greek world had begun to question traditional accounts of the gods and the nature of the world found in the epics of Homer and Hesiod. These philosophers, referred to as "Presocratics" because they lived before Sokrates, were independent thinkers who advanced many different theories about the nature of the world, the gods, and human beings. The first, Thales of Miletos (ca. 600), successfully predicted a solar eclipse and is said to have taught that the fundamental or first principle (Greek, *arche*) of everything was water. Other Presocratics rejected Thales' views, but substituted their own candidates for first principle. Anaximander, a student of Thales, said it was the "unlimited" or "infinite" (*apeiron*), and Anaximenes air. These early thinkers supported their views by arguing for their theories and attacking the theories of others, establishing the concept that philosophy entailed reasoned discourse. One could not just say that something was true; one needed to argue for it.

Among the most famous of the Presocratics were: Pythagoras of Samos (ca. 570–490), who was credited with discovering the Pythagorean theorem and the ratios underlying musical harmony; Parmenides of Elea (6th–5th century) who used logical argument to prove that reality as we see it is illusory; Herakleitos of Miletos (6th–5th century) who taught that all things are in flux and are really various forms of fire; Anaxagoras of Klazomenai (ca. 500–428), who said that in everything there are bits of everything else, and that the world is governed by a rational principle or "mind" (*nous*); Empedokles of Akragas (ca. 492–432), who taught that all things were made up of the four elements—earth, air, fire, and water—acted on by the forces of Love and Strife; and Leukippos of Miletos (fl. [flourished] 435) and Demokritos of Abdera (ca. 460–370s), who developed the notion that all things are made up of small, indivisible atoms.

SOKRATES

Sokrates (see Figure 8), who lived in Athens from 469 to 399, knew about the views of these philosophers, but ignored most of their work to focus on ethics, or how people should best lead their lives. Ethics had been a concern of some earlier Presocratics, but Sokrates pursued the topic with single-minded intensity. He wrote nothing himself, but Plato and Xenophon, both students of Sokrates and our main sources for knowledge of his teaching, make it clear that Sokrates' goal was to discover the best way for human beings to live. Plato relates in the *Apology*, his version of Sokrates' defense speech at his trial, that Sokrates was launched on his philosophical mission by a response of the Delphic oracle. Asked whether anyone was wiser than Sokrates, the oracle responded that there was not. Puzzled by this answer, Sokrates began to question his fellow Athenians who were reputed to be wise. Sokrates thus engaged in philosophy not by reading the works of other philosophers, but by talking with his fellow Athenians.

Sokrates lived at a time of great moral upheaval. Traditional concepts about the gods and morality had come under attack by another group of thinkers labeled the Sophists, or "wise men," so-called based on their reputation for wisdom earned by traveling around various Greek *poleis*, teaching for pay. These Sophists—the most famous of whom were Gorgias of Leontini, Sicily; and Protagoras of Abdera, Thrace—taught rhetoric, or the art of persuasion, and often promoted doctrines that challenged the existence of the gods and traditional conceptions of the virtues.

Judging from the dialogues of Plato and Xenophon, Sokrates tried to counter this sophistic relativism and clarify various moral concepts for himself and his interlocutors. Sokrates founded no school, did not take money for teaching, and had no formal students. Instead, he talked with his fellow Athenians from all walks of life—craftspeople, politicians, and poets—though he had a particular fondness for talking with young, upper-class Athenian males. Sokrates often began his philosophical conversations in innocent ways, asking his interlocutor questions to pique his interest and draw him further into discussion. This process of asking questions was called the Socratic *elenchos*, "refutation" or "cross-examination," also known as the "Socratic method."

The Socratic *elenchos* seems to have had at least two goals. First, it had a deflating purpose, to show the interlocuter that although he thought he knew what a virtue like justice or courage or friendship was, he was, in fact, mistaken. This negative use of the *elenchos* was consistent with the Delphic oracle's pronouncement that no mortal was wiser than Sokrates, interpreted to mean that everyone but Sokrates thought they knew things that, in fact, they did not. Sokrates began an *elenchos* by asking a "what is?" question, about some moral concept like courage, piety, self-control, friendship, or justice. The interlocutor would then propose a definition, and Sokrates, through an intricate series of questions and answers, would show that this definition contradicted other views the interlocutor held. According to Plato, Sokrates was almost always successful at showing the interlocutor that his view of the virtue they were investigating was inconsistent with his other beliefs.

Plato's *Euthyphro* at 7a–8b, when Sokrates asks Euthyphro what he thinks piety is, provides a good example of the *elenchos*. Euthyphro proposes the following definition: "What is dear to the gods is pious, what is not is impious." Sokrates shows Euthyphro the problems with this definition, which conflicts with the consequences of his other views. Since Euthyphro has claimed that the gods are in discord with one another, Sokrates shows that if the gods disagree, they must disagree about, among other things, which things are just and unjust. If they do, the same actions will be dear to some gods and hated by others. Thus, the same actions will be both pious—because they are loved by some gods—and impious—because they are not loved by other gods—which Euthyphro agrees is impossible. Euthyphro, refusing to give up his other belief that the gods are in a state of discord, gives up his attempted definition.

After this process was repeated a number of times, the interlocutor was often reduced to a state of *aporia*, of "being at a complete loss." The person, once sure he knew what justice or another virtue was, either was reduced to uncertainty, grew angry at Sokrates, or both. Sokrates hoped the process of the *elenchos* would stimulate others to see they did not know what they thought they knew, and force them to rethink their moral views. Frequently, however, this deflating effect of the *elenchos* made people resent Sokrates and his methods.

The second goal of the *elenchos* was more positive. Through the *elenchos*, Sokrates discovered a number of ethical propositions upon which he could base his actions. These ethical propositions included: (1) it is better to be harmed than to harm; (2) the just man can never be harmed; and (3) justice is always more beneficial than injustice. Sokrates found in his discussions that these and other moral propositions were never refuted, and thus that one should act on them, at least until someone could show him by argument that they were false. In this sense, then, Sokrates believed that the *elenchos* could provide ethical guidance to those who practiced it. As Sokrates says in Plato's *Apology*, "The unexamined life is not worth living for a human being," because only through examination can one find out what one's moral presuppositions are and how one should live one's life.

Sokrates' philosophizing was suddenly halted in 399, when he was put on trial for his life. There has been great controversy about why the Athenians put Sokrates to death. Many Athenians blamed Sokrates for the behavior of his acquaintances. Two of Sokrates' close associates, Kritias and Charmides, were part of the Thirty Tyrants, the oligarchical government set up by Sparta after the Peloponnesian War, and Alkibiades, the controversial Athenian general, had been a friend, pupil, and lover of Sokrates. In addition, Sokrates' constant questioning of others had made him many enemies, and many Athenians saw him as a destructive force who questioned traditional moral beliefs without offering any clear moral alternatives. Finally, Sokrates' own behavior in court may have seemed high-handed to the 501 jurors who heard the case. In Athenian courts, the accused defended himself, and was expected to appear contrite and throw himself on the mercy of the court. Sokrates was far from repentant in his defense speech, and instead of proposing the penalty that his prosecutors probably intended, exile from Athens, he proposed a monetary fine. Forced to choose between the prosecutors' proposed penalty of death and Sokrates' proposed fine, a majority of jurors voted for death.

PLATO

Philosophy was never the same in the Greek world after Sokrates' death. A number of writers were so struck by his way of life and felt his loss so greatly that they composed a new genre of literature, the Socratic dialogue, after his death. The most famous writer of dialogues and Sokrates' greatest student was Plato (429–347), who first absorbed and then transformed Socratic philosophy into his own. The exact relationship of Plato's doctrines to Sokrates' has been a matter of great dispute, and Plato has not made it easy in his writings to distinguish their views. With the exception of some letters attributed to him, Plato never writes in his own voice. The principal speaker in most of his dialogues is Sokrates.

Plato's dialogues are traditionally divided into three groups:

1. The early dialogues, where Sokrates interrogates his interlocutor about some virtue and the conversation ends in *aporia*. These dialogues provide much of what is presumed to have been the historical Sokrates' philosophical method and results. The early or "Socratic" dialogues include the *Euthyphro, Apology, Crito*, and *Protagoras*.

2. The middle dialogues, where Sokrates is still the main character, but many positive philosophic doctrines are proposed, including the doctrine of recollection, the doctrine of the forms (to be discussed below), and a more sophisticated psychology of the soul. Most scholars believe that in these dialogues Plato is using Sokrates as a spokesperson for his own philosophical beliefs. The middle dialogues include Plato's greatest philosophic and literary masterpieces: the *Phaedo, Republic, Symposium*, and *Phaedrus*.

3. The later dialogues, where Sokrates' role is reduced or is absent altogether, and in which Plato raises problems with his theory of forms and other doctrines. These dialogues include the *Parmenides, Statesman*, the *Laws*, Plato's second major depiction of an ideal state, and probably the *Timaeus*, about the origins and nature of the physical world.

Whereas Sokrates had been both philosopher and fully integrated into the life of his city, with Plato philosophy becomes separated from the ordinary life of the *polis*. Plato founded the Academy, a philosophical school just outside the city walls of Athens, which attracted students from all over the Greek world. Combining insights from Sokrates' work in ethics with the work of earlier philosophers like Herakleitos and Parmenides, Plato elaborated his own distinctive philosophical system. Accepting Herakleitos' view that the physical world is in a constant state of change and flux, Plato denied that true knowledge of the physical world was possible. But rather than deny the possibility of any knowledge, he proposed another realm, modeled on Parmenides's notion of the nature of reality, the world of the forms, which exists apart from this world and provides the source of knowledge of it.

For Plato, a deep connection exists between the realms of sense perception and of the invisible forms. All physical objects are made up of matter, which "participates in" the forms. To take an example that Plato uses, a physical bed is composed of matter that participates in the form of the bed. It is the form of the bed that makes the matter of any particular bed a bed, and makes the object intelligible to us as a bed. Any individual physical bed, however, is a better or worse bed to the extent that it approximates or falls short of the perfect form of the bed. This same framework holds for abstract concepts and the moral virtues. For example, objects are more or less "beautiful" to the extent that they participate in the form of beauty, and humans are more or less "just" to the extent they and their actions participate in the form of justice.

The doctrine of the forms was crucial to Plato's philosophy in a number of ways. First, in Plato's epistemology, or theory of knowledge, the doctrine allowed Plato to distinguish between opinion and knowledge. As he shows in the *Republic*, the philosopher, trained from childhood in the right desires and in the right subjects, could attain knowledge of the forms. Second, Plato believed that the forms of the moral virtues provided a firm basis for a science of ethics. For the philosopher, right action was ultimately not a matter of opinion, but knowledge based on the forms. Third, Plato's view of the forms led him to put great stress on the role that beauty and *eros* (desire or erotic love) can play in leading human beings to a knowledge of the forms. Particularly in the *Symposium*, he suggests that *eros*, aroused by beauty, can, under the right conditions, lead an individual from the love of individuals to the love and knowledge of the form of beauty itself, thus bridging the gap between the world of sense perception and the realm of the forms.

On the nature of the human soul, Plato disagreed with Sokrates, who apparently believed that the soul was unitary. Plato, however, taught that the soul was divided into three faculties: the appetitive part, which sought food, drink, and sex; the high-spirited part, which sought honor; and the rational part, which sought knowledge. In the *Republic*, Plato uses this psychological theory to divide his ideal state into three classes: the producers, guardians, and philosopher kings, each of which is characterized by the dominance of a different soul type. Plato's tripartite division of the soul allowed him to explain the problem of *akrasia*, or weakness of will; that is, people sometimes know what they ought to do but do something else when they allow one of the other parts of the soul to dominate the rational part.

Altogether, Plato not only expanded Sokrates' philosophical views, but he began a philosophical tradition of his own, Platonism, that had a major influence throughout antiquity as well as influence the development of Christianity and thinkers in the Middle Ages, the Renaissance, and into the present day.

ARISTOTLE

Plato's most famous student, Aristotle (384–322 B.C.E.), from Makedonia, studied at the Academy from age seventeen for twenty years until Plato's death in 347. When Plato died, Aristotle left Athens, living in various places, and was hired by Philip II of Makedon to tutor his son Alexander in 343. Returning to Athens in 335, Aristotle established his own school, the Lyceum, also known as the Peripatos. His followers were called Peripatetics. With Aristotle's school, philosophy became even more specialized as a discipline.

Aristotle's philosophical brilliance and range were phenomenal. Even as a student of Plato, he wrote philosophical dialogues (now lost) in which he disagreed with his teacher's fundamental views, but he is most famous for his philosophical treatises that span wide areas of thought. These treatises, originally notes of lectures he gave in the Lyceum, include works on logic, metaphysics, physics, ethics, psychology, biology, political science, rhetoric, and literary theory.

Aristotle brought significant advances to all these areas, illustrated by the following examples. He rejected Plato's doctrine of the forms and his views about the ideal state, concentrating instead on actual observations of the real world. Aristotle enunciated a system of logical reasoning: in metaphysics he sought to define the fundamental nature of substance, while in his physics he treated the first principles of nature. He analyzed the notions of change, place, and time, and set out his famous theory of four causes: the material, formal, efficient, and final causes. In psychology he developed a view of the soul as the "first actuality" of the body. Aristotle taught that all living entities have soul, including plants, animals, and humans. Humans share some aspects of the soul with plants and others with animals—such as nutrition, perception, imagination, and memory—but have a form of intelligence, the active intellect, that other living creatures lack. A keen observer of nature, he discussed the parts, structure, motion, and reproduction of animals in his biologies. His scientific works have been influential for more than 2,000 years.

In his ethical and political works, Aristotle focused on how to attain *eudaimonia* (happiness, human flourishing) at the individual (ethical) and community (political) levels. Aristotle defined *eudaimonia* as "an activity of the soul in accordance with virtue," and taught that the best way to attain it is by developing both moral virtues (including courage, justice, and self-control) and intellectual virtues (including science, art, practical wisdom, intuitive reason, and philosophic wisdom). One of Aristotle's most famous ethical doctrines was the "doctrine of the mean," in which he argued that every moral virtue is a mean in emotion and action between two vices. Courage, for example, is a mean, both in feelings and in action, between cowardice and rashness. At the end of the *Nicomachean Ethics*, Aristotle compares conceptions of happiness, and says that while the life of virtuous activity is a happy life, the life of philosophical contemplation is more blessed, even divine.

In his *Politics*, Aristotle addresses how to achieve happiness not just for an individual but for a community. Rejecting Plato's radical reshaping of the Greek *polis* in the *Republic*, he argues for more traditional *polis* forms, and tries to demonstrate that the best forms of constitution, and thus the best kinds of life, are to be found either under kingship or aristocracy. Aristotle's biological, ethical, and political works also reveal his own culturally bound limitations, as he uses these disciplines to "prove" the natural inferiority of women and slaves, ideas to have a pernicious influence on the development of Western thinking.

Finally, Aristotle also wrote important treatises on rhetoric and poetry. In the *Rhetoric*, Aristotle systematized earlier rhetorical theories and discussed techniques of persuasion, including shaping the character of the speaker, making emotional appeals, and using persuasive arguments. In the *Poetics*, Aristotle defends poetry and tragedy from Plato's attacks in the *Republic*, arguing that tragedy, as a form of *mimesis* (imitation), plays an important role in human life. He defines tragedy as a creative form that arouses the emotions of pity and fear and accomplishes a *katharsis* (purgation or purification) of these emotions, ostensibly bringing viewers to a new state of understanding.

Aristotle's philosophical range and output were incredibly vast, and his successors in the Lyceum, including Theophrastos of Eresos (ca. 372–286), carried on the peripatetic tradition. Although his works were not always known throughout antiquity, Aristotle's treatises were later very influential on Islamic philosophy and theology, and formed the philosophical basis of Medieval Christian Scholasticism. St. Thomas Aquinas (ca. 1225–1274 c.e.) helped integrate aspects of Aristotelian philosophy into Christianity, and Dante (1265–1321) called Aristotle "the master of those who know."

HELLENISTIC PHILOSOPHY

Aristotle died within a year of the death of his former pupil Alexander the Great, and the political upheaval throughout the Greek world brought about by Alexander and his successors was reflected by major changes in Greek philosophy. A new phase of ancient philosophy began, labeled "Hellenistic Philosophy," the period from the death of Alexander the Great in 323 to Octavian's defeat of Kleopatra in 31 B.C.E. As Greek *poleis* lost autonomy and were absorbed into the greater world of the Hellenistic kingdoms, many Greeks found philosophy helped them gain a much-needed sense of perspective on their changing world. Besides Platonism and Aristotelianism, new philosophical schools flourished, attracting wide attention and many followers, chief among them the Cynics, Cyrenaics, Neopythagoreans, Sceptics, Epicureans, and Stoics.

Among the many striking features of these schools was the role women played. In the *Republic*, Plato had advocated the equal education of men and women and imagined male and female philosopher kings studying philosophy and ruling his ideal state. But, overall, the participation of women in philosophy before the fourth century B.C.E. had been minimal. Some Greek philosophers, including Aristotle, had argued for the natural inferiority of women, compared to men, and women had had little opportunity to step outside their normal societal roles and take up the study of philosophy. This changed somewhat in the fourth century. Ancient sources report that some female students studied with Plato in the Academy, and women actively participated in several of the other schools, although they were always greatly outnumbered by their male counterparts. Unfortunately, later writers often downplayed women's importance in these philosophical schools because of inherent societal biases.

Characteristic of all the Hellenistic philosophies was a shift in focus from the good of the community to an emphasis on attaining individual happiness, which was defined differently by the different schools. The range of Hellenistic philosophies reflects the diversity of the period, one of the most distinctive being Cynicism, founded by Diogenes of Sinope (ca. 412–321), perhaps under the influence of Antisthenes, a follower of Sokrates. Nicknamed "the dog" (from the Greek *kuon*, from which the name "Cynic" derived), Diogenes shocked his contemporaries by his disregard of societal conventions, styling himself as "a Sokrates gone mad." Living in the Athenian *agora* ("marketplace"), he proclaimed and practiced a life of extreme simplicity and self-sufficiency, advocating the ideal of "life in accordance with nature," by which he meant living simply, like animals, or like humans before the rise of civilization. Hence his ideas of complete shamelessness, including performing natural functions like eating, urinating, defecating, and making love in public, which generated many stories about his teachings and outrageous behavior. Advocating a strict equality of the sexes, Cynicism attracted many followers, including a female Cynic philosopher, Hipparchia of Maroneia. Cynicism thus served as an important critique of contemporary culture, forcing people to question conventional, "normal" behavior.

The Cyrenaics, named after its founder's home, Aristippos of Kyrene (ca. 435–355), an associate of Sokrates, were famous for being hedonists (from *hedone*, "pleasure"), arguing that the chief goal in life was pleasure. Rather than meaning momentary pleasures, scholars believe that Aristippos meant that pleasure played a role in the attainment of happiness within a larger framework of self-control and long-term happiness. The Cyrenaics, like the Cynics, also valued the philosophical acumen of women: when Aristippos died, his daughter Arete headed the school.

Pythagoreanism (or Neopythagoreanism) was a Hellenistic evolution of the ideas of Pythagoras, who was regarded by his followers as the ideal philosopher, scientist, mathematician, and religious sage, and many philosophical doctrines were credited to him. He was most famously connected with a belief in the reincarnation of the soul, arguing that human souls suffered countless reincarnations into human and animal bodies, and teaching ways one could train and purify the soul. Women as well as men were active in the school, and among the surviving fragments are works attributed to female Pythagoreans, including Theano, Myia, and others. Apparently composed by women and addressed to a female audience, the writings of the female Pythagorean philosophers demonstrate the *harmonia*, balance, between men's and women's roles, and that ethical concerns about living right and well are as important to women as to men. Pythagoreanism was an important school throughout antiquity, particularly because Neopythagorean doctrines were conflated with Platonic ideas, since Plato had himself been influenced by Pythagorean teachings.

But the two major philosophical schools of the Hellenistic period were Epicureanism and Stoicism, both of which had a major impact on Roman and later Western ideas. Epicurus (341–270), an Athenian citizen born on the island of Samos, founded his school, called the Garden, at Athens around 307. Adapting the earlier philosophies of the Greek atomists, Leukippos and Demokritos, Epicurus taught and wrote prolifically. Unfortunately, the majority of his works have been lost. All that remains of his writings are three "epitomes" or outlines of his teachings in the form of letters about physics (*Letter to Herodotus*), ethics (*Letter to Menoeceus*), and meteorology and astronomy (*Letter to Pythocles*), and brief fragments of other works, most notably his major work, *On Nature*.

A strict materialist in his physics, Epicurus taught that nothing exists except atoms, the void, and compound bodies made up of atoms moving in the void. He held that the universe is infinite in all directions, and that an infinite number of atoms are moving constantly through space. These atoms come together in the void to create compound bodies and, thus, everything that exists. All compound bodies are impermanent, constantly coming into being and passing away. Only atoms and the void are eternal and indestructible, having no beginning and no end. Human beings, too, are made up of atoms. Epicurus distinguished the human body and soul, both made of atoms. The soul and body come into being together, work together throughout life, and at death, the soul atoms separate from the body atoms and scatter in different directions. Thus, Epicurus concluded that there was no afterlife, since the soul does not survive as an entity after death. Hence, there is no need to fear death, since nothing happens after death. Finally, although strict materialists, Epicureans were not atheists. Epicurus taught that the gods exist, but have nothing to do with our world and can do no physical harm to humans. The gods do, however, function as models of perfect happiness and tranquillity for Epicureans to emulate.

In ethics, Epicurus was a hedonist, teaching that the highest form of good is pleasure. However, the later popular view of an Epicurean as a profligate hedonist is a misleading distortion of Epicurus's views. Epicurus taught that the highest good in life is freedom from pain in the body and freedom from anxiety in the mind, which he called *ataraxia*, "untroubledness." The highest form of pleasure is the absence of pain, when the normal, healthy motions of the atoms of the body and soul occur. Epicurus believed the happiest life is easy for human beings to attain, but that human beings normally fail to attain it because they do not see that our basic needs for food, drink, shelter, and clothing are easy to meet. Humans instead usually desire objects—fancy food, large amounts of money, honor, public office—that are difficult to obtain and usually harmful to our happiness.

Epicurus taught that pleasure was also the basis for evaluating virtue and ethical behavior. It is important to be courageous, just, self-controlled, and live according to the standard Greek and Roman virtues, not because they are virtues, but because they are the means to the most pleasant life. For example, Epicurus wrote in *Principal Doctrine* 24, "Injustice is not a bad thing in its own right, but only because of the fear produced by the suspicion that one will not escape the notice of those assigned to punish such actions." In other words, justice is better than injustice because it contributes better to *ataraxia* and happiness.

The Garden, known as a community of friends, attracted men and women from all over the Greek world and from all walks of life, where they could live together in tranquillity, practicing the tenets of Epicureanism. The most famous of many women who lived there was Leontion, who wrote a philosophical treatise attacking the views of Theophrastos, Aristotle's successor in the Lyceum. Most famous of later Epicureans was the Roman poet Lucretius (90s–50s B.C.E.), whose epic poem, *On the Nature of Things*, forms our major source on Epicureanism.

The other major Hellenistic school of philosophy was Stoicism, founded by Zeno of Citium (ca. 334–261), who started his school around 300 B.C.E. in Athens. The Stoics were named after the famous "painted stoa" (*stoa poikile*) in Athens, where Zeno first started to teach. The Stoics became one of the most important of all ancient philosophical schools, best known for their Roman adherents, Seneca (ca. 4 B.C.E.–65 B.C.E.), Epictetus (mid-1st–2nd century C.E.), and the emperor Marcus Aurelius (121–180).

The goal of Stoicism was also tranquillity of mind, though Stoics' course for attaining it differed greatly from that of the Epicureans. The Stoics divided their philosophy into physics, ethics, and logic. In their physics, they taught that the world was a single, finite living creature, and maintained that all bodies are made up of an active and passive element. They identified the passive element (*to paschon* or *hyle*) as the matter of an object, and the active principle as fiery breath (*pneuma*). For example, a rock has a passive element (its matter or "stuff"), and an active element, the *pneuma* that permeates and organizes the rock, giving it its characteristic properties. The *pneuma* in animals and human beings is identified as soul. In the case of human beings, the soul or *pneuma* is attuned in such a way that it makes us rational and sets us off from other animals. The Stoics equated this *pneuma* that pervades all of nature with the divine *logos*, or rational principle, which organizes and controls the whole universe and which was also identified with god or Zeus. Thus, the Stoics believed that the world is divinely controlled, ruled by fate, and is the best of all possible worlds.

Consequently, in their ethics, the Stoics taught that the goal of all living creatures is "life in accordance with nature." This meant that adult humans must live in accordance with their rational nature. The Stoics argued that the only good for humans is virtue, the only evil vice. Only virtue can make a person truly happy, and only vice can make one miserable. All other things (including health, wealth, life, honor, and their opposites) are "indifferents"; that is, they make no difference in terms of human flourishing or happiness. In contrast to most mortals, whom the Stoics called "fools," only the sage, who possesses perfect virtue and knows how to live correctly and in accordance with nature, can perform virtuous activities and thus attain true happiness. All other humans fall short of true virtue and happiness, but can make gradual progress toward virtue.

Finally, the Stoic view of the emotions was different from what the modern term "stoic" implies. The Stoics said the sage would have feelings—just not excessive or irrational ones. Anger, elation, pity, fear, and other emotions were seen by the Stoics as mistakes in thinking, as when humans misinterpret "indifferents" like wealth or poverty as goods or evils. Not overcome by these irrational emotions, the Stoics maintained their goal of tranquillity through "rational passions" such as rational wishes and prudent caution.

CONCLUSION

The last phase of Platonism in antiquity, Neoplatonism, was initiated by Plotinus (204–270 C.E.) whose student, Porphyry, published Plotinus's philosophical essays in six books of *Enneads*, or "Nines" (so-called because each book is divided into nine parts). In the *Enneads* Plotinus combines Platonic, Aristotelian, and Stoic doctrine into a unified whole.

The work of Plotinus and Porphyry consolidated the ancient Platonic tradition, and passed it on to later ages. Their work influenced pagan and Christian writers of late antiquity, including St. Augustine (354–430), as well as Byzantine, Islamic, Medieval, and Renaissance thinkers. Though later Greek philosophies had in many ways moved far beyond Sokrates' ideas, the ethical questions, concerns, and investigations characterizing Sokrates' teaching continued to form the mainstay of subsequent philosophical inquiry.

SUGGESTIONS FOR FURTHER READING

Armstrong, A.H., ed. 1967. *The Cambridge History of Later Greek and Early Medieval Philosophy*. Cambridge: Cambridge University Press. An excellent collection of essays on various aspects of later Greek philosophy, with special emphases on the Platonic tradition, Plotinus, and the influence of Platonic and Aristotelian thought on Jewish, Christian, and early Islamic philosophy.

Barnes, Jonathan. 1982. *Aristotle*. Oxford and New York: Oxford University Press. An excellent introduction to and overview of major aspects of Aristotle's philosophy.

Branham, R. Bracht, and Marie-Odile Goulet-Cazé. 1996. *The Cynics: The Cynic Movement in Antiquity and Its Legacy*. Berkeley: University of California Press. A collection of essays on aspects of ancient Cynicism and its influence on later philosophies.

Brickhouse, Thomas, and Nicholas D. Smith. 2000. *The Philosophy of Socrates*. Boulder, Colo.: Westview Press. A recent overview covering many aspects of Socratic philosophy.

Guthrie, W.K.C. 1962–1981. *History of Greek Philosophy*. Vols. 1–6. Cambridge: Cambridge University Press. One of the leading overviews of ancient Greek philosophy from the Presocratics to Aristotle.

Inwood, Brad, and L.P. Gerson. 1997. *Hellenistic Philosophy: Introductory Readings*. 2d ed. Indianapolis and Cambridge: Hackett Publishing Company. An excellent selection of the writings of the Epicureans, Stoics, and Skeptics in English translation.

Kerferd, G.B. 1981. *The Sophistic Movement*. Cambridge: Cambridge University Press. The best short introduction to the lives and chief doctrines of the Sophists.

Kirk, G.S., J.E. Raven, and M. Schofield. 1983. *The Presocratic Philosophers*, 2d ed. Cambridge: Cambridge University Press. The standard edition of the writings of the Presocratic philosophers with analysis and interpretation.

Kraut, Richard. 1993. *Cambridge Companion to Plato*. Cambridge: Cambridge University Press. A first-rate collection of essays by leading scholars on various aspects of Plato's thought.

Long, A.A. 1986. *Hellenistic Philosophy*. 2d ed. Berkeley: University of California Press. An excellent, clear overview of the Stoics, Epicureans, and Skeptics.

———, ed. 1999. *The Cambridge Companion to Early Greek Philosophy*. Cambridge and New York: Cambridge University Press. A very useful collection of essays on the thought of the Presocratic philosophers and the Sophists.

Long, A.A., and D.N. Sedley. 1987. *The Hellenistic Philosophers*. 2 vols. Cambridge: Cambridge University Press. The standard edition of the Greek and Latin texts, with English translation and philosophical commentary on the Skeptics, the Epicureans, the Stoics, and the Academics.

Reeve, C.D.C. 1988. *Philosopher Kings: The Argument of Plato's Republic*. Princeton, N.J.: Princeton University Press. A clear and sophisticated reading of Plato's *Republic*.

———. 1989. *Socrates in the Apology: An Essay on Plato's Apology of Socrates*. Indianapolis and Cambridge: Hackett Publishing Company. An excellent introduction to Plato's *Apology* and Socratic thought.

Sharples, R.W. 1996. *Stoics, Epicureans, and Sceptics: An Introduction to Hellenistic Philosophy*. London and New York: Routledge. A thematic introduction to the major Hellenistic philosophical schools.

Snyder, Jane McIntosh. 1989. *The Woman and the Lyre: Women Writers in Classical Greece and Rome*. Carbondale and Edwardsville: Southern Illinois University Press. Contains a helpful chapter on "Women Philosophers of the Hellenistic and Roman Worlds."

Taylor, C.C.W. 1998. *Socrates*. Oxford and New York: Oxford University Press. A good, brief overview of Sokrates' life, philosophy, and influence on later philosophical thought.

Vlastos, Gregory. 1991. *Socrates: Ironist and Moral Philosopher*. Ithaca: Cornell University Press. A collection of essays on Socratic philosophy by one of the leading twentieth-century interpreters of Sokrates and Plato.

———. 1994. *Socratic Ethics*. Edited by M. Burnyeat. Cambridge: Cambridge University Press. A second collection of essays by Vlastos on aspects of Socratic philosophy, including a good introduction to the Socratic *elenchos*.

Waithe, Mary Ellen, ed. 1987. *A History of Women Philosophers, Volume 1: Ancient Women Philosophers, 600 B.C.–500 A.D.* Dordrecht, Netherlands; Boston; Lancaster, England: Martinus Nijhoff Publishers. A collection of essays on female philosophers in antiquity.

Ward, Julie K., ed. 1996. *Feminism and Ancient Philosophy.* New York and London: Routledge. Essays by leading scholars on the way different ancient philosophers viewed women's nature.

Zeyl, Donald J., ed. 1997. *Encyclopedia of Classical Philosophy.* Westport, CT: Greenwood Press. A handy and reliable guide to the leading figures and chief doctrines of ancient philosophy.

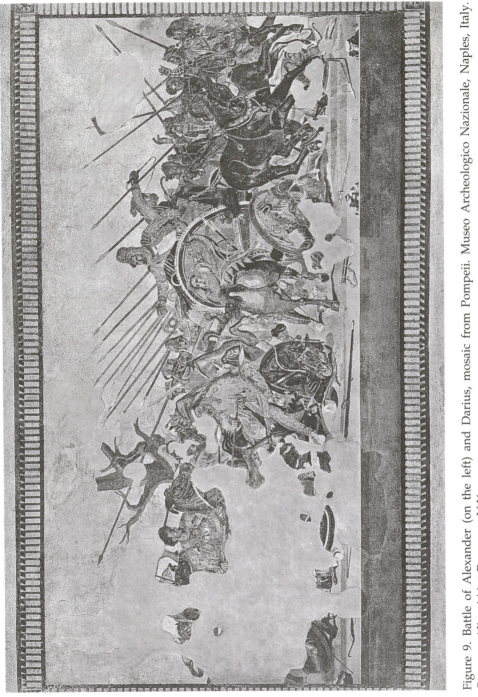

Figure 9. Battle of Alexander (on the left) and Darius, mosaic from Pompeii. Museo Archeologico Nazionale, Naples, Italy. Courtesy Alinari/Art Resource, N.Y.

9

Makedonian Conquests: Philip of Makedon and Alexander the Great

INTRODUCTION

The end of the Peloponnesian War did not bring peace. The first four decades of the fourth century B.C.E. saw different *poleis* pursuing imperialist policies of military and political hegemony. These conflicts aimed at control of Athenian or Spartan colonies along the coasts of Thessaly and the northern Aegean, control of Aegean islands, and alliances with Greek cities in Asia Minor. Athens's alliances shifted as first Sparta then Thebes held dominance, and jointly or separately each *polis* continued its treaties or conflicts with Persia. Athens led a second defensive league, but in response to renewed imperialist activities, several islands and Ionian cities revolted (357–355 B.C.E.).

Since the mid-seventh century B.C.E., another region had been gaining power in Greece: the northern kingdom of Makedonia. Although they spoke Greek, it is unclear whether the Makedonians were Greek or non-Greek peoples from bordering regions. Rather than the Greek *polis*, Makedonia maintained a monarchy, and by the end of the sixth century, the ruling Temenid dynasty, which claimed Greek descent, had established control over a vast region north of Thessaly. However, it was in turn conquered by Persia and aided Darius in his invasion of Greece. Even while subject to Persia, Makedonia maintained ideas of expansion, making expedient alliances through the fifth century, alternately aiding different sides during the Peloponnesian War.

In 359 Philip II gained power in Makedonia. The previous twelve years saw the defeat of the dominating powers of Sparta, at the Battle of Leuktra (371), and Thebes, at Mantinea (362). Despite various attempts at control, no Greek region had the power to do so, and Makedon was weakened by both internal and external conflicts. In his early teens, Philip spent two years as a hostage in Thebes, where he learned the key to the dominant *poleis*—their military: Athens, Sparta, Thebes all dominated through their armies.

Learning from his observations, upon gaining power, Philip strengthened the Makedonian kingdom, training and building up an army, modeling his phalanxes on Greek hoplite formation. He invented the pike, almost twenty feet long, twice the length of a hoplite spear, which created a more formidable offensive as well as defensive infantry front. Having created an ever more efficient fighting machine, Philip's forces became invincible, readily sweeping through northern Greek *poleis*, and he expanded his empire by conquering Illyria to the west and Thrace to the east. Occupying Thessaly and Phokis, Philip defeated the Greeks resisting his advance at the Battle of Chaironea (338), where his son Alexander fought courageously. Part of the resultant treaty recognized the right of the *poleis* to maintain their own governing systems even while under Makedonian domination, but the character of Greece would now change irrevocably. The Greek *poleis* were no longer sovereign, independent entities, but quasi-autonomous polities within a vast empire, which influenced how people thought about themselves and their world, and which soon would experience another dramatic shift with the conquests of Alexander.

In control of Greece and using vengeance against Persia as his pretext, Philip sent out an expeditionary invasion force, but he was murdered at Aigai near the Makedonian capital of Pella (336). His son and heir apparent, Alexander III (the Great), twenty years old, with the help of his mother Olympias, quickly gained control, eliminating his rivals. Alexander had been tutored by Aristotle, whose father had been court physician to Philip, and due to court intrigue he spent the year before his father's death in exile in Illyria. After becoming king, Alexander squashed a revolt by Thebes (335), destroying the city and enslaving the survivors. The severity of this punishment was meant to dampen any other thoughts of revolt. Alexander handled all opposition with this same ruthlessness, executing trusted companions and destroying whole cities for any resistance to his rule.

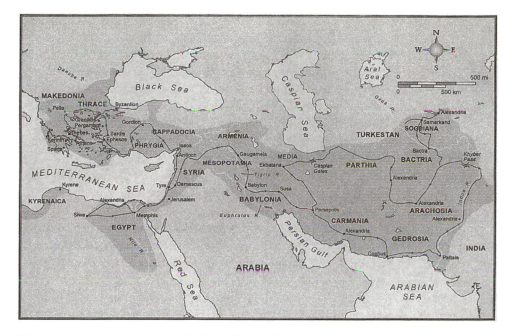

Map 2. Route and conquests of Alexander the Great, 323 B.C.E.

With Greece and lands to the north secured, leaving Antipater as viceroy in Makedonia, Alexander set out to accomplish his father's goal of conquering Persia (334). Thus began an eleven-year campaign that would alter the face of Greece and of many of the lands Alexander touched. Several accounts of this campaign were written after Alexander's death. While much of these near-contemporary accounts has been lost, they formed the basis for later works that have survived. Two works by Greek writers five centuries later provide important information about Alexander's life and his exploits: the biography by Plutarch (50–120 C.E.) and a seven-volume history by Arrian (86–160 C.E.), which was largely based on the history written by Alexander's general and close friend Ptolemy I (Chapter 10). In his history, Arrian saw himself immortalizing Alexander's deeds, as Homer had for Achilles. Hence, he, like his sources, eulogizes Alexander, praising him for his successful military campaigns and conquests while ignoring or minimizing his ruthlessness and heavy drinking.

Alexander amassed the largest military force ever to leave Greece: 43,000 infantry and 5,500 cavalry, supported by archery and javelin units. The core forces were Makedonian, supplemented by ethnically distinct companies. With this massive force, Alexander crossed the Hellespont (334); he easily overcame the Persian *satrapy* (province) and quickly occupied the Ionian Greek *poleis*. Routing their army, he defeated the Persian King Darius III at Issos (333), near the northeast corner of the Mediterranean Sea. Like the Athenians at Marathon, Alexander advantageously deployed a small number of his troops in a narrow plain, where the larger Persian forces were ineffective. With this overwhelming victory, Alexander controlled the Near East to the Euphrates River, replacing Persian *satraps* with his own, demonstrating his takeover of the Persian Empire while maintaining that empire's administrative organization.

Although Darius fled east, Alexander moved south through the Levant, capturing Phoenicia and Egypt (332), the latter offering no resistance. On the northern Egyptian coast he built Alexandria, which would become a commercial, cultural, and intellectual center in the coming centuries, the first of several new "Alexandrias" he would establish throughout his empire. In Egypt Alexander took a personal detour west to the Ammon oracle at Siwa, where he was acknowledged as son of Ammon, the Egyptian analogue of Zeus. This boosted Alexander's claims to divine descent, formerly through Herakles. But now, as an offspring of Zeus, he wanted to be worshipped as divine. However, his Greek and Makedonian troops refused to prostrate themselves before him, believing that gesture to be appropriate only for the gods.

Leaving Egypt, Alexander retraced his route north, conquering Mesopotamian cities with no resistance. He decisively defeated Darius at Gaugamela (331), again routing the Persian army and sending Darius fleeing. Again, rather than pursuing Darius, Alexander headed south, easily conquering Babylon and Susa. He seized the Persian capital of Persepolis and appropriated its wealth. After living there luxuriously for several months, he held an orgiastic drinking party as he burned it (330). After Darius was murdered by his own official, Bessus, Alexander directed his campaigns against Bessus, who declared himself the new Persian emperor, installed Persian-friendly *satraps*, and incited revolt.

Intent on further conquest, Alexander left his *satraps* to deal with Bessus in characteristically severe, exemplary fashion, while he moved east and north, conquering or resubjugating lands now part of Iran, Afghanistan, and India. Everywhere he massacred and uprooted the conquered populations, establishing Greek and Makedonian regional governors, sometimes alongside his appointed local *satraps*. He easily defeated Indian forces in the Punjab at the Hydaspes River (326), thus extending his empire 3,000 miles from his home. It had been eight years since Alexander began his campaign against Persia, which had become a steppingstone to further conquests. His troops' mutiny forced him to abandon plans to advance farther east, and he promised them they would return home.

On his return—south along the Indus River to the Arabian Sea, then west—Alexander continued his campaign of terror and conquest, sustaining a severe chest wound, and losing many men from heat and famine in the Gedrosian desert. Returning to Persepolis and Susa (324), he and eighty advisors married Persian noblewomen, and he eventually included Persian nobility in his innermost circle, thereby securing relations with already established local lines of power. While he prepared for his next conquest, the Persian Gulf, Arabian peninsula, and westward along the Mediterranean, confronting Carthage and Italy—one ancient writer suggests that he was intending to circumnavigate Africa—he died in Babylon in 323 at thirty-two years of age, the cause of his death disputed. Contemporaries claimed he was poisoned, but his secretary Eumenes wrote that complications from his chest wound exacerbated by excessive drinking caused his death.

With his invincible army, Alexander conquered the largest empire of the Near East, and he made it Greco-Makedonian. For this he earned the name *Alexander the Great*, and numerous coins, medallions, busts, and paintings depict him and his victories. The Hellenizing of the lands he conquered—by installing Greeks and Makedonians in occupied cities, and by building new cities populated with Hellenic peoples—gave its name to the period following Alexander's death, the *Hellenistic*, when Alexander's generals divided and fought for control of this Makedonian-Greek empire.

INTERPRETIVE ESSAY
Joseph Roisman

How should we judge Alexander? Was he, as one historian put it, an epoch maker? And even if he was, should he be condoned for this or condemned? The answer depends on one's historical perspective, which, in turn, is susceptible to contemporary notions and values. It is almost a cliché among Alexander's historians that every reader has her or his own Alexander. Indeed, opinions about Alexander have been divided from the time people started writing his history. The contemporary or near-contemporary accounts of his career include admiring comments as well as sharp criticism of his conduct, and ever since, a consensus of opinion about Alexander has eluded his historians. Early in the twentieth century, the British historian William W. Tarn romanticized the Makedonian king and made him a forerunner of both Jesus and French revolutionaries in his quest for harmony, equality, and universal peace. Nazi historians scolded Alexander for what they thought was his attempt to mix the races of his empire. For some post–World War II historians, he was a military genius and for others a despot who hit mercilessly at whomever he deemed a threat to himself. If, in the past, scholars depicted him as a civilizing force in Asia, today some regard him as a brutal conquistador. The ancient sources, our basis for any evaluation of the king, can be made to accommodate all these and other opinions as well.

Our information on Alexander is based chiefly on ancient literary accounts, which were written much later than the events they describe. The most important of them are Flavius Arrian's and Plutarch's biographies of the king (both second century C.E.), an incomplete history by the Roman historian Q. Curtius Rufus (first century C.E.), one volume of an extensive opus by the Greek historian Diodoros of Sicily (first century B.C.E.), and Justin's (third century C.E.) truncated version of Alexander's history by the Roman Pompeius Trogus (first century C.E.). Arrian and Plutarch draw a positive, even protective portrait of the king, while the other historians' attitudes range from less favorable to hostile. Over the years, modern Alexander scholars have tried to identify and classify the sources of these works according to their accuracy and bias. The results are impressive, though not always helpful. We are stuck with the capricious survival of secondary sources written by people who had their own views of the king, views that were likely to have influenced their choice of evidence. Nevertheless, the extant accounts are informative enough to help us mold our own opinion of Alexander. The following discussion of key issues in Alexander's story provides a basis for each reader to judge.

ALEXANDER, PHILIP, AND THE GREEKS

Many of the surviving accounts of Alexander are biographical and ascribe to the conqueror an exclusive claim to his accomplishments. This perspective is largely inaccurate or unfair. Alexander owed much of his greatness to his father, Philip II, who had consolidated the royal power in Makedonia, made the Makedonian army practically invincible, and subjugated Greece. Philip also initiated the preparations for war against Persia. But Philip's rule, both at home and abroad, was based on his personal charisma, rather than on the legitimacy of his rule or the stature of his country. Hence, when he was assassinated, the entire edifice he had built threatened to collapse. Alexander's swift reaction, one of the reasons for his military success, saved his life and his father's work. He gained the support of the leading Makedonian nobles, got rid of potential rivals, and then restored Makedonian power in the north, west, and finally against rebellious Thebes in the south.

The Athenian orator Demosthenes had contemptuously called Alexander a kid and a parody of a hero. Alexander had to prove to the Greek world that he was neither, so when the Thebans tested his resolve and power, he destroyed them. The sack of Thebes was a lesson for both conquered and conqueror. It proved that it paid to be a friend of the king or, at least, not to antagonize him. Greek opposition to Makedonian rule subsided into ineffective grumbling, and, when the Persians tried later to incite rebellion in Greece, they met with little success. The king, too, learned from the experience that terror could be a useful instrument of power.

Alexander also showed in his Greek campaign that he was an eclectic student of his father, as he simultaneously continued Philip's policies and deviated from them. He left the political and military settlements his father had established in Greece largely intact. The League of Korinth, which regulated the relationship between Makedonia and the Greek states and compelled the Greeks to preserve the status quo, was a useful political organization. Like his father, he cultivated ties with members of the local elites, and even in Thebes he spared the pro Makedonians. He would follow the same policy in Asia, where he established links with the Persian nobility. Unlike his father, however, who had spared Thebes after defeating it and Athens just three years earlier, Alexander destroyed his enemy. He also ignored his father's agreements when it served his purpose. Toward the end of his reign, he ordered Greek cities to take back their exiles, even though he and his father had promised not to interfere with the Greeks' autonomy. Alexander was his father's heir only up to a point.

Alexander's relationship with the Greeks was complex. Since the Makedonian royal house was Greek in origin, culture, and orientation, Alexander, when he saw fit, presented himself as Greek. Much of Alexander's propaganda was geared to showing the Greeks that his war was their war. Thus, the official goal of the campaign against Persia was to take vengeance on the Persians for their invasion of Makedonia and Greece in 480–479 B.C.E. He employed Greeks in his army and looked for Greek naval assistance, expecting that they would surely not support his enemy. Following his first triumph over the Persians, he sent back a dedication that declared it a victory of Alexander and the Greeks.

But the Greeks were also his subjects. When he conquered the coast of Asia Minor he faced the problem of how to deal with Greek cities that he claimed to have liberated from Persian rule. His solution was to give them autonomy, but have them ruled by governments friendly to him and supervised by a Makedonian governor. The taxes, formerly paid to the Persians, were now paid to him. The dualism of being both a partner and a ruler of the Greeks, a crusader against their enemy Persia and an enforcer of Makedonian power over them, was based on political considerations but also on authentic sentiments of affinity on his part. Yet many Greeks, and especially those whose power was curtailed by the Makedonians, had less than a charitable view of his attitude and goals. They were happy to see him campaign deeper and deeper into the heart of the Persian empire.

ALEXANDER'S AIMS

It is hard to know whether Alexander had grand plans of conquest when he crossed from Europe to Asia in 334. What is certain is that his war against the Persians was predictable, even destined. Earlier Greek campaigns in Asia Minor proved to be both militarily feasible and profitable. Greek intellectuals, such as Isokrates, called on various leaders to relieve Greece from its poverty and constant internal wars by directing aggression against Persia. Alexander's father had already dispatched an expeditionary force into Asia Minor. Yet even without these stimuli, Alexander was eager to pursue the war. Impatience with the sedentary administration of a kingdom characterized his entire career. First and foremost Alexander was a conqueror. There was something youthful and, for many contemporaries, heroic in his unremitting pursuit of military victories and collection of war prizes. Driven by an ambition to win as well as by the search for glory and excellence, and even by simple curiosity, Alexander kept pushing the boundaries of his progress farther and farther.

Alexander signaled the scope of his ambition quite early. After taking the coast of Asia Minor, he went inland to Gordion, where tradition claimed that whoever could untie the famous Gordian knot would rule Asia or the world. Alexander allegedly simply cut through it with his sword. If people still had doubts about his aims (including Alexander himself), they would have been put to rest after his first great victory over the Persian king Darius at Issos. When Darius offered to pay ransom for his captured family, Alexander declined and kept the royal family for himself. Even after Darius died and his self-proclaimed successor was eliminated, Alexander continued his march all the way to India. He probably intended to reach the ocean, which he believed to be not too far away, but was stopped by his reluctant soldiers. Yet his search for new wars and territories never stopped. On his return to Babylon, he began making plans for a campaign in the Arabian Peninsula, and possibly west against Carthage. Modern readers may disapprove of his insatiable and destructive appetite for conquest and fame, but in the eyes of many Greeks and Makedonians, this made him great. Like his model hero, Achilles, Alexander was invincible on the battlefield, a quality that legitimized and enhanced his superior status.

If military success made him distinguished, it also made his achievements personal and ephemeral. Alexander was the first and last king of both Makedonia and Persia. During a thirteen-year career, he both augmented and destroyed an empire that had lasted for over three centuries before his arrival.

THE WAR AGAINST THE PERSIANS

The Persians seem to have understood from the outset that, like Philip's rule, Alexander's power was rooted in personal charisma. His first great battle against the Persian governors of Asia Minor at Granikos showed that their goal was to eliminate him. There were rumors of Persian plots against his life. When all attempts failed, the Persian king decided to rely on his strengths, namely his superior numbers and naval power. Alexander was unable to challenge the Persians on the sea because his fleet, made up mostly of Greek ships, was unreliable. He chose to conquer the Persian navy on land by depriving it of bases of supply and support. He first took over the coastal cities of Asia Minor, then attacked the Phoenician city of Tyre and later Egypt. Following the retreat of the Phoenician and Egyptian fleets from the Aegean, the naval threat to Greece and Makedonia disappeared.

On land, Alexander relied on his excellent cavalry and infantry. The Persian cavalry was a worthy opponent, but the infantry was weak. Darius tried to compensate for his inferior infantry by recruiting Greek mercenaries and by mobilizing troops in great numbers. His strategy, however, shows that he was a prisoner of history. Especially in his last battle at Gaugamela, Darius imitated successful Persian battle plans of the past, while Alexander, both in his set-piece battles and in siege warfare, revealed inventiveness and the ability to improvise solutions to military challenges. The combination of a well-trained army and a courageous and skilled general was too much for a king who, in the final analysis, was an inept military commander. To a large extent, Alexander won his great battles because he met the right enemy.

ALEXANDER AND THE MAKEDONIAN ARMY

While the Persian army was an amalgamation of different units and peoples, Alexander's Makedonian troops formed a cohesive unit, which reflected the political and social structure of his homeland. The commanders belonged to the Makedonian elite and owed their position to the king and to their local power in Makedonia. The troops were recruited by region, but some major units were linked directly to the royal house from which they received lands. Common dialect and culture, and probably a sense of community, made the Makedonian army a distinct group. In it, social status and political power often corresponded to military rank, but since the King stood at the top of the pyramid, he could control promotions and demotions. Alexander used his officers not only for military assignments, but also as advisors on policy matters and to keep him company. Among them he found men who would support him in implementing his decisions and putting down opposition.

Alexander's relationship with his marshals was complicated by Philip's legacy, from whom Alexander inherited the army's chain of command. Most of Philip's generals transferred their loyalty to the young king, but Alexander felt more at ease with the men in his age group. Personal friendship and dependence on him made them trustworthy. At times he manipulated the tension that arose between the new, ambitious generals and the "old guard." Some court intrigues, including plots against Alexander's life, reflected the struggle between the old and the emerging elite. Eventually, the king completed the transfer of leadership over the army to the latter, who would reward him by breaking up the empire after his death and inheriting its fragments. During his reign, however, most of Alexander's appointees were loyal to him and supported his policies, including the contentious issues of his treatment of the Persians and his quest for superhuman status (see following discussion). In the relatively small confines of Alexander's court, issues of politics, military rank, administration, personal loyalties, and honor were often intertwined.

Just like the elite, the Makedonian troops played a political role because they were the Makedonian constituency. On special occasions, the army functioned as a political institution or a judicial court, although the king was able to control the results of their decisions. He enjoyed the prestige of his office and power, and the soldiers admired the leader who gave them so many victories and made them masters of the empire. Yet, Alexander was dependent on his soldiers too. When upset, they reminded him that his victories had been achieved through their blood and toil, and when they refused to march into India, Alexander had to yield. Partly to reduce his dependence on them, partly to solve the problem of dwindling Makedonian manpower, and partly to create a new power base for himself, Alexander turned to recruiting local Asian forces and incorporated them into the army. His Makedonian veterans disapproved of this policy, and when he discharged them and sent them home, they mutinied. This time Alexander did not give up, and the leaders of the mutiny were summarily executed. Alexander resolved to separate politics from the military, create an army more obedient to him, and thereby increase his control over the troops even more. He died, however, shortly afterward.

CONQUEROR AND CONQUERED

The question of Alexander's relationship with the conquered peoples was a delicate one. Nevertheless, it was an issue that turned contentious only later in the campaign. At first, Alexander's official policy toward the peoples of the Persian Empire was relatively straightforward. He had come to Asia to fight the Persians and free its peoples from the Persian yoke, whether they wished to be free of it or not. He was able to play the role of a liberator all the way to Egypt, where his paying respects to an Egyptian deity showed him as the antithesis of a former Persian king, who was reported to have offended local religious sentiments. Contemporary documents and later Egyptian sources identify Alexander as a Pharaoh and a son born miraculously to an Egyptian father. In Egypt, then, he was viewed not as a conqueror but as a legitimate ruler. The Makedonians did not object. Alexander's Egyptian monarchy raised no controversy because it did not threaten their status, as would his later military reforms and his claims to the Persian throne.

Egypt holds another key to Alexander's story. While in Egypt, Alexander made a major detour to visit the distant oracle of the Egyptian god Ammon in Siwa, a desert oasis. There, the priest confirmed that he was the son of Ammon, whom the Greeks identified with Zeus. In spite of the Egyptian locale, it was the Greek interpretation of the message that counted. Alexander was informed by a divine authority that he had a divine father just like other Greek heroes, including Herakles, the legendary ancestor of his royal house. It did not mean that he disowned Philip; at least, not yet. Herakles, and other mythical sons of Greek gods, had mortal fathers too. Yet the gap between the king and his men grew wider and would increase tension within the camp.

Alexander took his divine lineage seriously and was gravely offended if people poked fun at it. Moreover, like Herakles or Dionysos, both sons of Zeus who were deified, Alexander would eventually gain recognition of his divine status. The process was protracted and may not have been premeditated. It was motivated more by the wish for extraordinary honors than for political power, though the line between the two could be blurred. First came references, by Alexander himself and others, to Zeus/ Ammon as his father. Next, in central Asia, Alexander made an ill-judged attempt to combine his aspirations for divine status with his claim to inherit the Persian throne. Adopting Persian court procedure, he let it be known that he expected people to make obeisance to him. For the Asians, this honor proclaimed the elevated position of the king and his supreme power. Among the Greeks and the Makedonians, however, the act of prostration was reserved for the gods and, when performed for a mortal, suggested servility. It is hard to imagine that, in introducing prostration, Alexander was merely interested in unifying procedures in his court. He must have known what the act meant for the Makedonians and the Greeks. When his court historian led the opposition to the experiment, Alexander did not press the issue, for the moment.

But his quest for divine status continued. In India, he outperformed Dionysos and the top military feats ascribed to Herakles, proving that he had better credentials than those heroes to divine status. Finally, in 324, the Greek cities learned that he wished to establish a cult for himself as a god. It is possible that some Greek communities had already taken the initiative to give him divine honors, although other leading politicians and intellectuals ridiculed his cult. But Alexander had both contemporary notions of excellence and historical precedents on his side. Before his time, there had been prominent Greeks and Makedonians who were accorded divine honors: his father, Philip, had his statue carried in the company of the statues of the Olympian gods. Alexander's quest, then, was not groundbreaking, and, in his eyes and perhaps in the eyes of some of his contemporaries, he was fully justified in expecting such honors. After all, he had performed better than any mortal in battle, he had created the largest empire in the known world, and he was the son of a god. He was Alexander the Great, indeed.

The king expected Greeks and Makedonians to recognize his super-human status, but, as far as we can tell, he had no such expectations of the Persians or other conquered peoples. For honor, Alexander looked mostly to the west. This did not mean that he had no respect for the conquered or demanded none of them, only that he took it largely for granted. His attitude toward most of the peoples of the empire was based on political and utilitarian considerations. He wished them simply to accept his rule and to provide him with supplies, money, and manpower.

More complex were his relations with the Iranians and his claim to the Persian throne, because the Persians and their king were, until his arrival, the long established masters of the empire. In the wake of the battle of Issos, Alexander publicly declared his claim to be the sole king of Asia. After the battle of Gaugamela, Darius ceased to be a viable threat, and Alexander effectively became the ruler of the western half of the empire. It was then that he began cultivating his relationship with the local nobility. In Babylon he appointed as a *satrap* (governor) Mazaeus, who had been one of Darius's chief marshals. He continued his policy of filling government positions with local nobles in the Iranian heartland and beyond. Just as in Greece, Alexander ruled with the help of the local governing class and the threat of armed garrisons. He also adopted Persian court etiquette and even articles of Persian dress (and, according to one source, the Persian harem of 365 concubines). He even made a gesture of honor toward Cyrus the Great, the founder of the Persian empire. But his policy of establishing and legitimizing his power by both replacing and continuing the former government was limited in scope. As far as we know, he never ritualized his ascendance to the Persian throne or followed any Persian protocol that confirmed his rule of the empire. The reason was that, ultimately, the spear provided legitimacy.

Alexander's treatment of Persepolis is relevant here. He reached this venerable Persian city, which scholars have called the spiritual capital of Persia, in the winter of 331–330. He left it stripped of its riches and with many of its stately buildings in charred ruins. The question why Alexander sacked Persepolis has intrigued both ancient and modern historians. One suggestion is that he wished to announce to the Greeks that he was still carrying on a vengeful anti-Persian crusade. Other scholars perceive a message of terror directed at those Persians who intended to reject his claim to rule Asia. Since motives are hard to ascertain, it is better to look at actions. Alexander's conduct in Persepolis was that of a conqueror and destroyer, even if, as some ancient sources tell us, he allowed the destruction to happen under the influence of wine. Alexander showed in Persepolis that he did not need Persian approval of his rule.

Soon, however, he tried to narrow the gap between the conquered and the conquerors, elevating the status of the former and lowering that of the latter. As usual, the process was gradual. After Darius died, Alexander discharged the troops who had joined the campaign under the auspices of the Korinthian League, at the same time offering them employment as mercenaries. This made them accountable only to him. Partly by necessity, partly by choice, he increased his reliance on local chieftains in central Asia, and made a local woman, Roxane, his queen. When he returned to Susa in 324, the process of bonding the Iranians to his rule reached a symbolic climax. He married Darius's daughter as his second wife and had Makedonian and Greek members of his administration marry Iranian noblewomen. In spite of the enthusiastic endorsement of this event by some modern historians, who have seen in it an attempt to create a world of equal opportunities, the marriages actually confirmed the superior position of the conquerors. In the Greco-Makedonian world, men ruled, and in Susa all husbands came originally with Alexander and all wives from among the local elite. Yet, neither men nor women seem to have had much say in the formation of these political alliances. The master player and matchmaker was the king. When he died, the overwhelming majority of the Susa marriages were dissolved.

Alexander's incorporation of the local elite in his government and of local troops in his army aroused resentment among the conquering elite and army. The king dealt effectively with the grumbling of both. After all, there was no viable alternative to his rule, and the longer the campaign lasted, the greater grew his power as well as the dependence of the Makedonians on his decisions. With so much power in the hands of one man, personality counts. It is time to discuss Alexander's character.

PERSONALITY AND EMPIRE

Alexander's character has been of great interest for both ancient and modern historians, because, in an autocratic state, character issues have political ramifications. Moreover, Alexander's story can and has served as a paradigm of how people deal with huge success and power. In short, Alexander's career and conduct raise moral and philosophical questions. In ancient times the biographer Plutarch wrote two rhetorical pieces aiming to show that Alexander was successful not because of fate or luck but due to the soundness and strength of his character and his political vision. By contrast, the Roman historian Curtius Rufus describes how Alexander's character deteriorated and he became tyrannical, deceitful, and easily corrupted. Modern historians have added their judgments of the king, depicting him as a brute and a tyrant or as a gentleman and an officer.

Alexander's story provides enough material for both admirers and detractors, or for those who fail to make up their minds. He was generous, at times compassionate, intellectually curious, and highly competitive—a virtue in the eyes of the ancient elite. But he could be ruthless, lose his temper or sense of proportion, and, toward the end of his life, he drank too much. Some prominent individuals and entire communities paid with their lives because of Alexander's wrath. Alexander's character attributes also affected the nature and the course of his Asian campaign, which was guided not just by the power of circumstances but also by the power of his personality. His administrative policy illustrates the point.

Throughout much of his campaign, Alexander's method of administering the empire was fairly simple. He adopted the Persian system of *satrapies* and appointed governors who were assisted by troops and tax collectors. He also founded a number of cities called Alexandria and left Greek and Makedonian veterans in these and in other settlements. In most cases, Alexander's local arrangements were intended to maintain his rule in the area, but also, and more importantly, to allow him to march on. The push to move forward, to conquer in order to conquer some more, was a function of Alexander's personality. Yet, due to these temporary local arrangements, the administration of the entire empire was shaky. When he came back from the Indian campaign, he suspected some of his Iranian and Asian *satraps* of pursuing an independent policy and of corruption. He had them executed and ordered armies disbanded. Consequently, hordes of mercenaries roamed Asia and threatened the stability of the government. Already his conquests in the east were collapsing. His chief treasurer, Harpalus, fled the court with a huge sum of money. Alexander ordered the Greek cities to take back their exiles in hopes of finding a home for many of his mercenaries or unattached troops, but this action threatened stability in the Greek cities. Typically, however, Alexander did not focus on regaining lost ground or on consolidating the empire, but on his future Arabian campaign. Another war was more appealing and could overshadow present troubles. Alexander's administrative record is not one that calls for accolades.

How, then, is one to judge Alexander? By the scope of his conquests?

By the human price paid for them? By the legacy of a victor that could be emulated or should be feared? As the reader may have gathered by now, the answer is in the eyes of the beholder. History, however, has rendered its verdict. In the written accounts, artistic portraits, and popular imagination, Alexander III is identified as "the Great." History is not always right or just, but it is unlikely that Alexander will ever lose this title.

SUGGESTIONS FOR FURTHER READING

Ancient Sources

Arrian. *Anabasis*. Translated by Peter A. Brunt. 1976–1983. Cambridge, Mass.: Harvard University Press, Loeb Edition. The most informative ancient source on Alexander; a strong emphasis on military history with a favorable account of the king.

Diodorus of Sicily. *The Library of History*. Vol. 17. Translated by C.B. Welles. 1963. Cambridge, Mass.: Harvard University Press, Loeb Edition. A far less informative account than Arrian's, but it incorporates information not found in other sources.

Justin. *Epitome of the Philippic History of Pompeius Trogus*. Translated by J.C. Yardley. 1994. Atlanta: Scholars Press. A late abbreviation of a Roman account of Alexander originally written in the first century C.E.

Plutarch. *Life of Alexander*. Translated by B. Perrin. 1919. Cambridge, Mass.: Harvard University Press, Loeb Edition. Plutarch's interest in Alexander's character and personality make his treatment of the king's career selective; it is especially informative about life in the court and about variant versions of ancient histories of the king.

Quintus Curtius Rufus. *The History of Alexander*. Translated by J.C. Yardley. 1984. New York: Penguin Books. A Latin history of the king with distinctly rhetorical and moralistic tones. The book includes valuable information: Alexander is portrayed as progressively tyrannical.

Modern Studies

Badian, Ernst. 1960. "Harpalus." *Journal of Hellenic Studies* 81: 16–43. A most influential discussion of Alexander's court and policies toward the end of his reign.

———. 1985. "Alexander the Great." In *The Cambridge History of Iran*. Cambridge: Cambridge University Press. Vol. 2: 420–501, 897–903. A concise history of Alexander written by the "Dean" of Alexander studies, with special attention to the politics of the campaign.

Borza, Eugene N. 1990. *In the Shadow of Olympus: The Emergence of Makedon*. Princeton, N.J.: Princeton University Press. An analysis of Makedonian history before Alexander (including Philip) based on literary and archaeological evidence.

Bosworth, A.B. 1988. *Conquest and Empire: The Reign of Alexander the Great*. Cambridge: Cambridge University Press. The best textbook on Alexander to date, including a description of his campaign and discussion of key issues.

———. 1996. *Alexander and the East*. Oxford: Clarendon Press. An examination of Alexander's campaign in Central Asia, India, and the Gedrosian desert.

Carney, Elizabeth D. 1999. *Women and Monarchy in Macedonia*. Norman: University of Oklahoma Press. An extensive and readable discussion of all the women associated with the Makedonian monarchy.

Green, Peter. 1991. *Alexander of Makedon, 356–323 B.C.: A Historical Biography*. Berkeley: University of California Press. A highly readable account with a focus on Alexander's personality.

Hammond, N.G.L. 1980. *Alexander the Great, King, Commander, and Statesman*. Park Ridge, N.J.: Noyes Press. A favorable biography of the king with valuable discussions of his military accomplishments.

Holt, F. 1999. "Alexander the Great Today." *The Bulletin of Ancient History* 13, 3: 111–17. Alexander is unjustly criticized by modern historians. This study and that of Worthington are for readers interested in the questions of how deserving Alexander was of his title.

Price, Martin J. 1991. *The Coinage in the Name of Alexander the Great and Philip Arhridaeus*. Zurich: Classical Numismatic Group. The authoritative study of coins issued under Alexander and his immediate successor and their symbols.

Robinson, C.A., Jr. 1953. *The History of Alexander the Great*. Vol. 1. Providence, R.I.: Brown University Press. The only English translation of the fragments of Alexander's lost histories, but the translation is not always adequate.

Stewart, Andrew F. 1993. *Faces of Power: Alexander's Image and Hellenistic Politics*. Berkeley: University of California Press. A comprehensive study of the early artistic evidence on Alexander, which is highly relevant to the ideology and politics of his reign.

Stoneman, Richard. 1997. *Alexander the Great*. London and New York: Routledge. A readable discussion of Alexander's conquest.

Warry, John. 1995. *Warfare in the Classical World*. Norman: University of Oklahoma Press. A superbly illustrated, excellent description of all aspects of warfare in the ancient Greek and Roman world; see Chapters 5 and 6 on Alexander's warfare and among his successors.

Worthington, I. 1999. "How 'Great' Was Alexander?" *The Bulletin of Ancient History* 13, 2: 39–55. Alexander was not so great.

Figure 10. Bust of Kleopatra VII, first century C.E. Marble. Courtesy Staatliche Museen zu Berlin—Preussischer Kulturbesitz Antikensammlung.

10

Hellenistic Empires: Spread of Greek Culture and Rule to the Death of Kleopatra

INTRODUCTION

While Alexander's death (323) abruptly ended his drive for conquest and empire, the thirst for empire did not slacken, as his Makedonian generals quickly carved out their realms from Alexander's conquests: Ptolemy took Egypt and Kyrenaica; Seleukos, Babylonia; Antigonos, Asia Minor; Lysimakhos, Thrace; and Antipater the rest of Asia. Antipater's return to Makedonia, leaving Asia in Antigonos's control, quickly changed the initial division, setting a pattern for the next two centuries—the Hellenistic period. The conflicts in the twenty years following Alexander's death resulted in imperial divisions that would become, with shifting borders and alliances, the principal Hellenistic kingdoms: Makedonian, Seleukid, and Ptolemaic. Rulers of these separate dynasties fought continuously, either to maintain their holdings by subduing revolts and resisting encroachment, or to extend their territories through conquest and colonization, in time appealing to Rome to support faltering regimes. The constant warfare ceased only when conquered by an increasingly powerful Rome, beginning in the early second century B.C.E. with Makedonia. Extending during the next 150 years through Asia Minor, these conquests culminated with the defeat of Kleopatra VII (31 B.C.E.), the last Hellenistic ruler to succumb to Rome's military power.

Battles for the Makedonian throne were always bloody. Antipater's son Kassandros defeated Olympias, Philip II's first wife and Alexander's mother, whose murderous actions secured her son's and later favorites' accession to the throne. Kassandros ruled until his death (297), when Antigonos's son, Demetrios I, seized the throne (294–287) and established the Antigonid ruling line in Makedonia. The Antigonids were constantly battling with Seleukid and Ptolemaic rulers for control of the Aegean and eastern Mediterranean, dominance depending on the most recent military victors. During this time, the formerly powerful Greek *poleis*— Athens, Sparta, and Thebes—bristled at Makedonian domination, periodically rebelling against it, but rarely achieving a shadow of their former autonomy. Although often aimed at thwarting other powerful interests, Hellenistic rulers at times revived the Greek defensive leagues.

Closest to Italy, which it challenged, Makedonia was first to endure Roman conquest. Following its defeat of Carthage in two Punic Wars (264–241, 218–201), Rome declared war on Makedonia's king, Philip V (200), who had made alliances with the Carthaginian general Hannibal. After several victories, even decimating the Makedonian army (167), Rome annexed Makedonia (148) against fierce Makedonian resistance. After destroying Korinth, enslaving its inhabitants and pillaging its wealth, Rome annexed Greece in 146. Despite some failed attempts at revolt, the histories of Greece and Makedonia had become irrevocably linked to Rome's.

In the Near East, although Antigonos controlled the largest territory, his expansionist designs united the other generals who twice defeated him in battle. After Antigonos's death (301), Seleukos I expanded the Seleukid empire from the east, to Syria, founding Antioch on the Mediterranean coast (300), and after Lamakhos's death (281), to Asia Minor, thereby ruling the largest Hellenistic kingdom. His treaty with Chandragupta Maurya, founder of the Indian Mauryan dynasty, gained India as an ally to the east. Seleukos maintained Persian administrative procedures, incorporated Babylonian customs, and used Babylonian kingship as the basis for Seleukid. He supported worship of Babylonian deities and intermarrying with indigenous populations, practices continued by Seleukid kings, alternatively named Seleukos or Antiochos. Intent on reuniting Alexander's former conquests, Seleukos I was killed by Ptolemy I's eldest son as he proceeded to invade Makedon.

Seleukos's son, Antiochos I, continued his father's policies and acquisitions; he led a successful allied assault, repulsing the Celts, who were invading Makedonia, Greece, and Anatolia from the north. He built new cities, modernized infrastructures, and colonized the territory with Greek

and Makedonian settlers. Even when outlying regions revolted and began breaking away, establishing their own kingdoms, many did so on
the model of Hellenic rule and custom. Hence, the Seleukids, through
Greek-based colonization and through imitation by non-Greeks, fostered
the spread of Hellenic culture through western Asia.

By the early second century, several regions had seceded, of which
Parthia would become the most powerful, eventually defeating Rome's
army. Seleukid power deteriorated, due to internal dynastic conflicts and
foreign incursions by Rome, which acquired Anatolia, and by Parthia
which seized Babylon (141). Much reduced Seleukid rule lasted in Syria,
until it was taken by the Roman Pompey (64).

Upon Alexander's death, Ptolemy I (whose account of Alexander's exploits was Arrian's principal source) quickly seized control of Egypt,
ousting Alexander's minister there, and establishing the wealthiest and
most stable of the Hellenistic kingdoms. Beginning Greek dynastic rule
of Egypt—its rulers all named Ptolemy—Ptolemy I moved the capital to
Alexandria, whose political organization was modeled on the Greek *polis*,
allowing only Greeks and Makedonians to be citizens. But as a major
international hub, many noncitizen residents inhabited Alexandria, including Egyptians, Jews, and people of other ethnicities.

Ptolemy I built Alexandria into a major cosmopolitan center, which
eclipsed Athens and rivaled Rome. The over 300-foot lighthouse in its
harbor, Pharos, was considered one of the seven wonders of the ancient
world. The first two Ptolemies built the Alexandrian Library, eventually
the largest in the ancient world, holding 500,000 rolls. They also began
the "Museum," a scientific, philosophical, and literary research center,
which lasted almost seven centuries. The Ptolemies, and later the Romans, generously financed its directors, and its seminars drew intellectuals from all over, including the Ptolemies, who, down to Kleopatra VII,
engaged in these discussions. As the cultural hub of the Hellenistic
world, the city attracted poets who developed a distinctive poetic style,
called Alexandrian.

Like Seleukos, Ptolemy incorporated Egyptian customs, a practice increasingly followed by his descendants, who, at first, took on Egyptian
priestly roles and eventually proclaimed themselves deities, like the old
Egyptian pharoahs. Setting significant precedent was Ptolemy II (282–
246) who expanded Ptolemaic rule to its greatest extent, including Cyprus, Phoenicia, Syria, Anatolia, and the Greek islands. By marrying (as
his second wife) his full sister Arsinoe II, for which both were called
"Philadelphos" ("Sister- or Brother-loving"), he instituted Ptolemaic
brother-sister marriage alongside the royal political marriages regularly

practiced by the Hellenistic dynasties. Ptolemy II established a Greek royal cult for himself and Arsinoe, who assumed both Alexandrian and Egyptian priestly roles; he built Philadelphia, Egypt, for her, and held festivals honoring his parents and her after their deaths.

Arsinoe's influence over her brother was legendary in antiquity; it reflects also the power of Ptolemaic queens. Certainly, royal women everywhere may exert great influence, especially in manipulating, often violently, the succession for their sons, or as regent for their minor son, as Olympias, Alexander's mother, did. The Ptolemaic queens may have wielded even more power, enhanced by brother-sister marriage, by adopting Egyptian royal/sacred customs, and by their public benefactor roles. Many of them were honored by religious festivals, by being shown, singly or with the king, on coins and medallions, and by being immortalized by Alexandrian and Roman poets. Through the third century, Ptolemaic queens of Makedonian heritage were named Arsinoe or Berenike. By marrying Ptolemy V (193) Kleopatra I, daughter of the Seleukid king and possibly Persian wife, began new female namesakes.

Ptolemy II's successors had difficulty maintaining the dynasty's reach; others lost the Alexandrians' confidence, who forced some of them out. Ptolemaic rulers increasingly relied on Rome to bolster their rule, as did Kleopatra VII's father, Ptolemy XII. By the mid-first century, the political rivalries of Rome's generals were battled out in Asia Minor and Egypt. With Syria annexed in 64 and Parthia dominating the east, Roman interest centered on Egypt.

Ascending to the throne upon her father's death (51), Kleopatra VII ruled sometimes alone, sometimes with her younger brother or later with her son. She was the first after her father to take the title "God," further embedding her rule in Egyptian custom. An accomplished linguist—she frequently acted as her own diplomatic interpreter—she was the first Ptolemy to speak Egyptian. Politically astute, she made strategic alliances, first with Julius Caesar, accompanying him to Rome in 46, and by whom she had her first child, Ptolemy XV, Caesarion. Three years after Caesar's assassination (44), Kleopatra met Mark Antony in Syria, beginning a liaison that would last to their deaths a decade later.

Although the sexual dimensions of this affair have been emphasized since ancient times, often with denigrating intent, here again Kleopatra's alliances had political purposes: to secure and build up her realm, wealth, and military forces. With his initial victories in Asia Minor, Antony appeared to be the strongest of the Roman ruling triumvirate; should he have succeeded, the consolidation of Rome and Egypt would have made a formidable combination. But Octavian, Julius Caesar's great-nephew and adopted heir, emerged predominant, defeating the armies of Antony and Kleopatra at the Battle of Actium (31 B.C.E.). Octavian seized Alexandria the following year and annexed Egypt. Rather than becoming a Roman captive, Kleopatra killed herself, as did Antony. Thus ended the last of the Hellenistic kingdoms and of ancient Greek rule in the eastern Mediterranean.

INTERPRETIVE ESSAY
Carl G. Johnson

INTRODUCTION

One of the key problems in approaching the Hellenistic age (330–323 B.C.E.) is the lack of a defining literary tradition. For the Hellenistic age, there is no surviving Homer or Hesiod, Aeschylus or Sophocles, Thucydides or Euripides, Plato or Demosthenes, as was true of the Archaic and Classical periods. No single author or two authors put their stamp on this period; rather, the writings we do have reflect the broad diversity of this period that defies categorization. With no surviving ancient conception of what was at the core of this age of human civilization, by default, then, modern scholars have attempted to create their own definition. This has been the goal of Hellenistic studies from the nineteenth century to the present day. Before we survey the political, economic, social, and religious developments of this period, it is necessary to briefly review the scholarly trends that have dominated the field of Hellenistic studies. Thereby, we may be more cautious when examining what little has survived from antiquity.

With the conquest of the Persian Empire by Alexander the Great, the Greeks came into contact with many non-Greek nations and cultures of the Near East. The relation between the Greeks who became the ruling class in the newly founded Hellenistic kingdoms and their indigenous subjects has been examined for more than a century, and two concepts of these relations have dominated: that of a mixing of the Greek race and the natives of the Near East, a fusion of civilizations, namely "syncretism," and that of isolation of the races, and only superficial influence, namely the "coexistence" between races. Both concepts owe much to philosophical, intellectual and cultural trends of the nineteenth and twentieth centuries, and, in this way, Hellenistic studies mirrors contemporary thought.

SUMMARY OF NINETEENTH AND TWENTIETH CENTURY SCHOLARSHIP

It was J.G. Droysen, in his monumental *History of Hellenism* (1833–1843 C.E.), who advanced the notion of a "Hellenistic age," as distinct from the Classical period and the Roman Empire. This Hellenistic age represents, moreover, a fusion of Greek and Near Eastern elements, which formed a unique and distinctive Hellenistic culture. "Hellenistic" has always signified "like" but not the same as the Hellenic age (750–338 B.C.E.). According to Droysen, the Hellenistic age was characterized by the rise of a common civilization, a mixture ("fusion" or "syncretism") of East and West, non-Greek and Greek, that produced a "Hellenistic" civilization distinct from that of classical Greece. From the ruins of the Greek city-state and the complex cultures of the Near East rose new and vigorous empires and societies. This theory of the fusion of cultures, however, had another purpose: the meeting of Greek culture with that of the Jews, which resulted in the Christian era and civilization.

Droysen's ideas on the nature of Hellenistic culture were clearly the most influential into the first half of the twentieth century. A number of pivotal works refashioned his history, and the mass of new data coming from archaeology, papyrology, and epigraphy seemed to confirm these ideas about the mixed nature of the Hellenistic world. The key concepts of the "fusion-syncretism" argument are "Hellenization" and "Orientalization" (and more particularly "Egyptianization" in the case of Ptolemaic Egypt), the forces believed to be operating after Alexander's conquest of the Near East. "Hellenization," the spread of Hellenic culture, was depicted as a conscious policy by Alexander and his successors, namely, the transformation of "barbarian" into Greco-Makedonians, and vice versa, or in a more gentler form, the making of a new Greco-barbarian. Some twentieth century scholars portrayed Alexander the Great as desiring, through a fusion of "races," to join all mankind into a single brotherhood, thereby inspiring the dream of the Stoic Zeno. Such a vision of the father of the Hellenistic age added fuel to the belief that the Hellenistic monarchs, in Alexander's mold, also wished to Hellenize and fuse their subjects. But more recent work examining Alexander's policy of racial fusion has essentially demolished this idealistic vision.

Other scholars showed the inadequacies of the fusion view, pointing out the essential lack of cultural and social interaction of the Greco-Makedonian and indigenous peoples of the Near East, except in one area: religion. In particular, Egyptian papyrological and epigraphic sources depict two distinct societies—one Greco-Makedonian, based in the cities and towns with their Greco-Makedonian institutions, culture, and education; the other the indigenous Egyptians, found in the countryside (*chora*) and scattered temple complexes. The only contact between the two peoples occurred when Egyptians wished to improve their status by rising through the Greco-Makedonian–dominated military or government. Such a process involved their becoming "Greeks" through the adoption of Greek language and culture; that is, speaking Greek, knowing Homer, engaging in the gymnasia, and the like. This separation, or "coexistence," of peoples is supported by the plurality of laws and courts in Ptolemaic Egypt. Greco-Makedonians and Egyptians were judged in different courts, where there were different laws for each group, for the Greco-Makedonian cities and settlements, and for the *chora*.

Another modern concern bears significantly on Hellenistic studies: that of postcolonialism and European analysis of their own age of imperialism. Hellenistic historians of the first part of the twentieth century—English, German, French and American—all saw Hellenization, in the guise of the "white man's burden," as something good, and part of the development of what they characterized as the backward, primitive Near Eastern civilizations. After the Second World War, with the collapse of the European empires, this position was reversed, and scholars saw just the opposite: the Hellenistic empires were now more oppressive than beneficial, and their purpose was not the betterment of their subject population, but their exploitation. This trend continues to this day, fueled by the work of postcolonial scholars such as Edward Saïd. This trend has also helped give rise to studies that focus solely on the non-Greek elements of the Hellenistic world in an attempt to see the period not only through the eyes of the ruling classes but from the perspective of the ruled.

HISTORICAL SURVEY OF THE HELLENISTIC AGE

As previously noted, lack of a defining historical and literary tradition makes a reconstruction of the events of the Hellenistic period exceedingly difficult. Of surviving historical sources, the most important are Polybios (200–118 B.C.E.) and Diodoros (first century B.C.E.); unfortunately, both are in fragmentary form and do not preserve a continuous history. These sources are complemented by the biographies of Plutarch (ca. 50–120 C.E.), and by Latin authors, including Livy (59 B.C.E.–17 C.E.) and Justin's summary of Pompeius Trogos (ca. third century C.E.). Scholars have looked at filling in the gaps by examining papyrological, epigraphic, and numismatic sources, but in interpretating these materials, historians have encountered the same methodological problems as they have with literary sources.

The nature of information contained in these surviving sources also differs significantly. The literary historians—Polybios, Diodoros, Plutarch, Livy, and Justin's Trogos—tend to concentrate on political and military history, the lives of rulers, and court history. As a result, the picture of the period is dominated by kings and their battles. Fortunately, this picture is somewhat balanced by inscriptions and, in the case of Ptolemaic Egypt, papyri that give details of everyday life in the Hellenistic kingdoms and the concerns of ordinary people. Thus, we can also examine the social and economic realities of the Hellenistic world. Finally, as already noted, texts from non-Greek sources have also survived, the voice of those ruled by the Hellenistic monarchs. These included Aramaic and cuneiform inscriptions from the Seleukid empire; Jewish literature, such as the historical accounts of Philo and Josephus (both first century C.E.) and the apocryphal Books of the Maccabees; and Demotic papyri and hierogylphic texts that describe the life and views of the native Egyptian from the priesthood to the peasant farmer.

As is often quoted, when Alexander died he told his generals that he was leaving his empire to the strongest. This set the stage for the period following his death and the internecine struggles to establish what would become the three great Hellenistic kingdoms. From 323 to 301 B.C.E., these wars of the successors or Diadochoi were fought to control portions of Alexander's conquests. A number of Alexander's companions rose to prominence during them: Antigonos Monophthalmos ("one-eyed") strove to reunite Alexander's conquests, and was opposed by Lysimachos, Ptolemy, Seleukos, and Kassander, each of whom attempted to carve out his own "spear-won" kingdom. By 301 Antigonos Monophthalmos was dead, his son Demetrios Poliorketes ("sieger of cities") in permanent exile, and three great kingdoms had been established: that of Ptolemy in Egypt, of Seleukos in Syria and the Near East, and Lysimachos in Asia Minor and Thrace. By 281, further adjustments had been made. Makedonia and Greece were now part of the new Antigonid Kingdom, ruled by a grandson of Antigonos Monophthalmos, Antigonos Gonatas, and Lysimachos had fallen in the battle of Corupedium, his kingdom divided among Antigonos, Ptolemy, and Seleukos.

By 304 each general of Alexander's had proclaimed himself king of his territory, and Ptolemy I, Seleukos I, and Antigonos Gonatas had established dynasties, their descendants ruling for over 200 years. These monarchies were not national in the modern sense, but personal and absolute in the style of Philip II and Alexander. Despite being founded in foreign climes, they maintained a distinctive Greco-Makedonian character. The monarchies were supported by Greco-Makedonian administrators and armies, joined by businessmen, merchants, craftsmen, and farmers who flocked to the new successor kingdoms in hopes of making their fortunes. This migration from old Greece was greatly encouraged by the kings, who held out subsidies to all interested in helping them build their power. But at the heart of the king's power was his Greco-Makedonian army, and to pay that army the king had to raise income from his subject populations. This burden, as well as the burden placed by the royal opulence and patronage of the Hellenistic courts, caused significant distress among the indigenous peoples. Each kingdom faced its own unique challenges, and each kingdom was eventually swallowed up by Rome.

Finally, the Hellenistic kingship had considerable influence on the later Roman emperors, providing a model both of beneficent autocracy and of divine monarchy. Both the Ptolemies and Seleukids (but not significantly the Antigonids) proclaimed themselves as gods in their own lifetimes. And whereas the divinity of the Roman emperor would pose a problem for later Christians, it provided a common focus and justification of rule for the diverse polytheistic peoples of the Hellenistic Near East.

THE ANTIGONID KINGDOM

When both Philip Arrhidaeus and Alexander IV, the last of the Argeads (the traditional royal family of Makedonia, which included Philip II and Alexander the Great), were murdered by the Diadochoi, the throne of Makedonia was left open. This was claimed in turn by Kassander, Demetrios Poliorketes, and Antigonos Gonatas, who proved his worth as king by protecting Makedonia from a number of Gallic invasions. Antigonos Gonatas became the founder of the Antigonid dynasty, which has been, over the last 200 years, seen as a beneficent monarchy or a ruthless tyranny, depending on the scholarly point of view. Certainly in antiquity, the dynasty was little loved by Greek historians, such as Polybios, who desired a return to the freedom of the *poleis*.

Although not related to the Argeads, Antigonos Gonatas essentially had the same ambitions as Philip II: secure his own kingdom and dominate Greece. Unlike Philip II, the Antigonids never sought the conquest of Asia Minor and beyond. The control of Greece proved difficult enough. Although the great *poleis* of the Classical period—Athens, Sparta and Thebes—persisted in their dreams of autonomy and hegemony, new

leagues, such as that of the Aitolians and the Achaians of the northern
Peloponnesos were ultimately the undoing of the Antigonids. The un-
wise intervention by Philip V in the Second Punic War (218–202 B.C.E.)
on Hannibal's side, gave Rome a *standi locus* ("a place of standing") reason to intervene across the Adriatic, resulting in four Makedonian Wars
(215–146 B.C.E.).

In the end, the Antigonid monarchy was overthrown and Makedonia
became a province of the Roman Empire. Greece was fully embroiled in
this debacle as well. With Roman intervention, the Achaean League rose
in prominence. But because of grave misunderstandings on both sides,
doubtless due to cultural differences, the Achaean League brought war
to Greece, and like Makedon, it eventually was absorbed by Rome (146
B.C.E.). This confusing, tragic period, in which the Greeks lost their claims
to sovereignty, is the subject of Polybios's *Histories*. He attempted to explain to his fellow Greeks why this fall was inevitable and why it was
best to acquiesce with the new regime.

THE SELEUKID KINGDOM

Of all the Hellenistic kingdoms, that of Seleukos I most resembled that
of Alexander's initially. At its height it stretched from the Indus River
to the Aegean Sea and comprised dozens of peoples. But its size and
diversity were its undoing. Like the Persian Empire, it suffered repeated
revolts; only under strong kings like Antiochos III Megas ("the Great")
did it manage to exert any real control throughout the realm. During the
mid–third century, two important parts of the empire were lost. In Asia
Minor, the eunuch treasurer of Antiochos I, Eumenes I, and his nephew,
Attalos I, established what would be known as the Attalid kingdom with
its capital in Pergamon (263). And in Bactria, Diodotos I, a Greek *satrap*
of Antiochos II, established a dynasty (ca. 250).

The Seleukids were also embroiled in a series of wars with the Ptolemies over the disputed territory of Coile Syria ("Hollow" Syria, extending from modern Lebanon down through Israel and the Red Sea).
Eventually, the Maccabees would liberate Judea from the Seleukids as
well (143). That only two Seleukid kings died of natural causes is a testament to the history of this kingdom: its kings were perpetually engaged in suppressing rebellions and fighting off pretenders. The
Seleukids, pursuing the dream of Alexander, made an ill-considered bid
to liberate Greece from the recently arrived Romans. Antiochos III was
quickly driven from Greece, and then crippled by Rome at the Battle of
Magnesia (189). In the resulting treaty (Apamea), the Seleukids lost Asia

Minor, and, with the rise of Parthia in the east, from that point on, the empire went into decline. In 64 B.C.E., the Roman general Pompey made Syria, all that was left of the once great empire, into a Roman province.

Although surviving sources are scarcer for the Seleukids than for the Ptolemies of Egypt, our image of their kingship and rule is dominated by the fusion and coexistence arguments noted above. To some scholars, they retained a Greco-Makedonian character, remaining untouched by the non-Greek elements around them. The persecution of the Jews in the second century B.C.E. by Antiochos IV is seen as an example of the monarch's attempts to "Hellenize" the non-Greek populations of his diverse empire, including the forcible conversion of Jews and the defilement of the Temple in Jerusalem. Other scholars portray the Seleukids as seeking the active support of the indigenous populations of the empire (Syrians, Jews, Babylonians, Bactrians, etc.), pointing out that the queen of the founder, Seleukos I, and the mother of his heir, was non-Greek.

THE PTOLEMAIC KINGDOM

As weak territorially as the Seleukid kingdom was, so was the Ptolemaic kingdom strong. Its founder, Ptolemy I, realized that Egypt, protected by a cordon of territories—Coile Syria, Kyrene, and a strong presence in the Aegean—was virtually impregnable. This was proven historically: under Ptolemaic rule, Egypt only suffered two successful invasions. But despite possessing one of the richest kingdoms in the ancient world—a wealth based on the wheat crops of the Nile valley, as well as royally controlled monopolies—the Ptolemies were also harried by rebellion and dynastic quarrels. Egypt was the home of the ancient Pharaonic civilization. The indigenous Egyptians, led by their priesthood, had resisted foreign domination before by the Semitic Hyksos and the Persians. Now, under the pressure of severe economic exploitation, a policy demanded by the culture of Hellenistic kingship, dating from the second century B.C.E., Egypt was wracked by successive internal revolts.

The Ptolemies made some attempt to win over the priesthood and populace, but never understanding that successful rule in Egypt required ruling according to an Egyptian and not a Greco-Makedonian model, they failed. Hence, the question of whether there was a fusion of native Egyptian and Greco-Makedonian elements or, alternatively, a separation of both and coexistence, arises here as well. Scholars are deeply divided over whether the Ptolemies saw themselves and acted as Egyptian pharaohs. Certainly, they allowed themselves to be honored as such in the milieu of Egyptian temples and rituals, but in their Greek official documents and coins they always depict themselves as Greco-Makedonian kings. Remarkably, only one Ptolemy, Kleopatra VII, ever bothered to learn native Egyptian, a testament possibly to the dynasty's general indifference to and isolation from the native population they governed.

From the battle of Raphia (217 B.C.E.), the native population began to resist more adamantly the presence of the invader. Literature appeared, such as the "Oracle of the Potter," prophesying the end of Greco-Makedonian rule and the expulsion of the "Sons of Typhon." This is hardly the manner in which the enlightened Ptolemies wished themselves to be seen.

The Ptolemaic Empire was politically strong in the third century B.C.E., thriving under the kingship of Ptolemy II, who used his immense wealth to build the Library and Museum of Alexandria, and Ptolemy III, who successfully invaded the rival Seleukid kingdom. However, in the second and first centuries, the dynastic quarreling of weak and incompetent kings weakened the realm, exacerbated by the eventual intervention of Rome. Egypt enjoyed a brief political renaissance under the last Ptolemaic ruler, Kleopatra VII (see Figure 10). Alone among the Ptolemies, she knew the native language of her Egyptian subjects and successfully enlisted their support, ironically against the domination of another foreign invader: Rome. With the aid of Mark Antony, she almost restored Ptolemaic Egypt to its former glory, but the Battle of Actium (31 B.C.E.) not only sealed her fate but also that of her rule. The last Hellenistic kingdom became a Roman province.

HISTORICAL RETROSPECTIVE

A quick review of the political history of the Hellenistic period reveals two salient features: that the Mediterranean world under the Diadochoi empires was wracked by war, and that the indigenous populations were hostile to the rule of the Greco-Makedonian invaders. Although attempts were made by the Seleukids and the Ptolemies to placate the indigenous populations they controlled—by benefactions and by allowing the upper classes into the government—these had little effect on the larger population's enmity to the foreigners. After all, even the Syrian, the Jew, or the Egyptian who wished to be a part of the Greco-Makedonian ruling class had to enter on the conqueror's terms: learn Greek and act like a Greek. Otherwise, admittance was refused.

Moreover, the political and economic oppression of the Hellenistic monarchies would culminate in the aggressive, widespread Romanization of the Mediterranean. With that Romanization, the world would lose the heritage of Carthage, the Celts, Pharaonic Egypt, and all too nearly with the sack of Jerusalem by Titus (70 C.E.), that of the Jews. In face of the internal pressure of subject populations and the external pressure of Rome, the Hellenistic monarchies could not survive.

What many scholars of this period have tried to show is that the conquest of the Near East by the Diadochoi kings was a good thing and in the long run justifiable. This interpretive line contends that the cultural, intellectual, philosophical, and religious advances of this period, which became so essential to the Roman-Christian world, more than make up for the many failings of the Hellenistic age. The failings are striking by modern standards: the suppression of freedom in Greece by the Antigonids, the persecution of the Jews and other peoples in the Near East by the Seleukids, and the gross economic exploitation of the indigenous Egyptians by the Ptolemies. Reflecting the theoretical split between the fusionists and separatists, the former have argued that the unique cultural, scientific, and intellectual advancements of the period resulted directly from the fruitful mingling of the traditions of the Near East and Greece. Those propounding the coexistence theory, meanwhile, deny that there is any real influence on the traditions of Greece, arguing that the work of Hellenistic writers and thinkers owed a debt only to Classical Greece.

INTELLECTUAL AND SCIENTIFIC ADVANCES

Part of the ethos of Hellenistic kingship was to play the great patron, something that required a great income. All the dynasties supported the arts and sciences, but none more splendidly than the Ptolemies in Alexandria, and, in particular, through their creation and support of the famous Library and Museum. Established by Ptolemy II, the Library and Museum were a research institute based on the models of the Academy and Lyceum of Athens. The Ptolemies sponsored research of every kind, paying salaries and encouraging both abstract and applied research. The Library contained not only all of Greek literature but collected and translated non-Greek literature from the Near East, the *Septuagint* (Greek translation of the parts of Hebrew scripture, from the third century B.C.E.) being the best example. The Library and Museum, in the tradition of Plato and Aristotle, aimed both at the preservation of known knowledge and at accumulating new knowledge.

A number of important Hellenistic scholars and poets worked and studied at Alexandria, their research ensuring the continuity of the great works of Archaic and Classical Greece into the Roman and eventually modern worlds. Notable was Aristophanes (ca. 257–180 B.C.E.), the great literary critic and grammarian who edited the texts of many Greek poets, including Homer and Hesiod. The literature of this period reflects the societal trends seen also in sculpture, philosophy, and religion: the emphasis on the individual. With the decline of the Greek *polis* and its public political life, identity was now found within each person and not in the body politic, portrayed in concerns about the individual, not the community.

Three of the major Hellenistic poets were associated with the Library and Museum in Alexandria, hence called Alexandrian: Theokritos, Kallimakhos, and Apollonios of Rhodes. Theokritos (ca. 310–250 B.C.E.) was famous for his pastoral poetry and scenes of contemporary life. Kallimakhos (mid-third century), a polymath and a poet, wrote the *Aitia*, which described the origins of Greek rites and customs. Famous for his statement "a big book is a big evil," he wrote erudite hymns and epigrams, preferring short, intricate works to long, onerous ones. And Apollonios of Rhodes (b. ca. 295 B.C.E.) composed a new Greek epic, the *Argonautica*, about Jason's quest for the Golden Fleece. Although considered inferior to the works of the Classical period by some, all three Alexandrians had immense influence on Latin poets and served thereby as an important bridge between the cultures of Greece and Rome.

Other important poets of the period include the works of three women, all late fourth to third century B.C.E. Erinna, from an island near Rhodes, wrote poems about her childhood and her friend Baukis, who, like Erinna, died in her late teens. Anyte, from Tegea, wrote epigrammatic epitaphs for men, women, and animals, and dedicatory and pastoral poems, in which, like Theokritos, she displays her love of nature. Highly popular in the Roman period, Anyte was called the "female Homer." Nossis, from Locri, in southern Italy, wrote epigrams to goddesses and dedications to women, her work a deliberate evocation of the greatest of Greek female poets, Sappho. Finally, two other poets include Aratos of Soli (ca. 315–245 B.C.E.), who wrote a didactic *Phaenomena*, describing the nature of the stars, and Herodas (third century B.C.E.), whose mimes depict everyday life in Hellenistic Greek cities.

The Hellenistic age witnessed significant scientific advances in three areas: astronomy, mathematics, and medicine. Dominating the field of astronomy, Aristarchos of Samos (early third century), developed the heliocentric view of the universe, and by crude instrumentation was able to determine the sizes and distance of the sun and the moon. Equally spectacular were the achievements of Eratosthenes of Kyrene (276–194), who accurately calculated the earth's circumference.

Euclid's (ca. 300 B.C.E.) work on mathematics served as the basis for the field until the Renaissance. Archimedes (ca. 287–212) worked on geometry, physics, mechanics, and hydrostatics. Apollonios of Perga (late third century) was the great authority on conics. Lastly, mention must be made of Hero of Alexandria (first century C.E.), whose simple steam engine was never used as anything other than a toy.

In medicine in the third century B.C.E., Herophilus, working at Alexandria, advanced the knowledge of anatomy (through vivisection of criminals, according to legend), while Erasistratos discovered the capillaries and that the heart was the center of the circulatory system. Rival medical approaches were proposed by Philinus, who believed in clinical observation rather than theory, and by Asklepiades (first century B.C.E.) who promoted a more theoretical approach, based on Epicureanism. These scientists would profoundly influence Galen (ca. 130–200 C.E.), the most famous of Roman doctors.

PHILOSOPHICAL DEVELOPMENTS

Intellectually, the Hellenistic age began with Chaironeia (338 B.C.E.), the subjugation of Greece by Makedonia, and the end of Greek freedom. The artistic and cultural representations of the Classical period no longer satisfied the inhabitants of Alexander's new world. As a result, new philosophies and religions grew up in an attempt to fill the void created by the dissolution of the old *polis* world. In addition, closer contact between Greeks and non-Greeks (Syrians, Egyptians, and Jews) broke down the traditional barriers between Greek and "barbarian." A vision of humankind—not merely based on the Greek *polis*, but, in fact, on the whole world, the *kosmos*—arose, expressed most eloquently by the Syrian-Greek Zeno and the Cynics. It was Diogenes the Cynic who described himself as a citizen not of any particular city, but "of the world." However, despite the awareness of a greater world, the philosophies of the Stoics, Epicureans, and Cynics were founded on ideas of the old Greek world, so that the non-Greek influence is seen not so much in the content of their philosophies but in the impetus fueling the shift in fundamental outlook. (See Chapter 8.)

From the Socratic legacy of Plato and Aristotle now arose two new schools of thought with lasting influence that well reflect the shift in Hellenistic thinking: Stoicism and Epicureanism. Both were founded on earlier Greek schools of thought, drawing on ideas of the Presocratics, Sokrates, Plato, and Aristotle; both developed a view of the world that might provide relief in times of political and social upheaval; and both aimed at tranquillity of mind for the individual. Developed by Zeno of Citium (335–263) and his successor Kleanthes of Assos (331–231), Stoicism stressed the primacy of reason and the need to live according to nature, which entails duty to oneself, others, and the community. Importantly, Stoicism appealed to the pragmatic Romans, and in turn to Paul and the Christian fathers, continuing as the most influential of all ancient Greek philosophies into modern times.

The second school, founded by Epicurus (341–270), had as its ultimate goal *ataraxia*, "lack of disturbance" of mind and body, which got misunderstood in antiquity and later as the pursuit of pleasure. While Stoicism encouraged public activity and duty, Epicureans withdrew from the world, seeking instead the quiet obscurity of a few friends and the Garden. This flight from life and duty made it unattractive to the Romans, with the exception of a few famous aristocrats and the great philosophical poet, Lucretius, whose *On the Nature of Things* preserved Epicurus's ideas.

RELIGIOUS DEVELOPMENTS AND INDIGENOUS POPULATIONS

As noted above, this one area, religion, provides clear, unequivocable examples of fruitful interaction between the Greco-Makedonian world and that of the indigenous cultures of the Near East. Increasing contact with Egypt and the Near East accelerated the process of adoption of foreign religions, begun in the fifth century B.C.E. It is understandable that, as a polytheistic people, the Greco-Makedonians might be more receptive to religious practices than to other aspects of foreign culture. Two religions, that of Pharoanic Egypt and that of the Jews, had the most profound effect on the Hellenistic world and on Mediterranean civilization in general.

Promoted officially by the Ptolemies of Egypt, the Hellenized version of the worship of Isis (combined with a truly syncretic creation, the god Sarapis) spread throughout the entire Mediterranean, growing stronger in the Roman period. Particularly popular among mariners and merchants, the rites to Isis, like the Eleusinian and Orphic mysteries, offered hope of an afterlife, increasingly important in the individually oriented Hellenistic world. The influence of Judaism is more complicated. With the Diaspora following the Babylonian destruction of Jerusalem (586

B.C.E.), Jews settled throughout the Near East and Egypt. In this process, many lost their knowledge of Hebrew, and, hence, their connection to the Bible. This was particularly true of the Alexandrian Jews of the Hellenistic age, who commissioned a Greek version of the Bible, the *Septuagint* ("seventy" from its seventy translators). This translation, in turn, made the biblical culture available to non-Jews, and became important in the rise of Christianity.

CONCLUSION

It is clear that all these advances of the Hellenistic age, as well as its preservation of Archaic and Classical Greek culture, are essential in shaping the world that we live in. But what was the cost? Like the Parthenon, like Alexander's liberation, the price was high and paid for by those who had no choice. The Library of Alexandria, an extension of Ptolemaic patronage, was supported by the economic exploitation of the Egyptian people. The development of Stoicism, Cynicism, and Epicureanism can be seen as a response to the politically oppressed environment of old Greece. Scientific advancements were made that had little impact on the day-to-day life of the ordinary person—the steam engine remained a toy in the face of extensive and cheap slave labor. In this light, the cost seems unduly high. But that is for each generation to judge.

Other than the isolated cases of the worship of Isis-Sarapis and the translation of the *Septuagint*, there was not significant cross-cultural influence. Generally, Greco-Makedonians and the indigenous peoples they encountered did not mix. Nor was this the intent of the new ruling class. The monarchic ideals of the Ptolemies and Seleukids did not emphasize the modern notions of cultural, social, and political equality (even though, at times, it was politically expedient to play the benefactor and protector). Rather, they promoted the naked power and military success that made them true heirs of Alexander, and in which they were supported by their Greco-Makedonian followers. Hence, they did not explore the new cultural, philosophical, and religious aspects of the ancient societies they found, but simply exploited them.

Moreover, we must add that two other factors militated against cross-cultural interaction: xenophobia and hostility of the indigenous populations who faced foreign invaders who interfered with their ancient way of life. In addition, many peoples had traditions that barred the admission of the outsider, because of religious scruples or the barrier of language. The ancient religious and social constraints on both sides did not provide a fertile ground for a dynamic interchange. This, in fact, was tragic. The modern world, albeit fraught with its own limitations, has shown that deep and significant cultural interaction can indeed take place. It is the modern who looks back at the Hellenistic Age as a lost opportunity for the development of a true, universal, human culture.

SUGGESTIONS FOR FURTHER READING

Austin, M.M. 1981. *The Hellenistic World from Alexander to the Roman Conquest: A Selection of Ancient Sources in Translation*. Cambridge: Cambridge University Press. An excellent sourcebook of Hellenistic inscriptions and papyri in English with commentary and notes.

Bradford, Ernle. 2001. *Cleopatra*. London and New York: Penguin Books. This new biography examines Cleopatra's image as a result of the negative portrayals put forth by the Romans.

Davis, Norman, and Colin M. Kraay. 1973. *The Hellenistic Kingdoms: Portrait Coins and History*. London: Thames and Hudson. A pictorially rich and interesting account of the Hellenistic monarchs through the medium of coinage.

Eddy, Samuel Kennedy. 1961. *The King Is Dead: Studies in the Near Eastern Resistance to Hellenism 334–31 B.C.* Lincoln: University of Nebraska Press. The most comprehensive survey of the conflict between Greek and non-Greek during the Hellenistic period.

Fowler, Barbara Hughes, trans. 1990. *Hellenistic Poetry: An Anthology*. Madison: University of Wisconsin Press. An excellent introduction to the most important pieces of Hellenistic poetry.

Fraser, P.M. 1972. *Ptolemaic Alexandria*. 3 vols. Oxford: Oxford University Press. A detailed study of the greatest city of Ptolemaic Egypt and the Hellenistic World.

Green, Peter. 1990. *Alexander to Actium: The Historical Evolution of the Hellenistic Age*. Berkeley and Los Angeles: University of California Press. The best overall treatment of the Hellenistic period, written for both the scholar and the general public.

Gruen, Erich S. 1984. *The Hellenistic World and the Coming of Rome*. 2 vols. Berkeley and Los Angeles: University of California Press. This work best defines the extremely complex and contradictory relationship between Rome and the Greek Hellenistic World.

Hughes-Hallett, Lucy. 1990. *Cleopatra: Histories, Dreams and Distortions*. New York: Harper and Row. The author examines the public relations image-making by Cleopatra and others in putting forth her image.

Lewis, Naphtali. 1986. *Greeks in Ptolemaic Egypt: Case Studies in the Social History of the Hellenistic World*. Oxford: Oxford University Press. An excellent study of a few families and individuals of Ptolemaic Egypt, with particular reference to the question of coexistence and syncretism.

Lindsay, Jack. 1971. *Cleopatra*. London: Constable. A basic introduction to the last Ptolemaic queen based on the sources.

Long, A.A., and D.N. Sedley. 1987. *The Hellenistic Philosophers*. 2 vols. Cambridge: Cambridge University Press. The best survey of the various philosophical schools developed in the Hellenistic Age.

Pomeroy, Sarah B. 1984. *Women in Hellenistic Egypt from Alexander to Cleopatra.* New York: Shocken Books. An examination of the social, religious and political roles of women, in the Hellenistic period, Greek and non-Greek, slave, free and royal.

Sherwin-White, Susan, and Amelie Kuhrt. 1993. *From Samarkhand to Sardis: A New Approach to the Seleukid Empire.* Berkeley: University of California Press. An interpretation of the Hellenistic world not only from traditional Greek sources, but also from the point of view of the indigenous populations of the non-Greek world.

Appendix A

Glossary of Terms

Akropolis. "Height of the city"; in Athens, the rocky outcropping on which the Parthenon, Temple of Athena, was built; among the other sanctuaries on its slopes was the theater of Dionysos, where plays were performed.

Anatolia. Asia Minor, much of modern-day Turkey.

apella. The Assembly in Sparta.

archon. "Ruler"; in Athens, the city magistrates elected annually.

Attika. Region of Greece surrounding Athens.

autocracy. Rule by a single individual having complete power.

barbaros. Originally, a non-Greek speaker, eventually with derogatory meaning as our word "barbarian."

basileus, pl. *basileis.* "King," "chief," hereditary ruler.

Boiotia. Region of Greece surrounding Thebes.

boulê. In Athens, council of 400 established by Solon, expanded to 500 by Kleisthenes.

deme. A political unit, like a county.

dêmos. "People."

disenfranchisement. Taking away one's political rights.

Dorian. Designation for a group of Greeks, mostly western; Sparta was a major Dorian city; also refers to their dialect and customs which were somewhat different from those of Ionian Greeks.

dyarchy. Rule by two kings, as in Sparta.

ekklêsia. The Assembly in Athens.

Eleusinian Mysteries. Worship of Demeter and her daughter Persephone, the most important ancient Greek religious rites, offering blessedness in this life and after death.

ephor. In Sparta, the city magistrates.

Great or *City Dionysia.* The festival for Dionysos in March, at which tragedies and later comedies were produced.

hegemony. Rulership or control.

Hellas. Greece in Greek.

Hellenes. The Greeks' name for themselves.

helots. Spartan slaves, from the conquered Messenians.

homoioi. "Equals," the elite core of ruling Spartan men.

hoplite. A Greek infantry soldier.

imperialism, adj. *imperialist.* Quest for empire, often violent.

indigenous. Native.

Ionian. Designation for a group of Greeks, mostly eastern; Athens was a major Ionian city; more specifically, it refers to the Greek cities on the western Anatolian coast, modern Turkey.

Lakedaimon. The region around Sparta.

Lakonia. Another name for Sparta.

Lenaia. The festival for Dionysos in February, established in 440, at which comedies were produced.

metaphysics. "After physics," study of ultimate causes and the underlying nature of things.

mêtropoleis. "Mother city," the city sending out colonies.

Minoan. Pre-Greek civilization, centered on the islands of Crete and Thera (Santorini).

Minotaur. Mythological monster—half-bull, half-man—in the labyrinth of Crete, which killed Athenian youth until it was killed by Theseus, with the help of the Cretan princess Ariadne.

monarchy. Rule by a single king.

Mycenaean. The earliest Greek civilization, 1600–1150 B.C.E.

Neolithic. "Old Stone Age," dating from the beginning of agriculture.

oligarchy: Rule by a few.

oracle. Form of prophecy; the oracle of Apollo at Delphi, the most important of ancient Greek oracular sites.

padrone. Local men of authority who get their will enforced.

Panhellenism. "All Greek," a movement begun in the Archaic period to provide a common identity for all Greeks.

Peloponnesos (or *Peloponnese*). "Pelops' island," southern peninsula of Greece; principal cities include Sparta, Argos, Korinth, Olympia, Mykenai, Tiryns, Pylos.

phalanx. An ordered battle formation.

polis, pl. *poleis*. "City-state," the independent Greek political city.

polytheism, adj. *polytheistic*. Belief in many gods and goddesses.

prostration. Showing reverence by lying down on the ground before a ruler or deity.

protocol. Code of diplomatic or military procedural etiquette.

rhetoric. Art of persuasion or public speaking.

ribald. Graphic sexual humor.

satrap. Persian governor of a *satrapy*.

satrapy. An administrative district of the Persian empire.

scatological. Referring to excrement.

Thesmophoria. The oldest and most widespread women's rites for Demeter.

trireme. A Greek warship with three banks of oars.

tyranny. Originally, rule by a nonhereditary ruler; later referring to harsh, dictatorial rule.

tyrant. Originally, a nonhereditary ruler; later considered harsh and dictatorial.

xenophobia. Fear of strangers.

Appendix B

Timeline of Events

7000–3000 B.C.E.	**Neolithic**
3000–1150	**The Bronze Age**
3500–1400	Minoan
1628	Volcanic explosion on Thera (Santorini)
1600–1150	Mycenaean
1425–1230	height of Mycenaean civilization
ca. 1220	the legendary Trojan War
11th–9th c.	**The Dark Age**
8th–6th c.	**Archaic Period**
8th–7th c.	Greek colonization to the west and east
776	Olympic Games founded, their four-year cycle the common basis for Greek dating
late 8th c.	Poets Homer, *The Iliad*, *The Odyssey*, and Hesiod, *Theogony*, *Works and Days*
750–700	Pithekoussai cup graffito, first evidence of Greek writing
735–716	First Messenian War, Spartan conquest of Messenia

657–625	Kypselos tyrant of Korinth
mid-7th c.	Lykourgos's reforms in Sparta
ca. 650	Temple of Hera at Olympia begun
650–620	Second Messenian War, Spartan victory
mid to late 7th c.	Poets Alkman in Sparta, Sappho, Alkaios in Lesbos
632	Kylon's attempted tyranny in Athens; Megakles and Alkmaionid clan cursed and expelled from Athens
625–585	Periander tyrant of Korinth
621	Drakon's first written laws in Athens
ca. 600	First Greek coins found at Temple of Artemis at Ephesos
600–570	Kleisthenes tyrant of Sikyon
594	Solon *archon* in Athens, new laws and reforms
early 6th c.	Philosophers Thales, Anaximander
mid to late 6th c.	Philosophers Anaximenes, Xenophanes, Pythagoras
561–556, 546–527	Peisistratos tyrant of Athens
558–530	Cyrus founds and rules Persian Empire
545	Conquest of Ionian Greeks by Persians
535–522	Polykrates tyrant of Samos
534	First tragedy performed at the City Dionysia in Athens
527–510	Hippias tyrant of Athens
522–486	Darius's reign, third king of Persia
514	Hipparkhos murdered by Harmodios and Aristogeiton in Athens
510	Spartan King Kleomenes helps oust Hippias tyrant of Athens
508	Kleisthenes political reforms in Athens
5th–4th c.	**Classical Period**
late 6th to early 5th c.	Philosophers Parmenides, Herakleitos
499–494	Revolt of Ionian cities against Persians
498	Sardis burned by Ionians with help of Athens and Eretria

494	Battle of Lade, ending Ionian Revolt, Miletos destroyed
492	Themistokles *archon* in Athens
490	First Persian invasion of Greece under Persian King Darius, Greek victory at the Battle of Marathon
486	First comedy performed at the City Dionysia in Athens
486–464	Xerxes, fourth king of Persia
483	Discovery of silver mines at Laureion in Attika
480	Second Persian invasion of Greece under King Xerxes, Greek defeat at Thermopylai, Artemision, Athenian Akropolis burned; Greek victory at naval Battle of Salamis
479	Greek victories at Battles of Plataia, Mykale
478	Delian League founded as defense against Persia
early 5th c.	Tragedian Aeschylus, *Persians, Oresteia, Prometheus Bound*
5th c.	Philosophers Anaxagoras, Empedokles
470–413	Athenian general Nikias
469–399	Philosopher Sokrates
462	Ephialtes' political reforms in Athens
461–456	Long Walls built from Athens to its port, Peiraios
461–429	Perikles, general and political leader in Athens
ca. 460–post 400	Historian Thucydides
460–446	First Peloponnesian War between Athens and Spartan allies
456	Temple of Zeus at Olympia completed
454	Treasury of Delian League moved to Athens
451–403	Alkibiades, aristocrat and politician in Athens, Sparta, Persia
mid to late 5th c.	Plays of the tragedians, Sophocles, *Antigone, Oedipus the King*, and Euripides, *Medea, Hippolytos, Trojan Women, Bacchae*

448	Parthenon, Temple of Athena in Athens begun
445–426	Historian Herodotos active in Athens
440	Lenaia festival for comedies established in Athens
late 5th c.	Philosophers Leukippos, Demokritos—atomic theory; Sophists Protagoras, Gorgias; physician Hippokrates
431–404	Second Peloponnesian War between Athens and Sparta
430–426	Plague in Athens
429	Death of Perikles from plague
429–347	Philosopher Plato
427	Mytilene revolt against Athens, forced into submission
427–355	Historian Xenophon, *Anabasis, Memorabilia*
425	Athenians capture Pylos, trapping Spartan troops on nearby island of Sphakteria
424	Battle of Amphipolis, Thucydides exiled from Athens
421	Peace of Nikias between Athens and Sparta
416	Athens destroys the neutral island of Melos
415–413	Athens's attempted conquest of Sicily—the "Sicilian disaster"
413	Sparta renews the war, with a permanent fort at Dekeleia
late 5th to early 4th c.	Comic playwright Aristophanes, *Lysistrata, Birds, Frogs, Clouds*
412–321	Philosopher Diogenes the Cynic
411	Oligarchic revolutions in Athens
410	Democracy restored in Athens
406	Tragedians Sophocles and Euripides die
405	Athenian fleet destroyed at the Battle of Aigospotamoi
404	Athens surrenders to Sparta; rule of Thirty Tyrants in Athens
403	Democracy restored in Athens

399	Sokrates' trial and execution in Athens
395	Thucydides' *History of the Peloponnesian War* published
387	Plato founds the Academy
384–322	Philosopher Aristotle
386	The King's Peace recognizing Persian authority over Ionia
371	Thebans defeat Sparta at Battle of Leuktra
366	Peloponnesian League disbanded
362	Thebans defeated at Battle of Mantinea
359–336	Philip II King of Makedonia
357–355	Ionian revolt against second Athenian defensive league
356–323	Alexander the Great
343–342	Aristotle tutors Alexander in Makedonia
342–289	New Comedy playwright Menander
341–270	Philosopher Epicurus
338	Philip II defeats Greeks at Battle of Chaironea
336	Alexander becomes king of Makedonia
335	Alexander puts down revolt in Thebes, destroying the city
335	Aristotle founds the Lyceum
334–323	Alexander's conquests
334–261	Philosopher Zeno of Citium, founder of Stoicism
333	Alexander defeats Darius III at the Battle at the Issos River
331	Alexander founds Alexandria, Egypt
331	Alexander defeats Darius III at the Battle at Gaugamela
330	Alexander burns Persepolis
326	Alexander defeats Indians in the Punjab at the Hydaspes River
324	Alexander returns to Susa
323	Alexander dies in Babylon, 32 years old

323–330 B.C.E. **Hellenistic Period**

321–301	Antigonos rules Alexander's Asian conquests
321–282	Ptolemy I rules Egypt, establishing Ptolemaic dynasty
321–281	Seleukos I rules first Babylonia, eventually most of the Near East, establishing Seleukid empire
310	Zeno founds the Stoic school in Athens
310–250	Poet Theokritos
307	Epicurus founds the Garden in Athens
304	Antigonos, Ptolemy I, Seleukos I proclaim themselves kings
300	Ptolemy I builds Library and Museum in Alexandria
3rd century	Poets Kallimachos, Erinna, Anyte, Nossis; mime skits Herodas; novelist Apollonios, the *Argonautica*; mathematician Euclid; physicians Herophilus, Erasistratos; *Septuagint*, Bible in Greek
294–287	Demetrios I, king of Makedonia, establishes Antigonid dynasty
287–212	Mathematician, physicist Archimedes
282–246	Ptolemy II Philadelphos rules Egypt
281–261	Antiochos I rules Seleukid empire
276–194	Mathematician and geographer Eratosthenes
263	Eumenes I and Attalos I establish Attalid kingdom in Pergamon
215–146	Rome's four Makedonian wars
200–118	Historian Polybios
189	Rome defeats Antiochos III at Battle of Magnesia, annexes Asia Minor
148	Rome annexes Makedonia
146	Rome destroys Korinth, annexes Greece
143	Maccabees free Judaea from Seleukid rule
1st century	Historian Diodoros
64	Pompey captures Syria, end of Seleukid empire

Appendix C

Greek Gods and Goddesses

Aphrodite. Goddess of sexuality and erotic desire, worshipped by adult women and men.

Apollo. God of music, light, and prophecy, with a major oracular site at Delphi; in ritual he oversees maturation rites of young men.

Ares. God of war.

Artemis. Goddess of animals, the wild, hunting, and the young; in ritual she oversees maturation rites of young women and men.

Athena. Goddess of wisdom, war, crafts, patron deity of Athens; in ritual she oversees maturation rites of young women and men.

Demeter. Goddess of agriculture, grain, female fertility; worshipped mostly in adult women–only fertility festivals; together with her daughter Persephone, worshipped by men and women in the all-important Eleusinian Mysteries.

Dione. "The female Zeus," wife of Zeus in some accounts.

Dionysos. God of the cultivated vine, wine, male fertility, drama; like Demeter, worshipped in fertility-promoting rituals.

Eros. God of sexuality and erotic desire.

Gaia. "The Earth" Goddess, the original deity who gave birth to Ouranos ("Sky"), then mated with him to produce the second generation of deities.

Hades. God of the underworld, married to Persephone.

Hephaistos. God of fire, crafts; in mythology a lame god, son of Hera.

Hera. Goddess of marriage; worshipped mostly in adult women–only fertility festivals; in mythology, the wife of Zeus.

Hermes. Messenger God, associated with travelers, boundaries, inventiveness, scheming, thievery; escorts souls to the underworld.

Ishtar/Astarte. Semitic (Babylonian/Phoenician) Goddesses of sexuality and erotic desire, Near Eastern forerunners of the Greek Goddess Aphrodite.

Ouranos. "Sky" God, who, after being created by Gaia ("the Earth") mated with her to produce the second generation of deities.

Persephone. Goddess of the underworld, spring; in ritual she oversees maturation rites of young women; worshipped with her mother Demeter in the Eleusinian Mysteries.

Poseidon. God of the sea, earthquakes, horses.

Zeus. God of the sky, thunder, lightning; considered the chief of the gods; "married" to Hera, but begetting offspring by many other goddesses and mortal women.

Index

About the Editor and Contributors

WALTER G. ENGLERT is Omar and Althea Hoskins Professor of Classical Studies at Reed College. His works include *Epicurus and the Swerve on Voluntary Action* (1987), *Cicero: Pro Caelio* (1990), and "Stoics and Epicureans on the Nature of Suicide," *Proceedings of the Boston Area Colloquium in Ancient Philosophy* 10 (1994): 67–96. He is currently working on a translation of Lucretius's *De Rerum Natura*.

ROBERT GARLAND is Roy D. and Margaret B. Wooster Professor of the Classics at Colgate University. His most recent works include *The Eye of the Beholder: Deformity and Disability in the Graeco-Roman World* (1995) and *Daily Life of the Ancient Greeks* (Greenwood, 1998).

STEVEN HIRSCH is Associate Professor of Classics and History at Tufts University. He is the author of *The Friendship of the Barbarians: Xenophon and the Persian Empire* (1986) and co-author of *The Earth and Its Peoples: A Global History*, 2d ed. (2001).

CARL G. JOHNSON is Assistant Professor of Classical, Near Eastern, and Religious Studies at the University of British Columbia. His works include "The Divinization of the Ptolemies and the Gold Octodrachms Honoring Ptolemy III," *Phoenix* 53 (1999), and "Ptolemy V and the Rosetta Stone: The Egyptianization of the Ptolemaic Kingship," *Ancient So-*

ciety 26 (1995). He has a book in progress: *Royal Titulature and the Ptolemies: A Study of Image and Power (304–116 B.C.).*

JENNIFER LARSON is Associate Professor of Classics at Kent State University. She is the author of *Greek Heroine Cults* (1995) and *Greek Nymphs: Myth, Cult, Lore* (2001).

DONALD LATEINER is John R. Wright Professor of Greek and Humanities at Ohio Wesleyan University. He is the author of *The Historical Method of Herodotus* (1989) and *Sardonic Smile: Nonverbal Behavior in Homeric Epic* (1995).

JOHN W. I. LEE is Assistant Professor of History at the University of California at Santa Barbara. He is preparing a monograph on social organization and daily life in a fourth century B.C.E. Greek mercenary army.

JOSEPH ROISMAN is Professor of Classics at Colby College. He is the author of *The General Demosthenes and His Use of Military Surprise* (1993) and editor of *A Companion to Alexander the Great* (forthcoming).

F. E. ROMER is Associate Professor of Classics at the University of Arizona. He is the author of *Pomponius Mela's Description of the World* (1998) and numerous articles on Greek and Roman antiquity. He also has served as historical consultant for the University of Arizona excavations at Chianciano Terme and Lugnano in Teverina, Italy.

CAROL G. THOMAS is Professor of History at the University of Washington. She is the author, with Craig Conant, of *From Citadel to City State: The Transformation of Greece, 1200–700 B.C.E.* (1999) and *Progress into the Past: The Rediscovery of Mycenaean Civilization,* 2d ed. (1990), with William McDonald.

BELLA VIVANTE, Associate Professor in Humanities at the University of Arizona, is 2000–2001 Hennebach Visiting Professor in Humanities at the Colorado School of Mines. She has translated with notes Euripides' *Helen* in *Women on the Edge: Four Plays by Euripides* (1998), and is editor of *Women's Roles in Ancient Civilizations: A Reference Guide* (Greenwood, 1999).